The Collector's Encyclopedia of

AMERICAN DINNERWARE

The Collector's Encyclopedia of

AMERICAN DINNERWARE

by Jo Cunningham

COLLECTOR BOOKS
A Division of Schroeder Publishing Co., Inc.
P.O. BOX 3009 • PADUCAH, KENTUCKY 42001

The current values in this book should be used only as a guide. They are not intended to set prices, which vary from one section of the country to another. Auction prices as well as dealer prices vary greatly and are affected by condition as well as demand. Neither the Author nor the Publisher assumes responsibility for any losses that might be incurred as a result of consulting this guide.

ABOUT THE AUTHOR

Jo Cunningham resides in Springfield, Missouri, with her family. She has been active in collecting for many years and is a member of several national organizations pretaining to collecting.

Jo has authored several articles on collectibles published by leading trade papers. She is the author of *The Autumn Leaf Story*, and *Hall China Price Guide*.

You are welcome to write Jo but if you require an answer, you must enclose a self addressed stamped envelope. Jo Cunningham, 535 E. Normal, Springfield, MO 65807.

Searching For A Publisher?

We are always looking for knowledgeable people considered to be experts within their fields. If you feel that there is a real need for a book on your collectible subject and have a large comprehensive collection, contact Collector Books.

The *Collectors Encyclopedia of American Dinnerware* is respectfully dedicated to all of the men and women who labored in the American pottery industry and to all of those who treasure the fruits of their labor.

ACKNOWLEDGMENTS

Many people are responsible for a book of this nature. *The Collector's Encyclopedia of American Dinnerware* is actually a compilation of dinnerware pieces and pieces of information gained from letters, trade publications and conversations with pottery people. Without this special help this book simply could not have been.

My first "thank you's" must go to my family who have had to contend with a lot while this project was in the making. They have patiently stepped over dishes and stacks of papers for some time now. Of course, a special thank you has to go to my husband, Wayne. He has put up with a wife who forgets birthdays but can recite dates of pottery openings and closings, knows more about pottery people than her own background and whom he probably would not recognize without a phone dangling from one ear. Thank you, Wayne.

From scribbled notes on a plain yellow tablet, secretary Mary Beth Houser somehow made these same notes magically appear into a neat typewritten manuscript. Jenny Compton, English teacher, then took her red marking pencil and corrected the finished copy. Terry Graves, number one daughter, did many of my chores so that I could be free to work on this project. The next acknowledgment is an unusual one I know but, had it not been for the excellent medical care given to me this past year by Dr. Robert A. Sweet, I would not have had the opportunity to share these words with you - for that opportunity, I am especially grateful.

The beautiful photography in *The Collectors Encyclopedia of American Dinnerware* was done by Lonnie Bolding and Greg Ciccolo. Lonnie is a Springfield, Missouri graphics designer and photographer. Greg operates The Wild Goose Antiques in Boston, Massachusetts. Both young men are talented artists and deserve special thanks for their efforts.

Most of the pieces shown in the book are from the author's own collection of American dinnerware but many friends supplemented by sharing pieces to be photographed. The following people loaned pieces for this project: B. A. Wellman, John Moses, Greg Ciccolo, Bill Stratton, Bud and Evelyn Rhoades, Harold Shaw, Betty and Jim Cooper, Frank and Norma Hudson, Phyllis Bess, Mark Schliessmann, Lee Wagner.

Information was shared by the following people: Mrs. William H. Blair, Mrs. Howard Blair, Louise Wommack, Jay Block, Al Fridley, Maxine Nelson, John Moses, B. A. Wellman, Mrs. Dan Hoops, Betty Burley, Norris Schneider, Esther Regel, Harold Vogus, Paul Merwin, Allen Kleinbeck, Rex Cunningham, James Coffey, Robert Boyce, John T. Hall, Jim Lange, Charles Doll, Ed Carson, Harrison Keller, Dorothy Glass, Harry Blair Purinton, Pauline Cash, Ann Kerr, J. David Conley, Terri and Don Stanek, Phyllis Bess, Chester Wardeska, Betty Rice, Donna Frisbee, Harry Davis, Miles Bausch, Don Hoffmann, Bette Cooper, Eva Zeisel, William Gates and Joniece Frank. For any of those who may have inadvertantly been left out I beg your forgiveness and please know that your contribution to *The Collectors Encyclopedia of American Dinnerware* is sincerely appreciated.

Many of the pottery companies were, themselves, very helpful in providing historical and promotion material. Especially cooperative in providing material were Frankoma Pottery, The Haeger Company, Pfaltzgraff, Scio Pottery Company, and Western Stoneware Company.

I especially want to thank Mr. Norris Schneider for sharing with me his article, "Shawnee Pottery," from the *Zanes Time Recorder* dated October 16, 1960. Mr. Schneider is a nationally-known author, historian, and researcher of American pottery and potteries of the Zanesville area. Without his research and the sharing of that knowledge, there would be a great void in the history of pottery. My personal thanks go to this grand gentleman, truly the pioneer of American Pottery research.

PREFACE

"He who proposes to be an author should first be a student." John Dryden

Had I been content to rely on information and misinformation that is currently being circulated this book would have been completed many months ago. It was very important to me that I not rely on these sources and many months have been spent tracking records and dates, talking to pottery workers, and going through trade publications, catalogues and magazines. One thing I have learned for sure, this is just the tip of this vast subject.

Some information in *The Collectors Encyclopedia of American Dinnerware* is based on conversations with, and letters from, old-time pottery workers themselves. These fine people are the first to admit that memories of workdays some 30-40 years past may not be 100% accurate. Their contributions however, provide us with a far better insight into the great American Pottery Industry.

We hope to be able to acquaint you generally with pottery terms and production methods so you may understand the processes used in the making of dinnerware.

It is important for you to know that the pictures in this book represent only a minute portion of wares each company made over the years. There is no doubt enough ware made by each company to fill a separate volume.

The Collectors Encyclopedia of American Dinnerware is only the beginning. It will be many years, if not an impossible task, to learn "all" about the hundreds of potteries that spanned 100 years and turned out hundreds of dozens of pieces of pottery daily.

In each of the comparatively few companies represented here, the examples shown represent only a few pieces each of a dinnerware line. For each company shown, you may find many more colors, shapes and patterns. For each reprint that is shown here, there are in our files several more that could not be included. For these reasons, it would be unduly presumptious to consider this book to be the last word, or to insult the reader's intelligence by my claiming to be the authority. How could one person learn in an entire lifetime what transpired in the making of millions of pieces of dinnerware?

I do however, consider myself to be a serious student of the American Pottery Industry and admittedly that interest is all consuming. It is my sincere hope that you gain some bit of useful knowledge and understand that we are on the threshold of a new collecting field and that you will be able to forgive the errors that must be accepted as an inevitable part of pioneering.

CONTENTS

THE AMERICAN POTTERY INDUSTRY: A BRIEF HISTORY

Authorities have not been able to agree on an exact date or site of the first American-made pottery. They do generally agree, however, on the mid-1600's and the New York, New Jersey area. It has been proven that several potteries were in business by the mid-1700's.

Of more importance to us is the East Liverpool, Ohio, area as the beginning of the dinnerware industry, as we know it.

James Bennett came to America in 1834 at the age of 22. Early reports say he went to Jersey City and worked at a pottery as a packer. He left Jersey City in 1837 for Troy, Indiana and, after a year or so found himself on a steamboat where a chance meeting with a gentleman from East Liverpool convinced him of the rich clay deposits in the East Liverpool area - or so the story goes.

Bennett started to work on his pottery in the fall of 1839 and the first kiln was drawn in 1840. He was backed to some degree by Benjamin Harker, another important pioneer in the pottery industry. Isaac Knowles became the first "crockery salesman" buying two crates and selling it down the river. Mr. Bennett left the area in 1844 but by this time Benjamin Harker was in the pottery business and no doubt news of the clay deposits brought other potters to the area. These early potteries produced yellow ware, and white ware was not developed until 1879 when Harker, Knowles and Laughlin developed whiteware at about the same time. From this chance visit by James Bennett, the East Liverpool area evolved into the pottery manufacturing center of the United States.

Early white ware was not considered to be as good as English ware and backstamps were such to give the impression that American-made whiteware was English made. Homer Laughlin is credited with using the American Eagle with the British Lion on its back, in what we now know to be the first distinctive American backstamp.

The development of whiteware created a need for independent decorating shops and early ware was decorated in these shops. Other companies soon cropped up, filling the potteries' needs for machinery, saggers, pins and any clay products needed.

Many potteries were destroyed by floods and fires only to rebuild and "go under" in the Depression years. In looking back, it seems to me that the 1940's were the most active years for those manufacturers who had survived. The American public was buying American products. By the mid to late 1950's it was over for many potteries that had remained. Plastics and the return of imports were obstacles too large to overcome. In the course of one hundred years from James Bennett's first kiln drawn in 1840, the great American pottery industry struggled, fought, overcame floods and fires to reach the very heights of success, only to have the doors of failure end their struggle in the 1950's. At this time only a few pottery companies remain and little American-made dinnerware is available to the American consumer. Institutional ware makes up the major portion of the wares produced by existing potteries.

HOW DINNERWARE IS MADE

A piece of dinnerware has its beginning in the clay shop. All of the ingredients are carefully measured, mixed, and a thin paste called "slip" is made by the addition of water to the dry ingredients. The slip then goes through a sieve and an electromagnet removes all foreign particles. Excess liquid is removed and the clay comes out in a round flat pie crust shape. It then moves to the pug mill. The pug mill squeezes out air bubbles and converts "pie crusts" into fat heavy rolls.

Throwing, casting and jiggering are the three methods of shaping clay. A ball of clay is "thrown" on the center of a horizontal wheel and water is used as a lubricant to the worker's hands. Jiggering machines were developed to speed the shaping.

Casting is achieved by pouring the slip into plaster of paris molds and allowed to stand long enough for the plaster to absorb sufficient water. The clay forms a wall of pre-determined thickness inside the mold. Excess slip is poured off and the piece can be removed.

All hollow-ware or holloware is made in this manner. Pre-cast handles are pressed into place with slip and the "green-ware" is dried. The soft dishes are racked in rough tile baskets that move by conveyor through the kiln. The "bisque" or "biscuits" move to the glazing department and then to another firing. Some ware is decorated before glazing.

The decalomanias are held to a piece by varnish and the paper backing soaked off with water. Delicate presses could press designs with soft rubber engravings. Automatic liners make lines. Final firing burns off the varnish and oil in the paint or decalomanias and the bright colors of dinnerware emerge.

Inspectors cull out all along the line pieces failing to meet specifications. Some pieces not "making it" are dropped and broken in a large bin by the inspector. A final inspection is made before the pieces are shipped.

The "backstamp" is just what the name implies. A rubber stamp with the company's name or line name is used on the back of the pieces. Some companies used a date and other marks might signify a worker or factory location. Mr. Doll of the Mt. Clemens operation tells us that after 1938 none of their wares were marked due to the volume of their production.

It will be impossible to definitely identify all ware. All potteries sold seconds, thirds, and even firsts to different jobbers. It is conceivable that the same blanks were sold to several different jobbers or decorators who decorated the ware and stamped it with their own "backstamp." Potteries also sold their ware to other potteries and it is not uncommon to find two pottery names on the back of one piece.

From "On American Dinnerware", by Franklin Ullrey.

Automatic cup forming on Cupmaster jigger. Anchor Hocking - 1980

Newly formed and dried flatware is automatically removed from quadramatic jigger by use of suction. Anchor Hocking - 1980

Brushes remove dirt from bisque ware before glaze is applied. Anchor Hocking - 1980

Cup handles are cut from stem and hand finished. Anchor Hocking
- 1980

Handle finishing. Mold marks are smoothed and finished to fit contour
of cup. Anchor Hocking - 1980

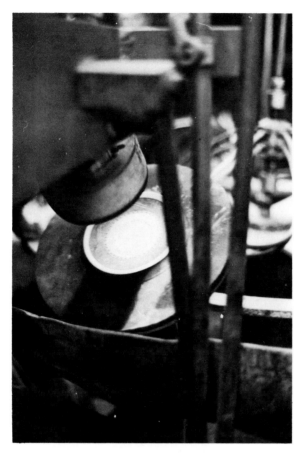

Underglaze stamp decorations are applied by machine, one color at a time. (pattern is Currier & Ives) Anchor Hocking - 1980

Hand application of mug handles. Anchor Hocking - 1980

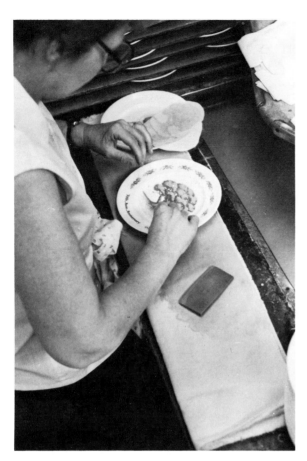

Overglaze decal being applied by hand. Special plate is for Avon Products. Anchor Hocking - 1980

Automatic Cup Lining Machine. Anchor Hocking - 1980

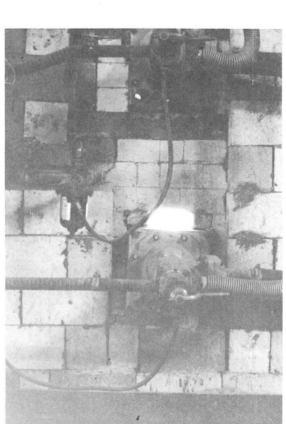

Looking into firebox of bisque kiln. Temperature inside is 2,300 degrees. Anchor Hocking - 1980

BACKSTAMPS

This is not a book of marks and some marks shown in this book are enlarged for your convenience. You will find many more marks used by these companies and you are invited to share unlisted marks by sending a sketch or copy to the author. This will help with identification in future books about the American pottery industry. Remember when writing, a self-addressed, stamped envelope is an absolute must if you want a reply.

You will find a variety of backstamps shown. Most are a design, company logo; some are in raised lettering like Cronin's Bake Oven; some are incised or cut in the clay before it is hardened and some are as colorful as a peacock which is exactly what was used on some of the Homer Laughlin Wells lines.

Sometimes the name on the bottom of a piece will be the pattern name but more times than not it is the shape name. Remember, there are approximately 150 different patterns on the Virginia Rose blank by Homer Laughlin and they all say Virginia Rose.

One can generally pick a production date out of the numbers on the back of a piece. Numbers can also be a code for factory location and at times provides information known only to the company. It doesn't take long for a dinnerware collector to become a confirmed "backstamp checker." Even though I know the pattern I still feel compelled to "double check." My family is somewhat appalled by my habit, especially when visiting or eating out. I soon developed a fast rule for dining out and that is to "backstamp check" before being served or after finishing your meal.

Mr. Robert Boyce formerly of the Harker operation tells us that backstamps did not have the significance that collectors attach to them. He also tells us a new backstamp was often used to promote some new pattern or line.

DESIGNERS

In the late 1930's and 1940's it was popular for dinnerware makers to contract with designers for a special shape or line. This idea carried over into the 1950's but later it is believed the major remaining potteries had their own "in-house" art-department and designers. Some names you will hear associated with American dinnerware are: Eva Zeisel, Russel Wright, Charles Murphy, Ben Siebel, Belle Kogan, Sascha Brastoff, Viktor Schreckengost, Don Schreckengost, Simon Slobodkin, Walter Teague, and J. Palin Thorley.

Eva Zeisel began designing in 1925. She designed aluminum ware, metal-craft frames, and cosmetic lines. Innovator of new shapes, she designed a line of china for Castleton, Red Wing, Butler Brothers, Hall China, and Western Stoneware. Mrs. Zeisel taught at Pratt Institute and was a well-known lecturer on functional design. Mrs. Zeisel came to the United States in 1938.

Russel Wright could well be called the Father of American modern design. Mr. Wright created a whole new concept, not only in dinnerware, but in functional furniture, silverware, radios and lawn furniture.

Russel Wright's American Modern dinnerware was introduced to the trade in 1938 and to the public in 1939. American Modern was made by the Steubenville Pottery in Steubenville, Ohio. Russel Wright designed a "plus pottery" line for Justin Tharaud, dinnerware for Tharaud, Steubenville, Harker, Sterling and Iroquois. He designed furniture, plastic dinnerware, stainless items and much more.

Charles Murphy was a graduate of the Cleveland School of Art. He went to Red Wing, Minnesota, to design for Red Wing in the 1940's, from the East Liverpool, Ohio, area. Charles Murphy designed for the Stetson Company for a brief period of time in the 1950's.

Ben Seibel designed Raymor for Roseville, Contempura for Steubenville, and Mr. Seibel's most recent design for American dinnerware was for The Haeger Pottery, Dundee, Illinois.

Belle Kogan was educated at Pratt Institute, Winold Reiss Studios and The Rhode Island School for Design. She studied in Europe in 1930-31. She designed in pottery, glass, plastics, wood, and silver, and also designed clocks and electrical appliances.

Sascha Brastoff designed mostly for California Potteries and designed several patterns for Winfield China.

Viktor Schreckengost was a native of Sebring, Ohio. His parents came to Sebring from Pennsylvania where their family had long been potters. Viktor Schreckengost was instructor in design at the Cleveland School of Art and had designed glass, stoves, pen sets, enamel furniture, and many other items. By 1934 his work had been exhibited at the Metropolitan Museum, Pennsylvania Museum, Akron Art Institute, Chicago Art Institute, and the Syracuse Museum.

He became chief designer for Limoges China Company in about 1938 and designed two new shapes, Americana and Diana. These shapes were decorated in many different ways and colors; Smoke, Coronet, Betsy Rose, Flame, Evening Star Esquire, Penthouse, Pueblo, Crocus Symphony and Hollywood. Frederick Rhead called Viktor's Limoge shapes as "... the most outstanding creative development by any American potter within the past year." (1934) Viktor Schreckengost studied in Vienna and then studied the people and architecture in Russia and Poland. He divided his time between being instructor at the Cleveland School of Art and serving as an assistant to Guy R. Cowan. Schreckengost later designed for Salem China, Salem, Ohio.

Don Schreckengost, brother of Viktor, designed for Homer Laughlin and the Hall China Company.

Simon Slobodkin designed for W. S. George and others. Walter Teague designed Conversation line for Taylor, Smith and Taylor. J. Palin Thorley designed the "E" line for Sears; Castle and Dogwood for Taylor, Smith and Taylor.

This is in no manner of speaking a complete list of designers nor is it a complete list of their works. Most designed not only dinnerware but many other items. I'm sure there will be much more written about these great artists who contributed so much to the great American pottery industry.

PRICING

In some of the ads for the trade you may see the mention of Sterling weight or Sterling pound. The Sterling system was a method of cost pricing or a series of price schedules used, rather than devising an individual price cost. It is thought to be a carry over from England. Some potteries phased the system out and others probably closed still using it.

I don't claim to understand how the system was devised but have been able to determine that cost of the ware was not based on the usual supplies, labor, etc. Taylor-Smith and Taylor was still using the Sterling pound method of pricing when Anchor Hocking purchased Taylor-Smith and Taylor but ceased to use it shortly after the purchase.

It is the sterling pound method of pricing that kept dinnerware pricing around the same dollar figure and not the idea that the manufacturers put their heads together. It was and still is a highly competitive business.

SHAPE NAMES

Most of the potteries had names for their dinnerware and bakeware lines; some potteries did not. Some had names for some lines and not the others.

By the same token, some collectors will be willing to learn shape names and others will not feel the importance of knowing any more than their pattern name.

It is much like shopping for clothing. If you are shopping for a blouse or shirt, find the style you like but not in "your best color," you know to search the racks for the same style in another color. The pottery industry used this same "basic pattern" method to make that shape seem different. On the basic ivory body of the same shape, they may have added a red or gold line. They might have then decided to use a floral decoration, a Mexican motif, a colonial lady, or just about any kind of decoration imaginable. They may have decided to use colored glazes, either bright or pastel solids, whatever had caught the fancy of the little lady whose kitchen was the center of her universe.

ADVERTISING PIECES

Hall China Old Crow punch bowl with cups and ladle. This particular set was given by National Distillers to bar owners on the opening of their new establishments in the 1950's.

Advertising pieces of all kinds have long been popular with collectors. Ad pieces were given away by a variety of businesses over the years. Groceries, furniture stores, cleaners, service stations and the potteries themselves gave away ash trays, plates, children's pieces, mugs, and like items to their customers.

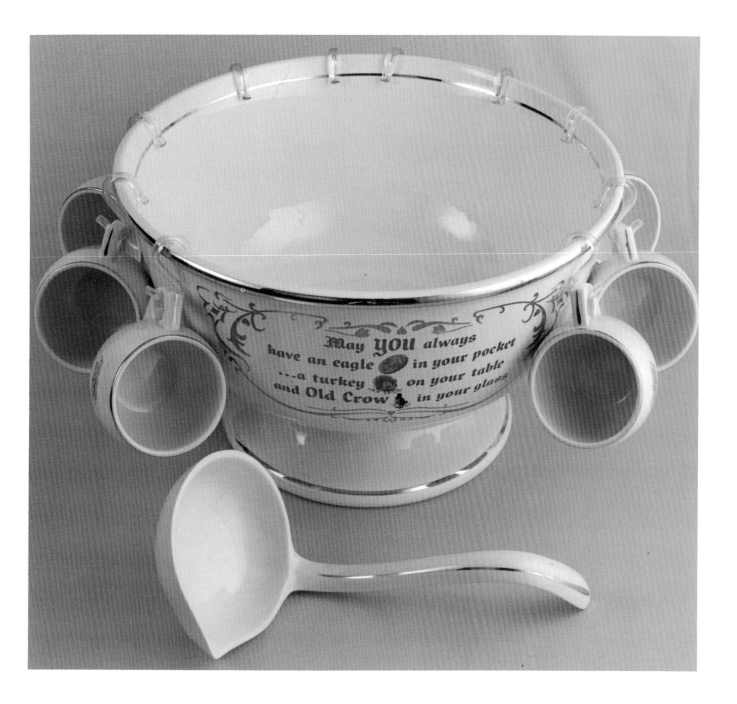

Row 1: O.E.S. & State souvenir cup, maker unknown, possibly made by the Harker Pottery. Toots Shor ash tray, made by Hall China. Lake Tower Inn ash tray, Royal China Company. Harkerware.

Row 2: Child's plate, maker unknown on back "Compliments Ash Furniture Co., East Ark's Largest." Child plate, maker unknown, on back, "We are glad you are here - Vance Furniture Company, Inc." Child's bowl, maker Continental Kilns on back, "Compliments of Leath's." Early Harker plate, "Pay Cash and Pay Less, Morris Bros." over early Harker semi-porcelain mark.

Row 3: Thompson plate, "compliments of Lacina's Bakery, 1943 South May Street." Hall China, Irish coffee mugs, Tri-State Pottery Festival and MacArthur Insurance, Sabin, deviled egg dish, "Retoff Package Liquors, Streator, Ill."

Row 4: Homer Laughlin Company, 1933, "Compliments of the New Bertschy Furniture Company . . ." Homer Laughlin blank overstamped by Sabin. "How about you doing the dishes tonight or how about buying me a Crosley automatic dishwasher," Harkerware Postmaster's Convention 1967.

My own personal favorite advertising piece is shown here. A Hall China #1273 Irish Coffee mug, white with black lettering and base commemorating the annual Glaze American Pottery Earthenware and China Show and Sale held each year in Springfield, Illinois, the fourth weekend in September.

Row 1: Harker zip code pencil holder, Harker 1920's creamer, grocery store, Taylor, Smith & Taylor's silhouette cup Hellick's coffee, early Harker plate grocery advertising on back, Steubenville "souvenir of KENJ."

Row 2: Harker covered refrigerator jug - Kelvinator, Harker stack set and rolling pin. The covered bowl is marked Sebring - may have been decorated by someone else.

Row 3: Hall China Sanka set; Laughlin Bell Savings and Loan Sit and Sip set includes mug and coaster.

Row 4: Crown Pottery plate, Harker Cherry pitcher and Crown plate - all grocery store give-a-ways. The name of the business may be found on the front of the pieces back or bottoms. I have a preference for these pieces with the business name placed where it can be seen.

I was somewhat surprised to learn that some of the mugs in the Sanka set were made in Japan. The Hall China Sanka mug has an ivory glaze, as compared to the white glaze on the "made in Japan." There are slight differences in color and placement of decals, slight differences in the handles and, of course, differences in the markings. The Hall China mug is marked, "made expressly for Sanka Brand Decaffeinated Coffee, furnished by Minners and Co., Inc., Hall China." The other mug is marked, "made expressly for Sanka® Brand De-Caffeinated Coffee, Made in Japan."

A variety of advertising ash trays made by The Harker Company, Chester, West Virginia.

Row 1: Reserved for a Wonderful Guy, King Cole, D FINE FOODS

Row 2: Be American, Harker China Company, Waterford Park

Row 3: Sunnyland's Fine Meats, Fontainebleau, Tennessee

Row 1: Yorktown shape plate, "Compliments of L. Miller Furniture and Stoves ..." Cakelifter, "W. C. Bunting, A Great Name in Pottery." "J. Horvath, city dressed meats and groceries ..." Maker unknown.

Row 2: Harker, "Friendly greetings, Sandner's, Mt. Olive, Ill., Dry Goods, Notions, Men's Clothing, 1930" - Jackson, Advertising Jackson China Company. Homer Laughlin - Century shape. Palestine Theatre, New York N.Y. The Limoges China Co. - on back, "Circulation success can be had with premiums more or less. Limoges China, when put to the test, gives better results than all the rest." Trenton Potteries Co.

Row 3: Crown Pottery, Best Wishes 1931, Syracuse China advertising ashtray, D. E. McNicol, East Liverpool, Ohio. Compliments of Mrs. J. D. Serfas.

AMERICAN CHINAWARE CORPORATION

An article appearing in *The Glass and Crockery Journal,* Vol. 107, 1929, lists the following companies as being part of the American Chinaware Corporation: *The Carrollton China Company,* Carrollton, Ohio; *Knowles, Taylor, Knowles,* East Liverpool, Ohio; *National China Company,* Salineville, Ohio; *Pope Gosser China Company,* Coshocton, Ohio; *Saxon China Company,* Sebring, Ohio; *E. H. Sebring China,* Sebring, Ohio; *Smith-Phillips,* East Liverpool, Ohio; and, *Strong Manufacturing Company* of Sebring. Strong manufacturing was an enamelware operation.

The Ohio Secretary of State could find no officers listed for the corporation. An article in a 1929 *Glass and Crockery Journal* announces the establishment of the American Chinaware Corporation "in Chicago under the supervision of Ray Cliff, formerly of Sebring." The new home offices and central location was to be the Terminal Tower Building in Cleveland, Ohio.

Also, from a 1929 *Crockery and Glass Journal,* another important announcement and that was the hiring of Joseph Thorley as designer and stylist for American Chinaware Corporation. Thorley came from a long line of Staffordshire "artists, sculptors and potters." His background before coming to America was impressive. Thorley had studied at the "College of Art, Stoke on Trent and at the Staffordshire College of Science." He was lecturer and teacher and served his ceramic apprenticeship at Josia Wedgèwood Pottery, coming to this country permanently in 1927. Securing such talent was quite a coup for the A. C. C. but even their well-laid plans and J. Thorley could not overcome the crash of 1929.

Information provided by the office of the Ohio Secretary of State shows that American Chinaware Corporation was formed November 23, 1928, and cancelled November 15, 1932. The principal location was listed as Beechwood Village, Ohio. No officers were listed either with the Secretary of State office or the Ohio Taxation Bureau.

Parent company of the American Chinaware Corporation was the Knowles, Taylor and Knowles. American Chinaware Corporation used the K. T. and K. plants in East Liverpool, Ohio, from 1929 to 1931.

1931 backstamp from a Pope-Gosser "Briar Rose" shape plate that also included American Chinaware Corporation backstamp.

BENNINGTON POTTERY

Bennington Potters was founded about 1949 in Bennington, Vermont, by David Gil. Mr. Gil is a graduate of Alfred University and considered to be a leader in the contemporary craft movement.

Bennington Potters is located on the site of the Norton Factory, founded in 1794. Early Bennington pieces are sought after by collectors.

Bennington Pottery made Honeycomb for The Block China Company in 1979. Oats, Brown Sugar, Blueberry, Block Bennington Honeycomb was also available in two deep tone colors, Blueberry and Brown Sugar.

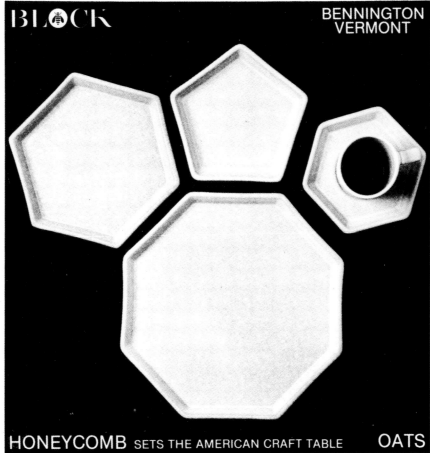

BLOCK BENNINGTON VERMONT

HONEYCOMB SETS THE AMERICAN CRAFT TABLE OATS

Block goes to Bennington for the trend in tableware: a handcraft look. Beehive shapes pressed in stoneware. Hand finished. Colors: Oats, Blueberry, Brown Sugar. $25 for 5-piece setting.

A recent Honeycomb sales brochure. Bennington Pottery made this shape for Block China Company.

The following two pages show a reproduction of the front and back sides of an eight page Bennington Pottery sales brochure, 1966-67.

bennington potters

1966-67   DESIGNS BY DAVID GIL AND YUSUKE AIDA

handcrafted dinnerware & artware

FAMOUS BENNINGTON DINNERWARE — Ovenproof and dishwasher safe. (From top, reading left to right)

D/1630 10 Cup Coffee Pot, 10¾" high $10.00	D/1628 Luncheon Plate, 8½" diameter $1.80	D/1634 Sugar Bowl, 4½" high $2.00
D/1639 Mug, 4¾" high, $1.50	D/1661 Bread & Butter, 6" diameter $1.00	D/1681 Tray, 5" x 9" $2.00
D/1682 Large Serving Platter, 16" x 9½" $12.00	D/1626 Cup, 2½" high $1.30	D/1683 Covered Butter, 8" x 3½" x 1½" high $4.00
D/1648 Serving Platter, 14" x 8½" $7.00	D/1627 Saucer, 6" diameter $.90	D/1667 Fruit Dish, 4½" diameter $1.40
D/1663 Large Bowl, 9" diameter, 3" high $6.00	D/1680 Gravy Boat ('. t stand), 9" x 5" $6.00	D/1641 Soup/Salad Bowl, 5½" diameter $1.70
D/1669 Buffet Plate, 10" diameter $2.50	D/1688 Ashtray, 4¼ iameter $1.50	D/1660 Salt & Pepper Set, 2½" high $2.50 pr.
D/1629 Dinner Plate, 9½" diameter $2.00	D/1635 Creamer, 3½' iigh $1.50	

All dinnerware is available in: MOUNTAIN BLUE, WHITE, VERMONT GREEN, RUST, TAWNY. (as illustrated by cups and saucers left to right) For information on sets, turn to Page 2.

BLAIR CERAMICS

Blair Ceramics, Incorporated, was founded in Ozark, Missouri, in 1946 by William Blair. Mr. Blair, an Ohioan, was a modernistic painter turned potter. He was a graduate of the Cleveland School of Art and furthered his art education in Europe. Mr. Blair returned to his native Ohio and eventually became involved with the Purinton Pottery Company.

Mr. Blair let his objections to the basic, round dinnerware shapes be known. He tried to influence some of the Ohio potteries to change the shape of their lines but was rejected.

Mr. Blair had visited the Ozarks earlier and liked the slower pace and, in 1945, moved to southern Missouri and spent the next year in preparations. The plant was opened in 1946 in Ozark, Missouri. A $15,000 kiln was shipped to the plant from West Virginia and during Blair's peak operational period the pottery employed up to 30 workers from the small town of Ozark.

Most Blair pieces are signed, and Blair dinnerware was shipped to all of the then 48 existing states, Hawaii, Cuba and Canada. Thirty-six hundred pieces were produced weekly during the peak period. Neiman-Marcus and Marshall-Field's were just two of the better known department stores seeking to stock Blair dinnerware.

Blair Ceramics closed in 1950's. Moulds for Blair's oven-proof dinnerware was purchased by a former Blair employee. The former employee tells us she has no future plans for the moulds.

Row 1: "Rick-Rack" bowl, Bamboo covered onion soup bowl, cup/saucer set, covered sugar.

Row 2: Bamboo 8″ square plate, coffee server (lid missing), creamer.

Row 3: Yellow Plaid divided serving plate.

Row 4: Bamboo square dinner plate, rectangular plate.

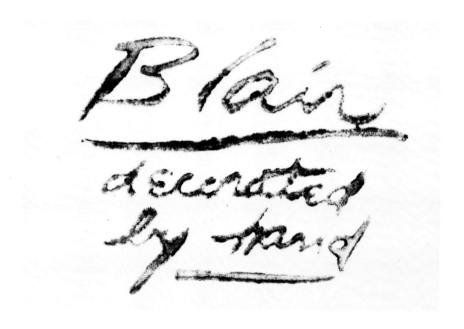

The most popular pattern Blair made, Gay Plaid or Plaid, was made continuously during Blair's brief operational period in Ozark, Missouri. Gay Plaid was nationally distributed to all parts of the United States. The twisted handles and leaf knobs are a unique feature of Blair ware.

Row 1: All Gay Plaid, cup/saucer, covered sugar, salt & pepper set, unusual closed handle cup/saucer set.

Row 2: Handled mug, creamer milk/utility pitcher, tumbler.

Row 3: Handled triangular bowl, water pitcher with ice lip, covered onion soup.

Row 4: Dinner plate, bowl, handled casserole.

A reprint of a 1948 advertisement featuring Blair's Autumn Leaf and Plaid dinnerware.

Row 1: Autumn Leaf nut dish, bowl, cup.

Row 2: Bird 6″ plate, unusual vinegar bottle needs stopper, salt and pepper, saucer does not have bird design.

Row 3: Bird celery dish, dinner plate.

Row 4: Divided vegetable, square plate.

"Bird" or "Primitive Bird", as it was sometimes called, came later on in Blair's Ozark career, with red base clay for the body, a scraffito bird made for an unusual combination. It is difficult to find "Bird" pieces that are not chipped. These pieces probably were not produced for any length of time and are truly the rarest of the Blair.

MAGAZINE   THURSDAY, MAY 26, 1949   ST. LOUIS POST-DISPATCH

Smart New Dishes From Ozark Country

Modernist Painter - Turned - Potter Creates Idea That Has Caught On Nationally.

MORE THAN 3600 PIECES OF DINNERWARE MOVE OUT OF THE BLAIR FACTORY AT OZARK, MO. EVERY WEEK.

MR. AND MRS. BILL BLAIR EXAMINE SOME OF THEIR HANDIWORK. BLAIR, FORMER PAINTER, STUDIED ART IN EUROPE.

By Ann Gray
A Special Correspondent of the Post-Dispatch

OZARK, Mo., May 26.

HERE in Ozark, a little hilltop town 50 miles north of the Arkansas border in the heart of the hill country, 39-year-old William H. Blair has created a set of dishes that may very well be making Mr. Wedgewood toss uneasily in his grave, but is charming American housewives who want something different in table settings as well as hats. Bill Blair is a modernist painter-turned-potter, a mild man with one prejudice: he considers the conventional circular plate, its bouquet rampant wreathed in mashed potatoes and gravy, not only an affront to the eye and the appetite but artistically old-fashioned as well. This gastronomical rebellion he has translated into a series of plates and platters planned like abstract

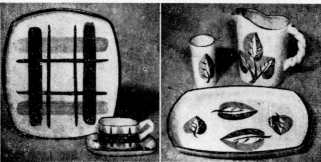

SHOWN ARE THE TWO PATTERNS TURNED OUT BY THE BLAIR FACTORY.

china mills. Blair perfected his designs and Higgins blueprinted the molds. By 1946 they had collected enough cash to kiss the Ohio kilns goodby.

★ ★ ★

SEVERAL years previously Blair had motored through the Ozarks, and had liked its rural quietude so well he had resolved to live there some day. In Ozark the two would-be potters found an empty motor car repair shop that was the right size and shape for what they had in mind. It took more than a year to make the place into a factory, including the installation of a $15,000 kiln shipped in from West Virginia. The factory is a small one, compared to the big fellows in Ohio, but the reputation of its dinnerware has grown all out of proportion to the scale of its operations. Thirty-two Ozark housewives and boys are employed in the mixing, molding, glazing, painting and kiln rooms. Blair works along with

Reprint from a 1949 *St. Louis Post Dispatch Magazine* section article.

BLOCK CHINA COMPANY

The Block China Company of New York is important to mention in that it is a distributor and not a manufacturer of dinnerware.

The Block Company was founded by J & I Block in the early 1930's and served as distributor for the Cameron Clay Products in Cameron, West Virginia. During the thirties, Block also bought from the Cronin China Company.

Jay L. Block of Block China Company graciously provided us with Block Company history. Mr. Block also provided us with brochures of both Bennington and Hall china that were made for and distributed by Block.

We also now know, through information provided by Mr. Block, that his father, founder of The Block China Company, distributed goods purchased from the Cronin China Company under the Pottery Guild name.

Pottery Guild pieces may be from a variety of makers. "Hostess Ware, handpainted in U. S. A.", will be found on some pieces. The Pottery Guild - Hostess Ware pieces were plentiful in the late thirties and early forties.

Liberty Hall American Ironstone was made by The Hall China Company for The Block China Company. Liberty Hall was made in Colonial White undecorated.

Martha's Vineyard - a green and grape color Vineleaf border decoration - solid green accessories.

Maine Village - shades of blue Early American rustic Village scene, solid blue accessories.

Mt. Vernon Honey & Brick Red tulip border decoration, solid honey colored accessories.

The following items were made in solid colors and Colonial White. Cup, 6½″ cereal soup, covered sugar, creamer, coffee pot, soup tureen - mid-1960's.

The UP-BEAT collection was made in the mid-1960's by The Hall China Company for The Block China Company. The Up-Beat collection was designed by Gerald Gulatta.

Toccata is described as "an explosion of fantasy flowers in the newest colors: ochre, orange, daffodil, ... with daffodil alone for accent."

Folk Song, "a lively, fresh theme, hand-painted look may be Scandinavian, Mediterranean and is American - Crafts ... blue on white, accent pieces in solid blue."

Impressions:

"Sings with color, blue and green that play a bold duet and vibrate together. The color newness, stressed with solid green."

Backstamps from Block China Company.

IMPRESSIONS, one of three patterns in new Up-Beat stackable stoneware dinnerware and coordinated glassware; offered in green and blue with green accessories. Retail: $25 for 45-piece set; in plain white, $20. Block China Company.

Reprint from a 1966 issue of China Glass Tablewares, used by permission.

LIBERTY HALL
AMERICAN IRONSTONE

LIBERTY HALL is authentic Ironstone, handmade in America by one of our oldest quality tableware factories, The Hall China Company.

The shape, decorations, and colors of LIBERTY HALL are Early Americana. Our Ironstone is dishwasher safe, ovenproof, and chip resistant to give you long years of carefree service.

		List Prices
1.	Dinner Plate 10¾"	$1.95
2.	Salad Plate 7½"	1.55
3.	Bread & Butter 6½"	1.15
4.	Tea Cup°	1.30
5.	Tea Saucer	.70
6.	Cereal Soup 6½"°	1.50
7.	Fruit Saucer 6"	1.00
8.	Luncheon Plate 8½"	1.65
9.	Rim Soup 9¼"	1.75
10.	Covered Sugar°	3.25
11.	Creamer°	2.50
12.	Coffee Pot°	5.50
13.	Round Baker 10¼"	3.00
14.	Platter 15½"	4.35
15.	Platter 17"	4.75
16.	Turkey Platter 19"	6.00
17.	Square Server 10½"	3.50
18.	Round Chop Plate 14"	5.00
19.	Soup Tureen°	7.50
20.	Sauceboat/Server	5.50

(°) Items are available in Colonial White or Solid Color Treatments Only.

LIBERTY HALL
AMERICAN IRONSTONE

COLONIAL WHITE—*Undecorated with a white traditional ironstone glaze.*

MARTHA'S VINEYARD—*Green and Grape color vineleaf border decoration, solid green accessories.*

MAINE VILLAGE—*Multi shades of blue, Early American rustic village scene, solid blue accessories.*

MT. VERNON—*Honey and Brick Red tulip border decoration, solid honey accessories.*

Martha's Vineyard • Maine Village • Mt. Vernon

Colonial White

Both sides of a Block China "fold top" card.

A step ahead of tomorrow—the Up-Beat Collection by Block. American — definitely: in mood, manner, material. Up-Beat is stoneware, made for Block by the Hall China Company.

Todays young swing shape: smooth, simple, uncluttered. Try stacking Up-Beat. Cup into saucer — solid, firm. Everything fits for easy storage, compact; a today word that's distinctly new in tableware. Designed by Gerald Gulotta. Young Americans have never seen a tableware more its own.

TOCCATA	FOLK SONG	IMPRESSIONS
An explosion of fantasy flowers in the newest colors: ochre, orange, daffodil, . . . with daffodil alone for accent.	A lively, fresh theme, hand-painted look may be Scandinavian, Mediterranean, and is American-crafts . . . Blue on white, accent pieces in solid blue.	Sings with color, blue and green that play a bold duet and vibrate together. The color newness stressed with solid green.

THE *UP-BEAT* COLLECTION

Front of a Block sales brochure.

Inside of a Block sales brochure.

CALIFORNIA POTTERIES

Collectors are just beginning to show an interest in California ware on a nationwide basis. The history of California potteries can be traced back to the Spanish fathers and the early missions. A whole volume or volumes will be needed to cover this vast subject, and we can only briefly touch on it in the space allotted here.

We will address ourselves to approximately 1927 when the use of talc in the body was introduced and this was also an approximate date for the introduction of color glazes on California ware. The natural abundance of some of the raw materials used in dinnerware account for the large number of manufacturers. In 1949 more than half of the dinnerware manufacturers were located in California.

California's "Big Five" were the *J. A. Bauer* plant established in 1909 in Los Angeles, California. Stoneware, flower containers and gardenlines were his mainstay until 1927 when he used color for kitchen bowls. Bauer's dinnerware line was added a few years later.

Gladding McBean & Company organized in 1875 as a sewer pipe manufacturer. Gladding McBean purchased Willis Prouty's formula for using talc as a basic ingredient. A ceramic engineer for Gladding McBean improved the Prouty formula and the process became known as "Malinite." They (Gladding McBean) began the pottery manufacturing phase in 1934. Frederic J. Grant was director. Their Franciscan ware was the first California ware to be marketed in eastern states. Their first dinnerware was El Patio.

Pacific Clay Products Company started making dinnerware in 1932. They, too, had formerly been sewer pipe manufacturers. Their art director was M. J. Lattie and they used very bright shades of reds, blues, greens and yellows and later added pastels.

Vernon Kilns began in 1916 when an Englishman named Paxon used European techniques. A fire destroyed the factory in December 1947, and the plant built to replace it was considered "the most modern ceramic plant in the world." G. Bennison became owner in 1931. Vernon Kilns is famous for their state plates popular with collectors.

Metlox Poppy Trail Manufacturing Company started making tableware, directed by President Willis Prouty (son of the Prouty credited with discovering the talc formula). Controlling interest was sold in 1946 and Metlox introduced its first popular line, California Ivy.

Catalina Pottery is credited with being the first California pottery to use color. Wm. Wrigley, Jr. built a small plant on Catalina Island and products were sold in a small shop on the pier. The company was purchased in 1937 by Gladding, McBean & Company. They continued to make the Catalina line until the war years.

Briefly, some other California names you may encounter are: American Ceramic Products Corporation made up of La Mirada and Winfield China. Winfield was marketed under "Gabriel" ware in 1949 and became so popular the La Mirada art ware line was dropped.

California Figurine Company founded by Max Weil (an important name in California ware). He purchased California Art Pottery line in 1945 and changed their name to Max Weil of California. A light new body was developed and Malay Bambu entered the dinnerware field in 1947.

Santa Anita Potteries began about 1939 and had a line of solid color as its first production items. It was purchased by National Silver Company.

Flintridge China Company, Pasadena, opened by Hogan and Mason in 1945.

M. C. Wentz started with $400 in mid-depression. Wentz later had a Westward Ho line manufactured by Wallace and designed by Till Goodan that was popular.

The pieces pictured are made by the Bauer plant. They are heavy, durable and fast becoming very collectible. Row 1 cup and saucer Ring pattern, tumbler Ring, 10″ dinner plate and mixing or utility bowl.

Row 1: Metlox Poppy Trail "Rooster" Sugar and Creamer, Vernon Kilns Organdie small plate and covered casserole.

Row 2: "Rooster" Metlox, "Winfield" Ash Tray, Dragon Flower 10″ dinner plate.

Row 3: Vernon Kilns coffee server, "Tam O'Shanter" two compartment bowl, "Homespun" Tumblers; Mrs. Nelson tells us there were six different color combinations, each with a different name.

Row 4: "Mayflower" by Vernon Kilns from 1940's to late 1950's. Mexican motif plate with backstamp in the shape of a mission bell. Vernon Kilns bowl.

Marks found on California Pottery.

Row 1: Unmarked and unidentified A.D. cup and saucer (looks like California ware), Vernon Kilns A.D. creamer and sugar, Vernon Kilns cup and saucer, creamer.

Row 2: Franciscan's Coronada pitcher, S. & P, covered sugar and covered coffee pot.

Row 3: Franciscan's Coronado gravy boat with attached liner. The plate, covered ¼ lb. butter, cannot positively be identified nor can the 2 pieces on the right - may be Metlox.

Row 4: Vernon Kilns brown (thirties) divided plate, cup and saucer, Franciscan water set.

Franciscan's swirl type pattern was called Coronada; Metlox's swirl is Yorkshire. (See Metlox reprint)

Fleur de Lis Vernon Kiln Plate.

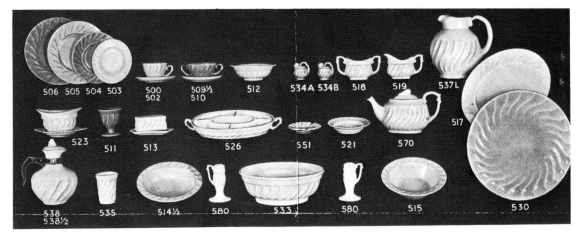

COLORS: Gloss Glazes, Vivid Colors: Delphinium Blue, Old Rose, Canary Yellow, Turquoise Blue, Poppy Orange and Rust.

Satin Glazes, Pastel Colors: Opaline Green, Powder Blue, Petal Pink, Pastel Yellow, Satin Turquoise, Peach and Satin Ivory.

YORKSHIRE

DINNERWARE ☆ BEVERAGEWARE ☆ KITCHENWARE

● Pintoria   COLORS: Gloss Glazes, Vivid Colors: Delphinium Blue, Old Rose, Canary Yellow, Turquoise Blue, Poppy Orange and Rust.

Poppytrail   POTTERY by METLOX   Poppytrail

Circa 1939 Metlox brochure

Catalina Plate

CANONSBURG POTTERY COMPANY

The Canonsburg Pottery was founded in 1900 by John George. John George was a nephew of W. S. George. The plant was first called Canonsburg China Company and they produced sanitary and hotel ware.

About 1909, the name was changed to Canonsburg Pottery Company and specialized in dinnerware, producing about 25,000 dozen pieces a week.

Steubenville's equipment and molds were sold to Canonsburg Pottery after Steubenville's closing in 1959. Adam Antique and Rose Point, two of Steubenville's popular patterns, were sold into the 1960's under the Steubenville name. A line called Partio was also sold in the 1960's under the Steubenville name, Canonsburg, Pennsylvania.

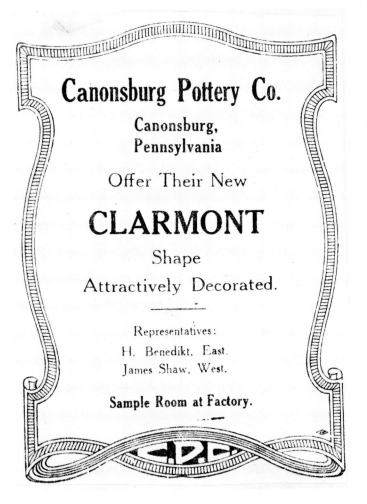

A very early cream pitcher with the Canonsburg China mark (also shown). The backstamp dates this piece to circa 1900-1909. A 1920's ad from the Canonsburg Pottery Company is also shown.

A Cannonsburg Pottery advertisemnt.

Canonsburg backstamps

CARIBE-STERLING CHINA COMPANY

The Puerto Rican government built a china facility in San Juan as part of their "operation Bootstrap," an economic development program. The facility was built for a group of investors headed by Mr. Earl Crane of the Iroquois China Company, Syracuse, New York, in about 1947-48. Earl Crane operated the facility until 1950 by which time he had exhausted the capital and the investment of the Puerto Rican government and shareholders. The shareholders began at this point to look for another "stateside manufacturer" to take over the operation.

It was at this point (fall of 1950) that the Sterling China Company of Wellsville, Ohio became involved. Sterling took an option, later exercised that option and began operating the facility in 1951. The plant had been designed as a hotelware operation. In the late 1950's Caribe made a casual dinnerware line. They used their regular hotelware body making for a superior product comparable only to Lenox's casual ware line.

Caribe made about 12 patterns in their casual dinnerware line, print transfer patterns, air brush, undecorated and line decorated ware. Advertising information of the day credits Caribe dinnerware as being designed by Carlos Montez. Carlos Montez was a made-up name for Ed Murphy who was the initiator of the Caribe dinnerware idea.

The Caribe line was not competitive and was phased out in about 1962-63. The plant was shut down in 1976 and liquidation nears completion.

The pieces that I have seen of Caribe are pleasing and of excellent quality, well worth a little extra search on the part of the collector.

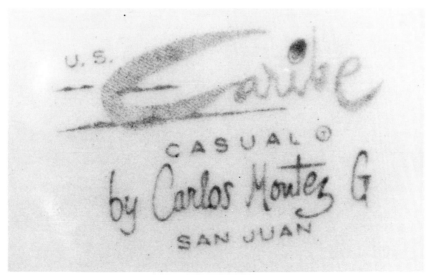

Backstamps from Caribe dinnerware.

The pattern name of this dinnerware is unknown but it is marked "Caribe Casual" by Carlos Montez G. San Juan." The dinnerware is from the collection of Allen Kleinbeck. The hotel ware coffee mug is marked only "Caribe".

Bonita

El Vuelo

CHILDREN'S PIECES

Juvenile decorated mugs, plates and other like pieces have long been a delight to search for and find. Whatever the reason for the attraction from bunny-shaped plates to mugs, "Jack and Jill" juvenile ware has always appealed to the collector. The American Pottery Industry contributed their share of play dishes and feeding sets with almost every major company producing such ware.

A variety of juvenile pieces from the collection of John Moses and B. A. Wellman.

Row 1: Edwin M. Knowles children's pieces, Elsie the Cow (may be Universal Cambridge) Hankscraft Bottlewarmer, maker unknown

Row 2: Harker Cameoware, Homer Laughlin plate made for International Silver.

Row 3: Marked "Excello" Mexican scene, Salem divided dish, Little Bo Peep.

Row 4: Pink Cameoware - Harker, Little Bo Peep, Hankscraft & Hankscraft clown maker unknown.

The Uncle Wiggily mug shown was "manufactured for The Wander Company, Chicago Makers of "Ovaltine." The copyright date was 1924 and sole maker was the Sebring Pottery Company.

THE CRONIN CHINA COMPANY

The forerunner of the Cronin China Company in Minerva, Ohio, was the Owen China Company built approximately in 1900. Dan Cronin moved his operation to Minerva and met an early death due to a riding accident. Surviving Cronin brothers managed the plant until it ceased operation in the fifties.

Mr. Dan Cronin and Mr. J. Block of Block China Company were friends. In the late thirties, Mr. Block founded the Pottery Guild and Cronin China Company supplied at least some of the pieces of Pottery Guild ware. The corporation for Pottery Guild was granted in 1938 and cancelled in 1946 in the State of New York.

Pottery Guild pieces are pictured under Pottery Guild. On some rare occasions a piece may be found with both the Cronin and Pottery Guild backstamps.

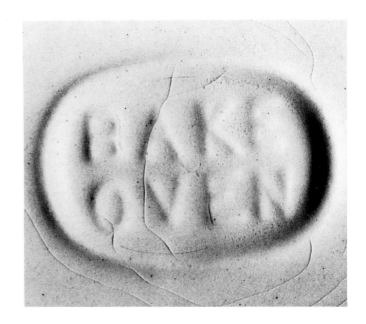

CROOKSVILLE CHINA COMPANY

A group of Crooksville, Ohio businessmen petitioned the Ohio Secretary of State for the purpose of granting a corporation for The Crooksville Art Pottery Company on January 9, 1902. S. H. Brown, W. H. Brown, W. J. Tague, A. P. Tague and Guy E. Crooks were the petitioners. Crooksville Art Pottery was formed to manufacture art ware "such as vases, flower pots and novelties."

The first stockholders' meeting was held on January 20, 1902, and the following offices were elected: President, J. L. Bennett; Vice-President, J. M. French; Secretary-Treasurer and General Manager was Guy E. Crooks. After reviewing the activities in East Liverpool the board decided to amend the articles of their incorporation and the name was changed to Crooksville China Company.

A plant site was found and the W. H. Showers Construction Company broke ground for the plant in March 1902.

William Tritt of Sebring, Ohio, was hired as General Superintendent and the first ware came out of the kiln in November of 1902. It was my pleasure to see one of those first pieces - a pitcher with one of the officer's name and date in gold. A personalized pitcher was made for each officer. By February 1903 the first ware was shipped by Pennsylvania Railroad. Mr. Tritt left Crooksville in 1910 when he moved to Niles, Ohio, to organize the Tritt China Company.

By 1923 business was such that more help was needed to oversee and Earl Crooks became Assistant Manager and S. L. Pitcock became Assistant Secretary and Treasurer. Harry Bennett was elected to become president following his father's death in approximately 1941. The final closing was 1959.

The "Yelo-Gren Cottage" outlet store for Crooksville China and the manufacturing plant.

The creamer and sugar with the "Country Home" scene are the only two pieces I have found. The "Fruits" blank was used with many different decals and I believe we can expect to find many more "Country Home" pieces.

A Crooksville backstamp.

This delicate pattern was well remembered by Crooksville workers as they nicknamed it "Spider." Many companies used a decal so similar to this one that in some instances the collector has to rely on shapes, backstamps and not the decal for identification. This Crooksville pattern was called other names by other stores and outlets. In this setting, everything but the creamer, sugar and gravy are on the La Grande shape. The sugar and creamer and gravy are on the Radisson shape. There are certainly many confusing factors in attempting to identify patterns and shapes of American dinnerware.

This pattern was listed in a 1940's wholesale catalogue as "Spring Blossom."

A Crooksville backstamp.

A letter from the Crooksville China Company to shareholders concerning final termination of the company, 1959.

ESTABLISHED 1902

THE CROOKSVILLE CHINA CO.

MAKERS OF

Dinner Ware

CROOKSVILLE, OHIO

NOTICE OF SHAREHOLDERS MEETING

Notice is hereby given that a meeting of the shareholders of The Crooksville China Company will be held at the office of the company on China Street, Crooksville, Ohio, on the 26th day of March, 1959, at 10:00 o'clock A.M., to consider and act upon the proposal for the final termination of the corporation, as set forth in the enclosed Memorandum.

By order of the Board of Directors.

Frank E. Bennett, Secretary

March 10, 1959

Waffle sets were very popular in the twenties and thirties. This 1929 Crooksville waffle set consists of six 8″ plates, one serving or utility plate, 11¼; one large covered jug for batter; one small covered jug for syrup, and six cup and saucer sets.

The shapes of the jugs are referred to by collectors as "duckbill." The jugs or pitchers set on the tray so, in some patterns are called batter sets.

Row 1: "Trellis" Iva-Glo plate 8″, utility tray 11¼″ handle to handle.

Row 2: "Trellis" covered batter pitcher 8″ tall with lid, syrup pitcher or jug 6″ with lid, "Trellis" cup saucer.

A Crooksville backstamp.

Row 1: 8 oz. tumbler, creamer, utility bowl 2 sizes and shapes both marked Pantry Bak-in.

Row 2: 8″ plate, glass tumbler, maker unknown, Pantry Bak-in 10″ pie baker.

Row 3: Handled serving tray 11-¾″, 10″ dinner plate.

Row 4: Platter 11½″, lid believed to fit flat spice jar, possibly part of kitchen, 6″ saucer.

$2.98

Sandwich and Bread Tray. Beautiful ivory colored china dish decorated with unique black silhouette figures. Handsome chromium plated frame in pierced and engraved design. Diameter 11¼ inches.
46 G 4337—We Pay Postage.........$2.98

$139 Candy or Relish Dish

Handsome pierced design chromium plated frame. Ivory colored China dish with black silhouette figures. Matches sandwich tray 46 G 4337. Diameter 6¾ inches. We Pay Postage. 46 G 4329 $1.39

1930-31 Wards sandwich and bread tray and candy dish in chrome plated frame.

Crooksville's Silhouette differs from Hall's and is easily recognized by the begging dog whose mouth appears to be watering. This appealing pattern is available in a wide variety of interesting pieces including tankards, pitchers, kitchen covered utility jars and covered refrigerator jars. Do not be surprised at any pieces you may find in "Silhouette". The pattern is from the early 1930's and was also used with a Farberware frame backstamped Provincial Ware. The decal was used in mid-1950's but the company that used the decal is unknown to me at this time.

A Crooksville backstamp.

Row 1: "Pheasant" on La Grande plate 9-¾″, mug with dog, "Hunting" on Iva-Lure plate 12″.

Row 2: Carnival on "Fruits" blank 9½″. "Little Bouquet" on La Grande, plate 9-¾″. Homestead in Winter on Iva-Lure chop plate 10″.

Row 1: Southern Belle on Coupe Shape 6-¾″ plate, Avenue saucer and covered sugar on pink coupe shape both early 1950's. Apple Blossom pattern on La Grande shape, Apple Blossom on Iva-Lure shape 6″ plate also 1950's (?)

Row 2: Apple Blossom pie baker 10″ marked Pantry-Bak-in, Apple Blossom 2-handled bean pot, Apple Blossom covered casserole 8″ Pantry Bak-In.

Row 3: "Rose Garland" utility bowl 3″ tall, "Rose Garland" vegetable dish 8″, "Rose Garland" gravy boat and liner. 1920's.

Row 4: "Medallion" saucer, "Border Rose" covered vegetable bowl and "Border Rose" platter 11½″. 1920's.

Row 1: "Posies" La Grande cup and saucer and utility bowl, "Oriental" "Gold Drape" creamer.

Row 2: California James Poppy on La Grande plate, Pantry-Bak-In covered casserole 8″ and plate 10″, (shape not known).

Row 3: "Blue Blossoms" bean pot, Apple Blossom coffee dripper both Pantry Bak-In line.

Row 4: "Blossoms" on "Fruits" blank plate 6-¾, "Roses" on "Birds" blank bowl 8-¾", "Kaleidoscope" on "Birds" blank soup bowl 8″.

PANTRY BAK-IN WARE

Rose tinted semi-porcelain, with pink, yellow and green floral design, and platinum edges.

3 Covered Refrigerator or utility Jars. Diameter 3⅞, 4⅞, 5⅞ in. Ship. wt. 5 lbs.

50 F 4940—
6-Pc. set **$1.59**

1½ Qt. Covered Casserole with 9½-inch Tray. Use tray when serving. Ship. wt. 8 lbs.

50 F 4942—
3-Pc. set **$1.25**

50 F 4943—
Same as 50 F-4942 but without tray. Ship. wt. 7 lbs. **98c**

10-In. Pie Plate
Ship. wt. 4 lbs.
50 F 4945. . 73c

A 1930's catalog reprint showing how Pantry Bak-in ware was originally sold.

Black Tulip hand-painted black on pink, designed by Arden Richards and made by The Crooksville China Company. Circa 1950's.

Crooksville workers tell me this was simply called "House." It may have been referred to at times as Cottage. Since it is a petit point pattern, "Petit Point House" seems to be a pleasing compromise. We picture it here to show the variety of shapes on which it was used. I believe the large 12-¾″ plate, the 9″ plate and server are part of a cake set.

Row 1: Petit Point (shape not known) casserole 7″, Petit Point plate 7¼″ La Grande with red lining, pie server.

Row 2: "Petit Point House" coupe plate "Pantry Bak-In," "Petit Point House" "Fruits" blank 9-¾″. "Petit Point House", plate 9-¾″, red outside trim and red inner lining.

Row 3: "Petit Point House" serving plate, coupe shape 12-¾″.

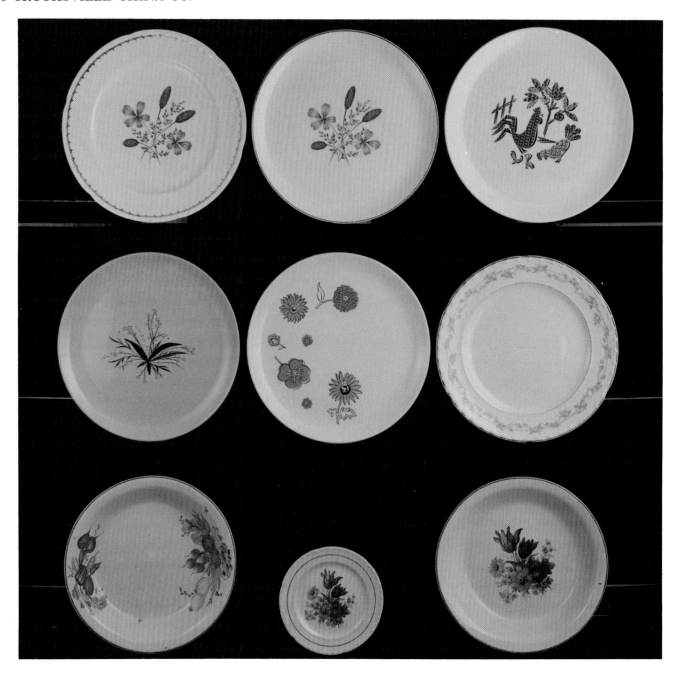

Row 1: Avenue on La Grande, dinner plate 10-¾, Avenue on Coupe shape dinner plate 10-¾, Calico Chick, coupe, dinner plate 10-¾.

Row 2: "Spray" on pink coupe, dinner plate 10-¾", Flower Fair, coupe, dinner plate 9", "Pink Border" on La Grande dinner plate.

Row 3: "Veggies" Pantry Bak-In pie baker 10", "Rust Bouquet" on La Grande, plate 9", "Rust Bouquet" pie baker 10".

Row 1: Flamingo or Hibiscus on Gray Lure plate, creamer, sugar, "Calico Flowers" creamer, sugar (lid missing) on Dartmouth shape.

Row 2: Trotter, coupe, dinner plate 10¼", Trotter cup and saucer, Scotch Plaid, coupe dinner plate 10¼".

Row 3: Trotter and Scotch Plaid, coupe shape plates.

Row 4: Willow coupe saucer, "Blossom Time" coupe plate 6", "Rose Garden" on Gray Lure, "Jessie" all 6" plates.

Row 1: Southern Belle on Iva Lure plate 7-¾, covered sugar, cup and saucer.

Row 2: Southern Bell on Iva Lure dinner plate 10″, Delmar Dianna coupe shape.

Row 3: Brilliance on coupe shape dinner plate 10¼″, Queen Rose or Dinner Rose, coupe, plate 9″, "Border Bouquet" La Grande.

Row 4: Ivy Vine, Swirl, Meadow Flowers, dinner plates 10¼ on Coupe shape.

CROWN POTTERY COMPANY

Crown Pottery had its beginning as early as 1882 when it was established by A. M. Beck. In 1884 it was taken over by Bennighof and Uhl. The 1892 Evansville, Indiana, City Directory mentions the incorporation of Crown Pottery in November of 1891 with H. V. Bennighof, President, Charles Uhl, Secretary, and S. P. Gillatt, Treasurer.

Other sources list the Flentke family as founding Crown in 1902 after an unsuccessful venture in Peoria, Illinois, but in our research we have been unable to connect the Flentke family as founders of The Crown Pottery. John Wendt took over the management of Crown in the early days and retired in 1952. Management was taken over at that time by a Mr. Lundquest who unsuccessfully attempted to halt the downward trend in business at Crown.

The pottery merged in the 1950's with Peerless Pottery, a maker of sanitary fixtures, and was finally closed in 1954.

A former Crown employee tells that to her knowledge there were no printed catalogues describing Crown. Sales were made by samples of ware carried by the salesmen. Crown made a semi-porcelain under glaze dinnerware with gold or platinum trims put on by hand. Patterns were not named but were known by numbers. New patterns came out each January and June.

Some of Crown's shape names were Jewel, Princess, Royal, Sovereign (see reprint) Majestic, Countess and Regent. All in keeping with the name "Crown." The ovenware line consisted of pie bakers, bowls, syrup pitchers and salt and pepper shakers.

The Princess shape was made mostly in plain white and fancy salad bowls, cake plates and servers, tea pots, salad plates, and juvenile items.

Crown also came out with a line of colored dinnerware in green, blue, tangerine, and brown. Coronada is the name of Crown's colored ware line made to compete with the Fiesta ware that was popular in the 1940's.

A Crown backstamp.

CROWN POTTERIES CO., EVANSVILLE, IND.

Crown's trademark.

FIRST QUALITY AMERICAN DINNERWARE

We use the finest imported clay in the manufacture of our dinnerware, giving it the remarkable high grade finish and glaze of highest quality China. Guaranteed not to craze. All decorations are carefully executed and thoroughly baked, assuring fine rich colorings. All pieces are first selection, no imperfect pieces in our stock. All of this Beautiful Dinnerware is manufactured in one of the largest representative potteries in the United States and is fully guaranteed.

42-PIECE COMPOSITION CONTAINS

6 Cups;
6 Saucers;
6 Fruits 5";
6 Bread and Butter Plates 6";
6 Dinner Plates 9";
6 Soup Plates 8";
1 Oval Open Vegetable Dish 9";
1 Round Open Vegetable Dish 9";
1 Platter 11";
1 Covered Sugar (2-pc.);
1 Creamer.

35-PIECE COMPOSITION CONTAINS

6 Cups;
6 Saucers;
6 Bread and Butter Plates 6";
6 Fruits 5";
6 Dinner Plates 9";
1 Round Open Vegetable Dish 9";
1 Platter 11";
1 Covered Sugar (2-pc.);
1 Creamer.

32-PIECE COMPOSITION CONTAINS

6 Cups;
6 Saucers;
6 Fruits 5";
6 Bread and Butter Plates 6";
6 Dinner Plates 9";
1 Round Open Vegetable Dish 9";
1 Platter 11".

COLORFUL INEXPENSIVE

THESE ARE IDEAL BREAKFAST AND LUNCHEON SETS

(A)   **NAVAJO PATTERN No. A6A/6157**

A colorful, gay Mexican design in a strictly modern trend. A shelf, draped with a Mexican shawl and holding a collection of Mexican pottery, fruit and flowers, all in vivid colors, forms the main decorative scheme. Each piece is finished with a bright red band on the rim. Each handle is traced to match. The Sovereign shape is used and this set is available in the 32, 35 and 42-Piece compositions listed above.

No. A6A/6157-32   32-Piece Set .... $ 8.30
No. A6A/6157-35   35-Piece Set 10.15
No. A6A/6157-42   42-Piece Set 12.70

(B)   **CROYDON PATTERN No. A6A/9327**

This splendid pattern is offered in the Sovereign shape, see illustration across top of page. The body of this ware is of imported clay and the set is decorated in a semi-border effect. The black trellis work is entwined with small red, pink and blue flowers and green foliage. Each piece is finished with gold line and all handles are traced in gold. A lovely set for breakfast or luncheon table use.

No. A6A/9327-32   32-Piece Set .... $ 8.80
No. A6A/9327-35   35-Piece Set 10.70
No. A6A/9327-42   42-Piece Set 13.45

(C)   **SWEDISH PATTERN No. A6A/7447**

Colorful set with Swedish Modern type decoration. Flowers are in lavender, blue, yellow and salmon colors, in modern effect. All pieces are finished with wide pastel harmonizing color band in choice of blue, pink or green colors and have fine matching line, specify. Made of imported clay on the Sovereign shape as illustrated across top of page.

No. A6A/7447-32   32-Piece Set .... $ 8.80
No. A6A/7447-35   35-Piece Set 10.70
No. A6A/7447-42   42-Piece Set 13.45

(D)   **BLUE BIRD PATTERN No. A6A/6007**

The decoration used on this pattern is called the good luck pattern. Consists of blue birds perched on a branch of delicate pink apple blossoms and natural green leaves. Each piece is finished with a harmonizing turquoise blue line. This set is made in the Sovereign shape as illustrated across the top of this page and the body is of imported clay, guaranteed against crazing. Our prices are most interesting.

No. A6A/6007-32   32-Piece Set .... $ 8.30
No. A6A/6007-35   35-Piece Set 10.15
No. A6A/6007-42   42-Piece Set 12.70

(E)   **WILD ROSE PATTERN No. A6A/4725**

Here is an elaborate yet inexpensive pattern that will do wonders for the breakfast or luncheon table. The attractive decoration consists of a cluster of Wild Roses and sheaths of Wheat joined at the base with a bunch of blue wild flowers. The shape is the ever popular Sovereign shape as illustrated across the top of this page and the body of this ware is made from imported clay. Truly a most interesting pattern.

No. A6A/4725-32   32-Piece Set .... $ 7.40
No. A6A/4725-35   35-Piece Set 9.00
No. A6A/4725-42   42-Piece Set 11.30

(F)   **PETIT POINT PATTERN No. A6A/9617**

A striking pattern of the sampler or cross stitch type. Center decoration is a bouquet of pink and yellow roses and foliage with an effect worked into it which gives the appearance of very fine needle work. Each piece is trimmed with a lace effect done in gold. Imported clay is used in fashioning the body of this set which is made in the handsome Sovereign shape illustrated across top of this page. Is unique and colorful.

No. A6A/9617-32   32-Piece Set .... $ 8.30
No. A6A/9617-35   35-Piece Set 10.15
No. A6A/9617-42   42-Piece Set 12.70

A reprint from a 1941 catalog.

Row 1: "Croyden" saucer, gravy boat, saucer.

Row 2: Monarch shape 9″ plate, cup and saucer, serving platter.

Row 3: Monarch shape serving bowl, cereal bowl, 6″ plate.

Row 4: "Autumn Leaf" covered jug, "Carriage" vegetable bowl.

A Crown Backstamp.

Row 1: Quena shape 6″ plate, Sovereign 6″ plate, Monarch 6″ plate, Monarch 6″ plate.

Row 2: Quena shape creamer, Oven Ware "Windmill" salt and pepper, "Windmill" pie baker 10″.

Row 3: Monarch 9″ plate, "Poppy" 9″ plate, Oven Ware "Bouquet" pie baker 10″.

Row 4: Quena shape 10″ plate, Oven Ware 9″ pie baker, Sovereign shape 9″ plate.

A Crown Pottery backstamp.

Charming First Quality American Dinnerware

We use the finest imported clay in the manufacture of our dinnerware, giving it the remarkable high grade finish and glaze of highest quality China. Guaranteed not to craze. All decorations are carefully executed and thoroughly baked, assuring fine rich colorings. All pieces are first selection, no imperfect pieces in our stock. All of this Beautiful Dinnerware is manufactured in one of the largest representative potteries in the United States and is fully guaranteed.

PRICES QUOTED ARE FOR 42, 54 AND 95-PIECE DINNER SETS
(Service for 6, 8 and 12 Persons)

42-PIECE COMPOSITION CONTAINS

6 Cups	6 Bread and Butter	1 Oval Open	1 Creamer		
6 Saucers	Plates 6"	Vegetable Dish 9"	1 Covered Sugar (2-pc.)		
6 Fruits 5"	6 Dinner Plates 9"	1 Round Open	1 Platter 11"		
	6 Soup Plates 8"	Vegetable Dish 9"			

54-PIECE COMPOSITION CONTAINS

8 Cups	8 Bread and Butter	1 Oval Open	1 Creamer
8 Saucers	Plates 6"	Vegetable Dish 9"	1 Covered Sugar (2-pc.)
8 Fruits 5"	8 Dinner Plates 9"	1 Round Open	1 Platter 13"
	8 Soup Plates 8"	Vegetable Dish 9"	

95-PIECE COMPOSITION CONTAINS

12 Cups	12 Fruits 5"	12 Pie Plates 7"	1 Oval Open	1 Round Open	1 Covered Vegetable
12 Saucers	12 Bread and Butter	12 Dinner Plates 9"	Vegetable Dish 9"	Vegetable Dish 9"	Dish (2-pc.)
	Plates 6"	12 Soup Plates 8"			1 Gravy Boat

1 Creamer	1 Platter 11"
1 Covered Sugar (2-pc.)	1 Platter 15"
1 Pickle Dish	

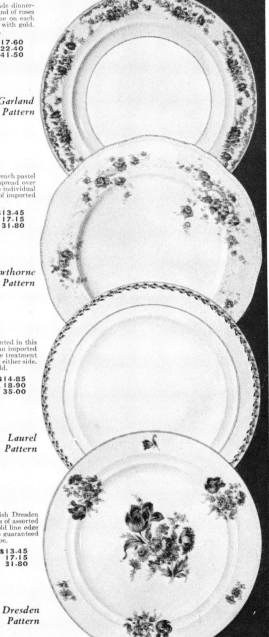

GARLAND PATTERN No. A6A/7277

You can set a very charming table with this lovely American made dinnerware for it is colorful and attractive. The design is a dainty garland of roses in natural colors done over a rich wide Ivory band with gold line on each edge of band. Edges and handles of all pieces are deftly treated with gold. Made on our popular Monarch shape with body of imported clay.

No. A6A/7277-42	42-Piece Set	$17.60
No. A6A/7277-54	54-Piece Set	22.40
No. A6A/7277-95	95-Piece Set	41.50

Garland Pattern

HAWTHORNE PATTERN No. A6A/8517

In this exquisite American made set of dinnerware we present a French pastel design of pink and blue hawthorne flowers which are profusely spread over the face of each piece. Of particular interest is the contour of the individual pieces which are made on our celebrated Qena shape with body of imported clay. Edges and handles of all pieces are cleverly traced in gold.

No. A6A/8517-42	42-Piece Set	$13.45
No. A6A/8517-54	54-Piece Set	17.15
No. A6A/8517-95	95-Piece Set	31.80

Hawthorne Pattern

LAUREL PATTERN No. A6A/9177

A most attractive combination of Black and Gold colors is presented in this handsome set of American dinnerware which is fashioned with an imported clay body on our smart Monarch shape. The effective decorative treatment consists of a laurel wreath design done in black with a gold line on either side. Edges and handles of all pieces are skillfully traced in bright gold.

No. A6A/9177-42	42-Piece Set	$14.85
No. A6A/9177-54	54-Piece Set	18.90
No. A6A/9177-95	95-Piece Set	35.00

Laurel Pattern

DRESDEN PATTERN No. A6A/8817

This lovely set of American dinnerware has a beautiful English Dresden type of decoration with all pieces elaborately covered with sprays of assorted flowers in their natural colors. Each piece is finished with a gold line edge and gold traced handles. Body is made of imported clay and is guaranteed against crazing. This ware is made on our popular Monarch shape.

No. A6A/8817-42	42-Piece Set	$13.45
No. A6A/8817-54	54-Piece Set	17.15
No. A6A/8817-95	95-Piece Set	31.80

Dresden Pattern

1941 Fort Dearborn catalog. Monarch and Quena shapes by Crown.

CUNNINGHAM AND PICKETT

The first listing in the Alliance, Ohio, city directory was for James A. Pickett residence in 1940. In 1941, Cunningham and Pickett was listed on Prospect Street with N. A. Cunningham. By 1961, Cunningham and Pickett was in a multiple warehouse on Main Street in Alliance. They either went out of business in the 1960's or moved, as there is no further listing. Cunningham and Pickett was not a manufacturer but a distributor or jobber for many items.

You will find many dinnerware pieces marked Cunningham and Pickett.

Cunningham and Pickett backstamps.

FRANKOMA

Frankoma was founded by John Frank. Frank came to Oklahoma from Chicago in 1927. In 1933 he started a "studio" pottery in Norman, Oklahoma, and equipped it with one small kiln, a butter churn for mixing clay, a fruit jar for grinding glazes, and a few other crude tools. He continued teaching until enough ware was produced to prove that a product could be made of Oklahoma clays that was a contribution to art and ceramics and still salable.

He resigned his teaching position in 1936 and he and Grace Lee, his wife, set out on their new venture. Oklahoma clays were used and by 1938 the "studio" was moved to Sapulpa where it is still located.

Frankoma is manufactured by a once-fired process - clay body and colored glaze are fused and fired at the maturing point of the clay and tempered as it slowly cools.

Wagonwheel is one of Frankoma's most popular lines over the years.

Frankoma backstamp.

WAGON WHEELS
Pattern

AVAILABLE IN: Desert Gold and Prairie Green.

A reprint of a Frankoma ad.

FRENCH SAXON CHINA COMPANY

During the early part of the Depression, W. V. Oliver liquidated his assets and put the money into several different banks, most of which had failed. His entire available assets amounted to $1200 and faith in his abilities. It was at this point in his life he decided to buy Saxon, one of the Sebring potteries that was in the hands of the bank. Oliver took a thousand of the $1200 to board members, and they accepted his offer. Now, Mr. Oliver had $200 left and needed to get the pottery operational. He went back to the banks where he had lost his money (some had reopened) and borrowed money.

The French-Saxon Company was opened. Vern Oliver was accustomed to "different beginnings." He had attended school only six months, left home at the age of ten. His first job was delivering newspapers, then he went to work in a pottery. He became sales manager of Sebring Manufacturing Company composed of the French China Company, the Saxon China Company and Sebring Manufacturing Company. It was the Saxon plant that Oliver bought in 1934. With the help of Duncan Curtis, who handled French-Saxon's ware exclusively, the pottery was soon underway.

Vern Oliver passed away in 1963.

An article in the 1964 April issue of *China, Glass and Tablewares* reports that Royal China purchased the French-Saxon Company of Sebring, Ohio. At that time (1964) Royalon, Inc. had manufacturing facilities in Sebring, East Palestine, Ohio, and Logansport, Indiana.

The French Saxon shape shown is their Zephyr shape colored glaze dinnerware line popular in the mid-1930's. A wide assortment of decals was added on an ivory body in the late 1930's to the "already popular Zephyr shape" by French Saxon. Poppy, Petit Point and other decorations are found on Zephyr shape. The pieces shown are from the collection of BA Wellman. Mr. Wellman tells us that, when French Saxon added colors to this line, the name was changed to Rancho.

Backstamps from the French Saxon China Company.

Row 1: Rancho maroon 10″ dinner plate, chartreuse 9″ luncheon plate, dessert plate 7″ dark green.

Row 2: Rancho 5½″ bowl, creamer, matching tumbler by Federal 12 oz., cup/saucer, bowl 6½″.

Row 3: Granada Tangerine plate 9″, cup and saucer, green creamer, shaker, green covered sugar.

Catalog advertisement for Granada.

W. S. GEORGE COMPANY

W. S. George was hired by the Sebring brothers to run the Ohio China Company in East Palestine, Ohio, in the mid-1890's. The Sebrings had been given $25,000 by the East Palestine townspeople plus free land to put up the Ohio building.

W. S. George managed to purchase the East Palestine Pottery Company in East Palestine by 1904. Soon after he is said to have suffered health problems. He later recovered and built a plant at Canonsburg and Kittanig, Pennsylvania, and a second plant in East Palestine that was known as the W. S. George #4 Plant.

Mr. George hoped to leave each one of his sons a pottery but only one son was interested in the pottery business. Some pieces will be marked Cavitt-Shaw Division of W. S. George. It is believed that Cavitt and Shaw were both family names. Cavitt-Shaw did not prove to be successful.

One of W. S. George's most popular patterns with collectors is Shortcake (see reprint) on the Ranchero shape.

Mr. Paul Merwin, retired newspaperman from East Palestine, has been very helpful with East Palestine's early history and shares the following early remembrances of W. S. George. We quote from a letter from Mr. Paul Merwin, dated December 19, 1979, and reprinted with written permission.

"Mr. George was a colorful personality, a boxer, a super salesman and also a humanitarian. When business was slow, he would get on the train and sell. He always insisted his workers had a good Christmas pay — he would tell his foremen, make the ware, stockpile it if need be, I will sell it myself if necessary. At a meeting of officials of the United Presbyterian Church, held at Westminster College in New Wilmington, Pennsylvania, in the 1920's, the need for $125,000 was voiced by the missionary leaders to erect a hospital in Ethiopia. Mr. George rose to his feet and told the group, 'I'll take care of that item myself, let us proceed to the next order of business.' As a youngster, I recall him riding past our home in a silver-colored Pierce-Arrow, complete with chaffeur. He always sat in the back, behind a plate glass partition. He knew most of his employees by first name, would walk through the plants frequently, perhaps stopping at work benches to show an apprentice the 'right way to do things.'"

The W. S. George plant went out of business in the late 1950's. The Royal China operation used the W. S. George facility for a time for additional production.

Row 1: "Blossoms" Lido sugar with cover, shaker and creamer, shaker Lido Dalyrymple or Blushing Rose.

Row 2: "Blossoms" on Lido dinner plate 10″, cup and saucer, flat soup 8″.

Row 3: "Mexi-Lido," "Mexi-Gren" vegetable bowl and saucer, Shortcake shakers, coffee-server.

Row 4: "Plain-Jane" Lido 10″ dinner, "Bouquet" 10″ dinner, "Flower Rim" Lido 10″ dinner.

Shortcake decal was also used in 1952 on W. S. George Times Square shape.

W. S. George trademark.

The shapes or official pattern name of the W. S. George pieces shown are unknown to me at this time. The "Petalware" plates are similar to W. S. George's Elmhurst shape introduced in 1939.

Elmhurst was introduced in 1939 in six pastel shades of blue, pink, yellow, Apple green, Maple sugar and turquoise. Elmhurst shape had been previously introduced in 1937 but not in pastel glazes. In a 1937 trade publication, Elmhurst was described as having a "thinner body, delightfully modern and having a shape that harmonizes with new decal decorations."

W. S. George used the same shape shaker with several different shapes of patterns.

"Sailing" on Georgette shape.

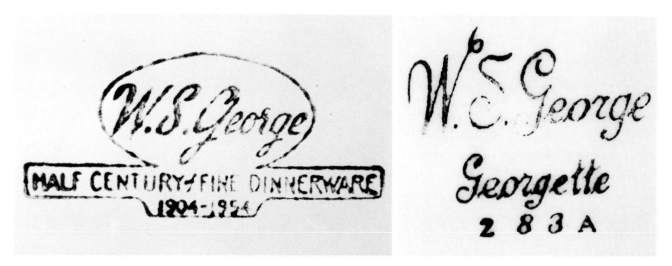

W. S. George backstamps.

"PETALWARE" AND RAINBOW

Row 1: "Petalware" maroon plate 9″, Ivory bowl 5½″, Petalware dark green plate 9″.

Row 2: "Petalware" pink plate 7½″, covered pink sugar, cup light blue, saucer light green.

Row 3: All Rainbow saucer yellow, green cup, egg cup blue, bowl 5″, bowl 5½″ pink.

Circa late 1930's.

Row 1: Peach Blossom on Lido plate 8″, (may be Smart Flowers), Lido plate 8″.

Row 2: Breakfast Nook, Rainbow plate 9″, "Poppy", Rainbow shape, platter 11½″, "Petit Point Rose" Fleurette shape, dinner 10″.

Row 3: All "Rainbow" on Rainbow shape; green plate 8″, blue bowl 4½″, pumpkin plate 8″.

Row 4: "Bird" Derwood shape plate 9″, Bluebird, Derwood shape 6″, "Roses" gravy boat attached liner, soup bowl 8″, Bolero Shape.

Breakfast Nook on the Lido shape was introduced in late 1931 or early 1932. It was advertised in the trade papers as being "delicate and feminine", done in an antique "yelo-tinge" glaze.

By March of 1932, Breakfast Nook was being promoted by a large Chicago department store as "Springtime" and a special sales promotion was used via direct mail and newspaper advertising. An entire window of the store on Chicago's State Street was devoted to a "Springtime" display.

This happened frequently in the matter of dinnerware names. Workers called a pattern one thing, the management another, and so on down the line. It is also the reason that each pattern shown in this book will have a name so that collectors will have a means of communication about this ware.

We did not have an example of Breakfast Nook on the Lido shape but on Row 2, number 1, the Breakfast Nook decal is used on W. S. George's Rainbow shape.

W. S. George Backstamp.

W. S. George Backstamp.

"Springtime"

It is in the air—it seems to be blowing into the cheerful open window of this lovely pattern. Here is a 32-piece service for six in a new shape. The base color is soft mellow ivory with silver edge—the design in natural colors, delicate and refined.

6 luncheon plates   6 fruit dishes
6 bread and butter plates   1 platter
6 tea cups and 6 saucers   1 baker

Unusual value   C 907 $5.95 postpaid

Daniel Low & Company

204 Essex Street, Salem, Mass.

Send for our complete catalog

A 1940's magazine ad for W. S. George.

.. popular priced

SEARS 5-POINT DINNERWARE

Guarantee

1. We Guarantee Perfect Quality! Dinnerware is selected four times...in clay...after first firing...after glaze firing...after firing of decoration.

2. We Guarantee Replacement of any piece broken in delivery! Packed, like eggs, in a special carton, your set will arrive safe and sound.

3. We Guarantee Savings up to 40% over others' prices for dinnerware of equal quality and decoration.

4. We Guarantee Open Stock! You can add and replace in every pattern as long as it is made!

5. We Guarantee Satisfaction! Sears dinnerware meets every claim...or your money will be refunded.

NEVILLE

SHORTCAKE

GASCON

BEST... 32-piece Set
Your Choice $5⁶⁹

Artistic and costlier shapes. Note the graceful holloware pieces. Border and spray patterns combining the more expensive colors. Appropriate for either informal snacks or for formal entertaining.

Neville
Simple, narrow border is the keynote of elegance and dignity. Tiny pink rosebuds and Gold lines accent the tan, green and black border. Ivory color glaze over finest quality American semi-porcelain; four times selected.
35 L 04449—32-piece set, 53-piece set, or Sugar and Creamer set.
35 LM 4449—95-pc. set.

Shortcake
Vivid with the beauty of luscious red strawberries and green leaves. Smart modern shape, with honey color glaze, red line trim. First quality American semi-porcelain. Four times selected. See matching pieces below.
35 L 04422—32-piece set, 53-piece set, or Sugar and Creamer set.
35 LM 4422—95-pc. set.

Gascon
Picture your table set with the brilliant blue flowers and gray leaves of Gascon. Modern ridged shape—off-white glaze. Finest quality American semi-porcelain. All sets have 9-in. plates; 95-pc. set has 11 and 13-in. platters.
35 L 04423—32-piece set, 53-piece set, or Sugar and Creamer set.
35 LM 4423—95-pc. set.

All sets available as listed below. State catalog number and size of set

32-piece set. Service for six.	Shipping weight, 20 pounds. Mailable.......	$5.69
Sugar and Creamer set.	Shipping weight, 3 pounds...............	1.43
53-piece set. Service for eight.	Shipping weight, 35 pounds. Mailable......	10.95
95-piece set. Service for twelve.	Shipping weight, 67 pounds. Not mailable...	20.95

Shortcake matching extra pieces
35 L 04422—State piece. Match your Shortcake dinnerware.

8-cup Coffee Pot. Shipping weight, 2 pounds........................	$1.29
Salt and Pepper Shaker. Shipping weight, 1 pound. Pair...........	49c
10-inch Salad Bowl (not illustrated). Shipping weight, 2 pounds...........	75c

What "four times selected" means for you:
1. Selected in clay—to insure perfect shape and flawless surfaces.
2. Selected after first firing—for perfect unblemished pieces.
3. Selected after glaze firing—for smooth, even craze-proof finish.
4. Selected after decoration firing for perfection of pattern and color uniformity.

12-piece Bargain Set $1³⁹
Regular Price $2.10

Cat-Tail Cups and Saucers
Look at this saving. You pay 71c less than the open stock prices at right for this set of six tea cups and tea saucers in the popular Cat-Tail pattern. Finest quality oven and craze-proof semi-porcelain.
35 L 04466—Shipping weight, 6 pounds........$1.39

Open Stock
For Set Composition See Page 697K

It's easy to replace pieces you've broken, to build a set as your family grows, or to make up a set of your own from Sears Open Stock. You save 40% at Sears low open stock prices.
* Dinner Plates, 9¾-in., and Platter, 15-in., not available in "Gascon" (No. 35L04423).

Open stock prices for Dinnerware on these two pages

Item—Approximate Sizes State Catalog Number and Item Wanted	Shpg. Wt.	35 L 04414 35 L 04453 35 L 04462 Cat-Tail	35 L 04442 35 L 04457 35 L 04458	35 L 04422 35 L 04423 35 L 04449
◆6 Tea Cups................	5 lbs.	$1.32	$1.32	$1.38	$1.50
◆6 Tea Saucers.............	5 lbs.	.78	.78	.84	.90
◆6 Bread and Butter Plates, 6 inches..	5 lbs.	.84	.84	.90	1.02
◆6 Pie or Salad Plates, 7 inches.......	8 lbs.	1.08	1.08	1.14	1.26
◆6 Dinner Plates, 9 inches........	11 lbs.	1.56	1.56	1.68	1.86
◆6 Large Dinner Plates, 9¾ inches....	12 lbs.	1.80	1.80	1.98	2.16*
◆6 Soup Plates, 7½ inches.........	9 lbs.	1.56	1.56	1.68	1.86
◆6 Cream Soup Dishes..........	6 lbs.	1.74	1.74	1.98	2.34
◆6 Sauce Dishes, 5¼ inches.......	5 lbs.	.78	.78	.84	.90
◆1 Covered Sugar Bowl..........	2 lbs.	.83	.83	.87	.91
◆1 Cream Pitcher.............	2 lbs.	.42	.42	.46	.52
◆1 Covered Vegetable Dish......	4 lbs.	1.43	1.43	1.49	1.69
◆1 Gravy Boat.............	3 lbs.	.59	.59	.63	.69
◆1 Gravy Boat Stand.........	1 lb.	.40	.40	.42	.44
◆1 Small Platter, 11 inches.......	4 lbs.	.45	.45	.47	.49
◆1 Medium Platter, 13 inches......	5 lbs.	.71	.71	.75	.84
◆1 Large Platter, 15 inches......	6 lbs.	1.19	1.19	1.25	1.29*
◆1 Round Open Vegetable Dish.....	3 lbs.	.49	.49	.53	.57
◆1 Oval Open Vegetable Dish......	3 lbs.	.49	.49	.53	.57

◆Order and pay postage on open stock from Mail Order House nearest you. Shipped from Chicago, Philadelphia or Los Angeles.

PAGE 697H . DINNERWARE

A catalog reprint from Sears, Roebuck and Company showing Shortcake by W. S. George.

Row 1: Shaker, Ranchero shape Wampum decal (designed by Simon Slobodkin) Iroquois Red sugar, Ranchero shape, Wheat coffee server, Ranchero Iroquois Red creamer, Shortcake on Lido shaker.

Row 2: "Flower Trim" on Lido, "Floral" egg cup, Lido bowl (decal called Breakfast Knook by Canonsburg Pottery), Egg cup "Tiny Roses". Lido - Cynthia (same decal on Bolero shape is called Peach Blossom).

Row 3: Rosita pattern on Ranchero - Cavitt Show - division of W. S. George. Introduced in 1946, Lido shaker, (may be Blue Dawn) Lido "Floral", Lido Ivory plain cream soup and liner, Lido - after dinner with saucer, Lido "Rust Floral" cup.

W. S. George backstamps.

W. S. George backstamp.

A 1940's magazine ad for W. S. George.

W. S. George backstamp.

GONDER

Again we are indebted to Mr. Norris Schneider for sharing his research by Lawton Gonder and the Gonder Ceramic Arts, Incorporated by way of an article written by Mr. Schneider that appeared in Zanes, *Times Signal,* September 15-22, 1957.

Lawton Gonder quite literally grew up with potteries and pottery people. He went to work at the Ohio Pottery Company at the age of 13 running molds and casting handles. He went to work in 1915 for American Encaustic Tiling Company in the research department where he remained for 11 years. After a variety of different jobs, Gonder bought the former Zane Pottery Company and named it Gonder Ceramic Arts, Incorporated. Gonder manufactured a higher price art pottery. Two of his ideas that set him apart were flambe glazes described by Mr. Schneider as looking "like flame red with streaks of yellow." The other "innovation" was a gold crackle finish.

Not much dinnerware came out of the Gonder operation that we know of but what Gonder did manufacture is unique in styling, being very heavy and thick. La Gonda was made in the early 1950's.

Row 1: La Gonda, aqua cup, yellow saucer, covered yellow sugar, aqua bowl 4¼.
Row 2: Covered pink creamer, aqua shaker, pink 8½ luncheon plate.

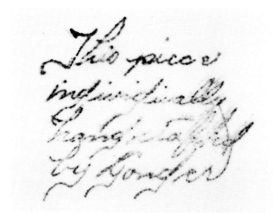

Gonder backstamps.

HAEGER POTTERIES

The Haeger Pottery was established in Dundee, Illinois, in 1871 as the Dundee Brick Yard. While Haeger is not primarily a dinnerware manufacturer, their earliest record of a dinnerware line dates back to 1919. Tableware and Teaware were the two early lines. Haeger also had a children's tableware line with plate, cereal bowl, pitcher mug and plate. Tableware and Teaware came in blue, rose, yellow and green. In a 1927 catalogue, the ware is shown in rich semi-matte black, Chinese blue, French blue, Meregreen, Ivory and Mulberry.

A more recent and modern design in *Today's World* is burnt orange and sandstone, made by the Haeger Pottery and designed by Ben Seibel. Another dinnerware line, Country Classics, made in Stone Gray and Taupe, designed by the Chief of Haegers design division, C. Glenn Richardson.

Photograph from a Haeger catalog, provided by the company.

THE HALL CHINA COMPANY

The Hall China Company was founded on August 14, 1903, in East Liverpool, Ohio, by Robert Hall. Thirty-three potters were employed and the first chinaware to bear the name of Hall was bedpans and combinets. The small company struggled for survival and whatever plans Mr. Hall had for its future were never known. Robert Hall died in 1904.

On Mr. Hall's death, his son, Robert Taggart Hall, became manager. He experimented tirelessly to develop a glaze that would withstand the heat required for "bisque-firing." This single-fire process had been used during the Ming dynasty and this was all Mr. Hall had to go on, that it had been done before. Robert Taggart Hall developed the first leadless glaze in 1911. The pieces that came out of the kiln were strong, non-porous and crazeproof. Temperatures used in the firing were 2400° F.

World War I gave The Hall China Company an opportunity to furnish ware to the institutional trade and they maintained this trade after the war. At this time, Hall became the world's largest manufacturer of decorated teapots and launched a campaign to educate the American housewife as to the proper methods of brewing tea. The proper pot was, of course, a Hall.

Continued success and obsolete equipment prompted the management to build a new factory in the east end of East Liverpool, Ohio. The plant was completed in 1930 and is still in operation at that site. Mr. John T. Hall is president and general manager. Hall also operates a plant in Gilmer, Texas and has plans for building a plant at another site in Texas.

Wild Rose.

Row 1: "Basket" is one of three stackette refrigerator sets #296. There was only a small amount of this decal used. You will find other items with this decal, salt & pepper and whatever made from 1932 to 1960 but not a big market. (2) "Cut-A-Way" open jug made in six sizes with or without covers and decorated with #488 decal. Numbers 282 - 283 - 284 - 285 - 286 - 287 made for general retail trade, dating back to 1930. A good seller.

Fantasy jug. Fantasy can be found in several pieces and dates back to late 1930's and early 1940's. These jugs were made in these numbers, smallest #1631, 1632, 1633 and largest 1634.

Row 2: Clover decal, #286 jug; several items with this decal were made for retail trade. Probably 1940-60. #633 Ball Water Jug, Cobalt Blue, Blue Blossom. Other items recalled in this pattern #964 custard, 3110 teapot, 633 jug, 1188 open grease pot, 1186 salt, 1187 pepper, 782 bean pot, 938 & 939 casserole, 966 - 967 - 968 bowls, 887 covered syrup jug. Late 1930's, early 1940's. A large open batter bowl with handle #884 cooker jar and several other items.

Row 3: Eva Zeisel, Bouquet Hallcraft jug. Forman pie baker - bought elsewhere and decorated by Hall.

Row 4: Canary bake pan made for Manning Bowman frame, mid 30-31, #1831 tea jar - made in many colors and decorations.

Hall backstamps.

Row 1: Thorley jug #1540, 1538, 1536.

Row 2: E-Shape dinner plate 10″, platter 10″, Monticello.

Row 3: E-Shape Monticello cup & saucer, covered sugar, covered round vegetable bowl.

Row 4: Mt. Vernon all-china coffee dripper made exclusively for Sears.

The Thorley jugs on Row 1 are thin and are described as "Almost China" by an ex-Hall worker. J. Palin Thorley was a designer for The Hall Co. in the 1940's. The Thorley jugs were made only in white with gold trim. If you look closely at the Sears E-shape dinnerware reprint you will see "Duncan Phyfe" styled candleholders designed by Mr. Thorley for Hall.

Hall Monticello backstamp.

A catalog reprint from Sears, featuring Richmond, Monticello, and Mt. Vernon.

CAMEO ROSE - E-SHAPE

Cameo Rose was made exclusively for the Jewel Tea Company by The Hall China Company, East Liverpool, Ohio. It was available in the Jewel Home Shopping Service Catalogues in open stock into the early seventies. It is already a very popular pattern with collectors. A word of caution: the cup handles tend to "pop-off", check for glued or mended handles.

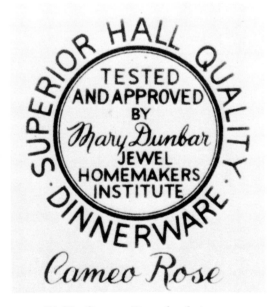

Hall's Cameo Rose backstamp.

Save up to 19% on Cameo Rose

(D) "Cameo Rose." Now available at reduced prices! We will be discontinuing this pattern soon, so take advantage of this opportunity to purchase lovely "Cameo Rose" ware at special prices. Superior quality semi-vitreous ware has a hard-fired, non-porous glaze...will not fade or craze. Decorative rose bud and leaf border with gold line trim frames the single White rose.

16-Piece Breakfast Starter Set includes: 4 cups, 4 saucers, 4 fruit dishes and 4 breakfast plates.
*5R 1. Was 10.95....Now 8.88

16-Pc. Dinner Starter Set includes: 4 cups, 4 saucers, 4 fruit dishes and 4 dinner plates.
*5R 52. Was 11.95...Now 9.88

53-Piece Service for 8. (See composition of set listed at right above.)
*5R 53. Was 42.95. Now 35.88

53-Pc. Set consists of 8 cups, 8 saucers, 8 fruit dishes, 8 bread & butter, 8 salad and 8 dinner plates plus large platter, oval vegetable dish, covered sugar bowl and creamer.

Open Stock	Cat. No.	Was	Now
Cup	*5R 2	.90	.76
Saucer, 6"	*5R 4	.50	.42
Bread & Butter, 6½" .	*5R 6	.60	.51
Salad Plate, 6½". . . .	*5R 7	.80	.68
Pie Plate, 8"	*5R 8	.95	.81
Breakfast Plate, 9¼".	*5R 9	1.10	.93
Dinner Plate, 10" . . .	*5R 10	1.45	1.23
Small Platter, 11½". .	*5R 11	1.90	1.61
Large Platter, 13¼". .	*5R 13	3.10	2.63
Fruit Dish, 5¼"	*5R 15	.55	.47
Cereal Dish, 6¼" . . .	*5R 16	.95	.81
Soup-Coupe, 8"	*5R 17	1.10	.93
Sugar Bowl Complete .	*5R 18	3.90	3.31
Creamer.	*5R 21	2.00	1.70
Oval Veg. Dish, 10½"	*5R 25	2.85	2.42
Cov. Veg. Dish.	*5R 26	7.50	6.37
Gravy Boat.	*5R 29	3.10	2.63
Pickle Dish, 9"	*5R 30	1.50	1.27
Round Veg. Dish, 8¾"	*5R 32	2.85	2.42
Salt Shaker.	*5R 38	1.10	.93
Pepper Shaker.	*5R 39	1.10	.93
Cream Soup	*5R 40	2.25	1.91
Tid-Bit Tray.	*5R 42	4.75	4.04
Cov. Butter Dish, ¼lb	*5R 43	2.25	1.91
Cov. Tea Pot, 6-cup. .	*5R 51	5.50	4.67

A catalog reprint showing Cameo Rose by Hall China Company and the prices.

Row 1: All Cameo Rose - cup/saucer, sauce dish 5-¾", creamer, covered sugar.

Row 2: Covered vegetable dish 8-¾" across top, salt & pepper set table size, teapot.

Row 3: Cameo Rose dinnerplate 10", 3 tier tid-bit server, 10-¾" bottom 7-¾" center, 6½" top, plate 7-¾".

This pattern has been previously called Fuji. Whether this is an official name or not is unknown to me but it is a fitting enough name for the decal.

Row 1: Fuji creamer and covered sugar, electric coffee maker and server.

Row 2: Petite Marmite (pronounced marmeat) in chrome frame for hot water. Ice can be packed in the Manning-Bowman frame for keeping cold foods.

Row 1: Open sugar, Sani-Grid shape #2293, Rose Parade, cadet blue/white handles #2286 salt and #2287 pepper. Rose Parade, cadet blue ball jug #633.

Row 2: Wildfire, (Sprig), Pear Shape #1186 salt, Wildfire, covered drippings jar #988, Pear shape pepper shakers #1187.

Row 3: Wildfire Border utility bowl #2277, Border coffeemaker #3075. The #3075 was a special item for the Great American Tea Company. The lid has an S on lid.

Row 4: Petunia, Pear shape #1186 handled salt shaker - Petunia decal was used from 1932 - 1969. Thistle bowls, Heather Rose salad bowl #3078.

ORANGE POPPY

decal #414 made for The American Tea Company.

Row 1: Orange Poppy #1186 range salt, #1187 pepper shaker, #361 custard, marmalade jar, liner (lid missing).

Row 2: Poppy #633 ball jug, #3116 Do-Nut teapot, #286 open jug, #3116 Do-Nut teapot, #286 open jug.

Row 3: Poppy #78 Round Casserole 8″, plate 7″, round jar (lid missing) not marked and not Hall's.

Expect to find many other pieces in Orange Poppy, both in Hall China and accessory items. There is an Orange Poppy tablecloth and also step-on metal trash can.

2-cup teapot (Boston shape) used in the corporate offices of the Jewel Home Shopping Service. Only six or eight known and not ever nationally distributed.

HALL CHINA AUTUMN LEAF

Autumn Leaf is the most popular dinnerware pattern ever produced at the Hall plant. Autumn Leaf was made by Hall for the Jewel Tea Company from 1933 until 1976. Not all pieces were made continuously during that time.

This is but a sampling of the many different pieces made in this pattern. In many of the dinnerware patterns one is able to find matching glassware and tinware. In the case of the popular Autumn Leaf, plastic items and linens are also sought after by collectors.

Autumn Leaf was an exclusive line made only for Jewel and sold only through the Jewel Companies. The decal, however, was not exclusive and was found on pieces made by just about every major manufacturer of dinnerware in the early 1930's. The decal became exclusive at some later point.

Hall China backstamps.

Row 1: 3-piece condiment jar, cream soup, teacup, St. Denis cup.

Row 2: Gravy boat, tea pot (also promoted as a 4-cup dripolator), 1-pound covered butter dish.

Row 3: St. Denis saucer, sifter (NOT HALL), regular saucer.

Row 4: 10″ dinner plate, bud vase, Libbey frosted glass, ball jug.

All Hall China "Autumn Leaf" pieces will have the Mary Dunbar name included in the backstamp. The fluted vase shown is the only one found to date. It is believed to be a sample item only.

Hall China backstamps.

Row 1: Serenade D Shape 8″ plate, Serenade tea cup, D Shape creamer, Serenade D Shape 4″ bowl.

Row 2: Serenade 9″ "D" Shape plate, Serenade #34 New York 6-cup tea pot, #3063 coffee pot - (metal dripper missing).

Row 3: Wheat, covered kitchen jars #1382, made for R. H. Macy in the 1930's. (The kitchen set consists of sugar, tea, coffee, flour and salt & pepper shakers.) The jars were made in several colors and decorations for the retail trade.

Row 4: All of Row 4 is Bittersweet. Bittersweet, Pear shape #1186 salt, covered drippings jar #488, covered casserole #298, Marmite #474.

All of the pieces on Row 4 were very good sellers for many years. These pieces may be found in several different colors and decorations. The shapes date back to the 1930's.

Hall China: All Crocus decal #6130 platinum lines, made since about 1938 and sold to retail trade and some tea companies. The decals were cut in pieces to get the maximum use. The cut pieces are called Sprig and the complete decal was called a border decal. Some stores and gas stations used Crocus as premium.

Row 1: Creamer, border decal #3123, sugar, border, #3122, beverage mug border #598, D-Shape creamer, Sprig, D-Shape covered sugar Sprig decal.

Row 2: Gravy boat D-Shape Sprig, covered drippings jar #488 Sprig, salt & pepper #1186 and #1187 border.

Row 3: Jug #633 Sprig, New York teapot #34 border decal, coffee pot #3063 border.

Row 4: Bowl #278 (part of set) Sprig, pretzel jar #584 border, casserole #298 Sprig.

Crocus, St. Denis cup is just one of the more recent finds in the Crocus pattern. The Crocus St. Denis cup is from the collection of Don and Irma Brewer. The Brewer's also have a beautiful soup tureen in the Crocus pattern.

ALL CROCUS DECAL #6138
SPRIG LAYOUT, D-SHAPE
PLATINUM LINES

Row 1: Sprig Crocus cup and saucer, sauce dish, plate 6″.

Row 2: Round vegetable bowl 9″, oval vegetable bowl coupe soupe 8″.

Row 3: Plate 9″, plate 8″, plate 7″.

Row 4: Platter 12″, platter 10″.

HALL Superior Quality KITCHENWARE

3 Piece Mixing Bowl Set

Beauty and utility are the outstanding features of this Hall China bowl set. Decorated with the lovely Crocus pattern and gleaming platinum bands. Crazeproof, stainproof, extremely durable, easy to clean. Useful for mixing, serving, baking, storing. Approved by Good Housekeeping.

The large size holds 3½ quarts, and is 8⅝″ across.
The middle size holds 2 quarts, and is 7½″ across.
The small size holds 1 quart, and is 6¼″ across.

SILHOUETTE

Silhouette was a premium item of The Cook Coffee Company and also of The Standard Coffee Company in the 1930's and 1940's. Do not be surprised at any piece you may find with Silhouette decal. Both Hall China and Taylor, Smith and Taylor used this pattern. The Harker Company made the rolling pins.

Row 1: Silhouette shelf paper, Harker rolling pin, glass pitcher probably McBeth Evans.

Row 2: Wax paper dispenser, shakers (metal).

Row 3: Match box, potato masher and whip with wooden handles, sifter.

Row 4: Tray (metal).

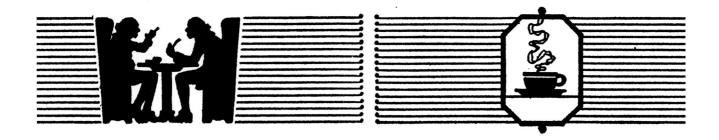

SILHOUETTE

Silhouette shelf paper. Many accessory Pieces were designed to go with Hall China but were not made by Hall.

Reproduction of actual "Salesmen's Route Cards" for Cook Coffee Company, Detroit, Michigan, dated 7/31/42.

Westinghouse Electrical Appliances

Limited Supply   Limited Supply

WESTINGHOUSE
FOOD CRAFTER
Illustrated at Left

EE4165 .... **$37.50**

(Suggested Retail Price $26.95)

Food Crafter with beaters and two Hall Fireproof China bowls; permanently attached rubber armored cord with soft-rubber unbreakable attachment plug; for AC or DC operation.

- Built-in power unit.
- No extra gear needed for attachments.
- Beaters are easily inserted, locking into place automatically.
- Beaters drop out at the touch of button but will not fall into bowl.
- Food Crafter Motor—non-radio interfering.
- Approved by Underwriters Laboratory.

From a 1940's wholesale catalogue. Hall made several items for Westinghouse during these years. Refrigerator sets and baking pans for roasters were just some of the items made for Westinghouse during this period.

Hallcraft was a line designed for Hall China Company by Eva Zeisel. The Classic Shape came in a myriad of patterns plus Hallcraft white. Some Holloware pieces were available in Satin Black or Satin Grey. The holloware pieces available in Black Satin finish were: salt and pepper, A.D. cream and sugar, 6-cup coffee pot, 6-cup teapot, gravy boat, 12 oz. sugar and 13 oz. creamer, A.D. cup, tea cup. Available also in Grey finish were: salt & pepper, A.D. sugar 6 oz., A.D. cream 6 oz., coffee pot 6-cup, teapot 6-cup, gravy boat, sugar 12 oz., cream 13 oz., A.D. saucer, tea saucer.

HALLCRAFT

CLASSIC SHAPE

by Eva Zeisel

MIDHURST CHINA SALES CORPORATION

712 SOUTH OLIVE STREET • LOS ANGELES 14, CALIFORNIA • MAdison 3-4297

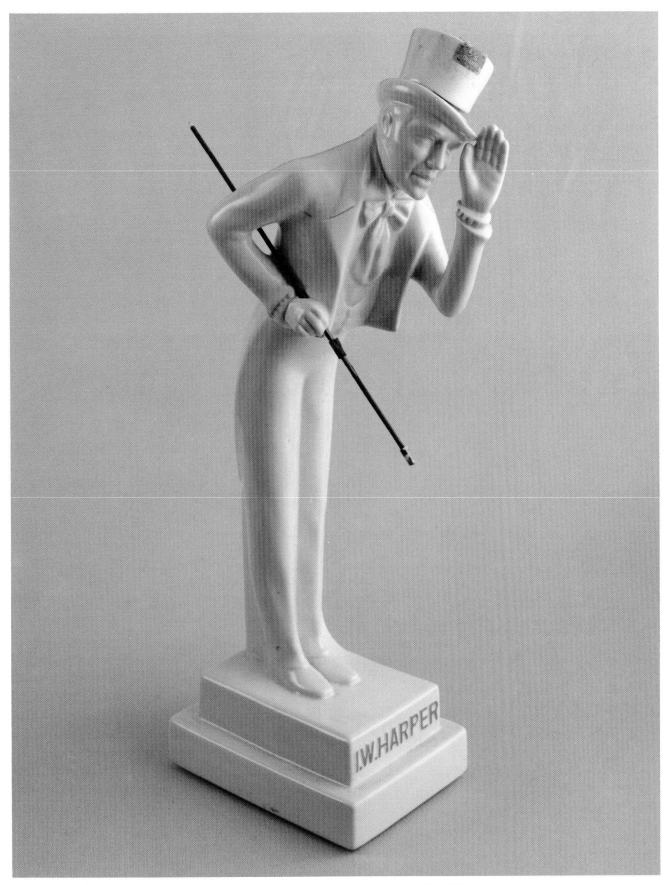

I. W. HARPER DECANTER

Not dinnerware but a striking example of other items made by the American pottery industry. Hall China made several different figural bottles over a period of about 25 years.

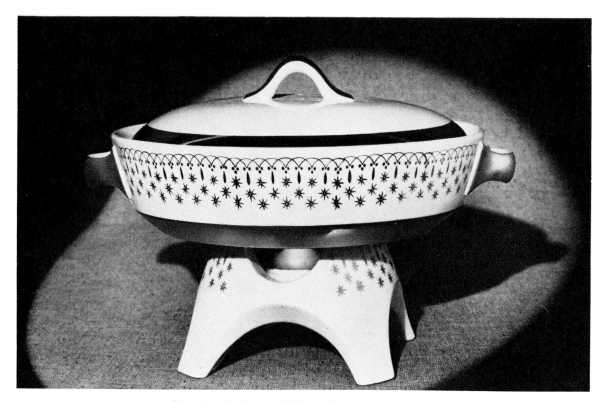

Reprinted from *China, Glass & Tableware,* Clifton, New Jersey.

Flare Ware Gold Lace made by the Hall China Company in the 1960's. Other known pieces are #1765 coffee server with brass warmer teapot, coffee urn, 3-pt. casserole, cookie jar, 3-piece bowl set and salad bowl.

Guaranteed against cracking under ordinary oven conditions is this colorful plaid china, for kitchen or buffet service, including two covered dishes and mixing bowls which might double for fruit or salad. (Hall China Company)

A 1932 ad for Hall's China.

1927 Cattail Hall Coffee service

HARKER POTTERY

The Harker Company had its beginning in 1840 when Benjamin Harker, an English slater (roofer) came to America and bought a farm for $3,600 on the banks of the Ohio River at East Liverpool, Ohio. The farm had extensive clay deposits and for a year or so, Harker sold clays to James Bennett who was later to found the Bennett Pottery Company. It occurred to Harker that he might make pots and ceased to sell to Bennett. In 1840, he and his sons, George and Benjamin, Jr., built a kiln and soon were transporting yellow-ware dishes by boats and wagons.

Soon after the new business was underway, Benjamin Harker died and his sons took over the operation. All was well until the Civil War. One brother was drafted and the other brother died leaving the small pottery without a head. At this time, a brother-in-law, David Boyce, took over the operation for the remaining Harker brother. David Boyce was married to Jane Harker, sister of the Harker boys.

After the war, the remaining Harker boy returned to the pottery but the name of Boyce was to remain an important name to the Harker operation from that time on.

Harker began making whiteware in 1879. There was quite a celebration of Harker employees and employers when the first kiln of whiteware was drawn. Harkers and their employees ferried to Rock Springs where they celebrated by consuming 10 kegs of beer and dancing to the music of the East Liverpool brass band.

The pottery was put into very bad financial straits by a severe flood in 1884. Workers were paid by check and had to hold those checks until the bank balance covered them but the Harker Company boasts that none of their workers missed a pay period. Charles R. Boyce is given credit for the growth and success of The Harker Company. Robert E. Boyce, oldest son of Charles, joined the company in 1923 and became the factory's ceramic engineer in 1927. David G. Boyce, another son, began selling dinnerware in the summer of 1923 and was later to serve as president of The Harker Company.

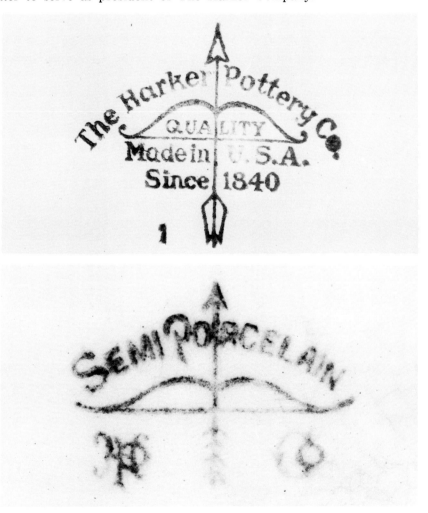

Harker backstamps.

By 1931, the company was relocated in new quarters in Chester, West Virginia, across the river from the East Liverpool site. It was felt that the threat of floods was too great at the old site. In 1965, the Harker organization is said to have employed 300 people and was capable at full production of turning out some 25-million pieces of dinnerware annually. In 1945 they also introduced their exclusive process using copper engraving device. The decorations themselves are in white and are carved from engobe colors. Engobe is "white or colored slip applied to earthenware after as a support for a glaze or enamel." Collectors refer to this Harkerware as "Cameoware." It was made in a variety of base colors with White Rose in blue being most common.

The Jeanette Glass Company bought Harker and closed it down in March of 1972. Another company, Ohio Stoneware, Inc., made crock-pot liners in the building until it was totally destroyed by a fire in September of 1975.

"The oldest pottery in America" is used on some Harker backstamps. While Harker was one of the oldest continuously run dinnerware plants and certainly one of the oldest in the East Liverpool, Ohio, area it can hardly lay claim to being the oldest pottery in America.

The corporate name for the Harker operation was Harker Pottery. The name of Harker China was used in the 1950's to identify and probably to promote their chinaware line.

HARKER - MALLOW

One of Harker's most attractive decals, in my opinion, is Mallow. Mallow is pictured here in a wire rack and lids. Several of the Harker individual custards or bakers can still be found in their original racks.

"ROSE SPRAY"

Rose Spray is an all-over pattern of tiny pink flowers tinged with yellow. The trim is a flat grey. Some handles have gold trim. Rose Spray was reportedly made for one of the Harker girls. The set boasts of a wide variety of serving pieces.

Shown are top left to right:
 9″ breakfast plate, 6″ round dessert, 8″ serving bowl, tab handle bowl, creme soup (2 handles).

Lower left:
 Creamer, 10″ dinner, square 7″ salad plate, cup and saucer.

Row 1: Regal pitcher "Blue Blossoms," pepper shaker, "Rosebud," Early pitcher Dutch children.

Row 2: Regal pitcher "Boyce" gold trim handle, "Cherry Trim" plate, "Basket" plate.

Row 3: "English Countryside," individual custards, tall jar.

Row 4: "Jessica" large utility bowl, Snack plate "Brim."

Harker Hot Oven backstamps.

Row 1: Shakers and server may not be Harker products. Cronin used this decal and the server especially looks like a Cronin product.

Row 2: 7″ Regal pitcher "Fruits," meat platter "Cherry Blossom."

Row 3: Meat platter, cake lifter, pie server, rolling pin.

Row 4: 9″ plate Autumn Leaf marked Columbia chinaware. Individual Autumn Leaf casserole, large utility bowl.

COLUMBIA CHINAWARE

Columbia Chinaware was a sales organization owned by The Harker Pottery Company and operated by Harker. The Columbia Chinaware was in business approximately from 1935 to 1955. Not only did they have Harker dinnerware and baking ware but other items including enamel ware, glass and aluminum items. The sales organization (Columbia Chinaware) generally went into smaller towns and not the larger cities. Mr. Boyce told me that letters from customers had stated they preferred Columbia products more than Harker. An amusing bit of trivia in view of the fact that Columbia and Harker were one and the same. There is a remote possibility that wares sold by Columbia other than dinnerware were marked Columbia in some way. At this point, that is conjecture and not based on fact.

Harker Columbia backstamp.

Columbia Chinaware was a sales subsidiary of the Harker Pottery Company.

Row 1: "Amy" sugar and creamer, server, individual casserole, individual bean pot or casserole.

Row 2: "Amy" plates in a variety of sizes.

Row 3: "Amy" teapot, scoop (hard to find in any pattern), fork, spoon, meat platter, rolling pin.

Row 4: "Amy" "High-Rise" jug with lid, tab handle soup, utility bowl, 3-bowl stack set with lid.

Harker Bakerite backstamp.

MALLOW AND "PANSY"

Row 1: "Pansy" 6″ bowl and pepper. Mallow Lard covered jar and covered jug.

Row 2: Mallow 8″ plate, serving spoon, 7½″ bowl.

Row 3: Mallow utility bowl 10″ across top.

Row 4: Mallow 12″ utility or serving plate, Still Mallow, more ornate treatment.

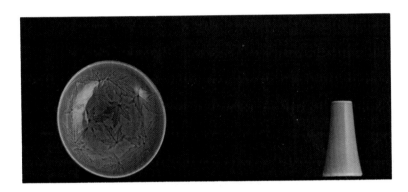

HARKER'S WOOD SONG

Honey Brown, Dawn Grey and Glacier White were colors introduced on Wood Song by The Harker Pottery in 1960. Honey Brown is shown and it is an appealing color and interesting pattern indeed. The pattern is said to be patterned "from real life Ohio Vally maple leaves comes authentic and permanent reproduction (real leaves actually impregnated into unfired clay) accomplished by a secret and exclusive process." And of course this is advertising copy from some prolific copy writer. Mr. Boyce tells us that actual leaves may have been used for an original design for a mold. Wood Song is a very pleasing pattern.

Row 1: Server and spoon.

Row 2: Utility bowl, 7″ plate.

Row 3: "Ruffled Tulip" covered bowl (may be part of a stack set), "Ruffled Tulip" utility or serving tray 11-¾″, covered Ruffled Tulip "Arches" pitcher with lid.

Row 4: "Lisa" "Arches" utility bowl, "Becky" utility bowl. Florist bowl made for florists trade "Poppy."

A Harker Royal Gadroon backstamp. (See page 132)

HARKER HOT OVEN LINE
"PETIT POINT ROSE"

Just about every American manufacturer of dinnerware used a petit point type of decal on one or more of their lines. The most popular type of petit-point seemingly was of roses or flowers. Other designs were used, however, and it will be interesting to see just what was made in Petit Point.

Notice, please, the variations in the decals shown. For the sake of communication, we will refer to the more ornate and detailed decal as *"Petit Point Rose #1"* and the other will be called *"Petit Point Rose #2"*. There will be pieces that will seemingly not fit into either category and we will refer to those pieces as *"Petit Point Rose"*.

"PETIT POINT ROSE" AND "ROSE I & II"

Row 1 : *"Rose II"* cake server, *"Rose II",* individual custard, "Rose" individual custard, *"Rose I"* cake server.

Row 2: "Rose II" utility bowl 6″ deep, 11½″ across top, *"Rose II"* 8″ covered casserole.

Row 3: *"Rose I"* 9″ pie baker and matching rolling pin. *"Rose I"* 6″ plate, *"Rose II"* 9″ pie baker and matching rolling pin.

Row 4: *"Rose II"* utility bowl, small 3-¾″ deep, 6″ wide across top, middle bowl 3½″ deep, 6½″ across top, larger bowl, 4-¾″ deep, 7½″ across top.

Harker's Royal Gadroon shape was achieved by spraying slip on the surface and wiping the gadroon edge. The Chesterton line was actually the Royal Gadroon shape offered in gray, green, yellow, pink and blue. It was not popular in the pink and blue colors.

Paté sur paté was achieved by spraying engobe with a mask or using a mask after drying to blast the design. This method cut through the engobe, eliminating decals.

Puritan was another name for the Royal Gadroon shape to identify it from decorated Royal Gadroon. Puritan was plain white and attractive without decals.

Mr. Boyce says that Royal Gadroon ash trays were sold by the thousands from 1945 - 1965. They sold to hotels, etc., for 15¢ each and up depending on quantity. (See advertising pieces)

Royal Gadroon shape - assorted decals.

CAMEOWARE

Cameoware had its beginning about 1935. George Bauer, formerly of the Bennett Pottery in Baltimore, and Harker's own design department are credited with Cameoware "engobe process" designs. Many engobe process patterns were used on a variety of shapes.

One of the most popular "engobe process" designs was White Rose. The rolling pin was available with the design for a few cents more. The engobe process, as it was explained to me by Jim Lange, Harker worker, is as follows:

"First, a rubber stamp would be cut in the desired pattern. The stamp had a cloth base and after repetitive uses would have to be discarded because fuzziness would appear on the fringe of the same.

This method was abandoned after a few years and sandblasting was the method used. When sandblasting was used, a copper mask was placed over the bisque and blasted with sand, leaving the imprint of the design.

In the original process, the rubber stamp was glued to the bisque, then dipped. When the glaze dried, the stamp would be removed with a tweezer by a worker and the process started again. Cameoware was not only hand-dipped but sent through a spray (dipping) machine.

The tops of the salt & pepper shakers and ends of rolling pins were covered with wax, so the glaze would not adhere, then stamp applied to the designated area, then dipped. The wax part was then sponged."

Blue and white seemingly were the most popular colors in Cameoware.

"Carv - Kraft was a name invented for Montgomery Ward to avoid the use of the name Cameo which was used on the regular department store trade. White Rose was a Montgomery Ward exclusive."

Reprinted from a Montgomery Ward catalogue. 1941.

Row 1: Cameo Shellware cup and saucer, White Rose drippings jar, pepper shaker, Carv-Kraft White Rose cup/saucer set.

Row 2: Shellware 9″ plate, covered jugs 3 sizes.

Row 3: White Rose teapot, covered Cameo Rose covered casserole, Cameo Rose pitcher (cover missing).

Row 4: Cameo Rose utility plate 11-¾″, Cameo Rose meat platter, White Rose Carv-Kraft pie baker.

The small jar on row 1 is backstamped Modern Age, one of the backstamps we overlooked. The same shape jug on row 3 is marked Bakerite. The same Bakerite backstamp can also be found on early Wellsville pieces.

A 1940's advertisement for Cameo.

Cameoware backstamps.

Row 1: Cameo Rose shakers pink, Cameo Rose rolling pin pink w/white handles.

Row 2: Cameo Rose salad set yellow, spoon and fork yellow w/white.

Row 3: Cameo Rose plate gray, "Vine" plate tan, Wheat plate beige, Rooster plate beige called Engraved Rooster or Cock-o-the-Morn.

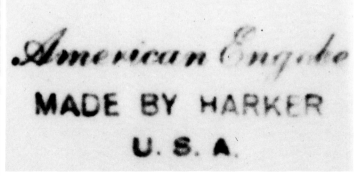

Harker backstamps.

Harker Holly plate was made prior to 1932 at the original plant on the river road in East Liverpool, Ohio. The Holly plate has an early backstamp.

White Clover was designed by the famous Russel Wright. There are many pieces to be found in this set. White Clover was made in Meadow Green, Coral Sand, Golden Spice and Charcoal. Russel Wright's signature is lightly incised in the back of the White Clover pieces. Not all of the pieces have the clover design. A 16-piece starter set sold for $9.95. The address, shown in the 1954 ad, was a mailing address only for the Harker plant.

Reprinted from *China, Glass & Tableware,* Clifton, New Jersey.

An ad for a Russel Wright designed clock.

None of the shakers are marked and I am not totally convinced that all shakers with this shape belong to Harker. For now we will assume they are but leave the door open for corrections.

Harker workers we talked to remember the pattern on Rows 2 and 3 as having an "Indian-sounding name" but were unable to recall what it was called.

Row 1: "Cherry" utility salt & pepper set, "Calico Tulip" individual baking dish, creamer and covered sugar.

Row 2: "Deco-Dahlia" 6″ utility jug, 5¼″ ash tray, 10″ pie baker and server.

Row 3: "Deco: Dahlia" 12″ utility plate, set of six custards in wire rack.

Row 4: "Cottage" covered casserole, fork, 8¼″ plate.

ALADDIN—our new low, squattily rounded shape, combines the best features of modern and traditional in a wide range of attractive patterns. Shown above is TEAL ROSE, a large bold floral design destined to be among the year's most sensational profit makers.

THE *Harker*
POTTERY COMPANY
The Oldest Pottery in America
EAST LIVERPOOL, OHIO
★★★★★★★★★★★★★★★★★★★★★★★★★

A 1952 ad showing Teal Rose on Aladdin shape.

COUNTRYSIDE, IVY, *BIRDS AND FLOWERS*

Row 1: Pepper Shaker, Rolling Pin, Server.

Row 2: Utility jug on "arches" shape 5½″, fork, scoop, utility bowl 10″ across top.

Row 3: Ivy on Regal shape pitcher 7″ tall, *"Birds and Flowers"* on Regal shape 8″ tall.

Row 4: Ivy 12″ utility serving plate, *"Birds and Flowers"* 12″ utility plate.

A 1966 Harker ad.

RED APPLE I & II

Red Apple was the name used by Harker workers for this decal. Again, for the sake of communication and ease of advertising, the small continuous decal will be referred to as Red Apple 1. The larger decal will be referred to as Red Apple 2. Dessert or cake sets were sometimes made up of utility plates, servers and 6″ dessert plates. The bowl, spoon and 8 small bowls were purchased as a berry set. It isn't known if it came as a berry set from the factory.

Row 1: Red Apple 2, creamer or utility pitcher (lid missing), custard marked Bakerite, sugar (lid missing), Red Apple 1 teapot (lid missing).

Row 2: Red Apple 2 swirl 9″ bowl with red trim, serving spoon and berry bowl. Hot plate.

Row 3: Red Apple 2 utility bowl 10″ across top, Red Apple 1 (Modern Age) covered utility pitcher. The 1st pitcher on the top row, the utility pitcher and one of the utility trays on the 4th row probably made up a batter set.

Row 4: Red Apple 1, utility serving plate 12″, server, Red Apple 1 utility serving plate.

These pieces are shown to point out one decal's use on five and possibly more shapes. This was not uncommon for companies to get the best mileage possible out of what was on hand or was popular. This particular decal is found on lines by other companies.

Row 1: Red Border 6″ plate, gold trim oval bowl 9″, plate with gold 6″.

Row 2: Utility plate 12½″, Royal Gadroon plate 8″.

Row 3: Pastel Tulip pie baker 10″, Pastel Tulip cake plate 11″.

Row 4: Pastel Tulip on Gadroon shape 9″ plate, Unmarked milk pitcher may be Hall's Princeton jug, utility bowl 10″ across top.

Harker Pate sur Pate backstamp. (See page 147)

Row 1: Chesterton creamer, gravy boat, decaled creamer.

Row 2: "Ivy Vine" platter, 8″ plate, saucer, teapot.

Row 3: "Springtime" 10″ plate, saucer, 9″ plate.

Row 4: Teal "Paté sur Paté" 9″ plate, saucer, saucer, 9″ plate.

HARKER CHESTERTON SERIES
GENUINE AMERICAN IRONSTONE

Reminiscent of an English countryside...beautifully tailored and color coordinated to enhance any decor. Harker's underglaze process guarantees each piece oven proof, detergent proof, dishwasher safe.

Reprint from a Harker brochure.

Row 1: "Basket" creamer, Shellridge covered sugar, Shellridge creamer.

Row 2: "Royal Rose" cake set.

Row 3: "Slender Leaf" 8″ plate, "Slender Leaf" serving plate.

Row 4: "Rosettes" plates, part of set.

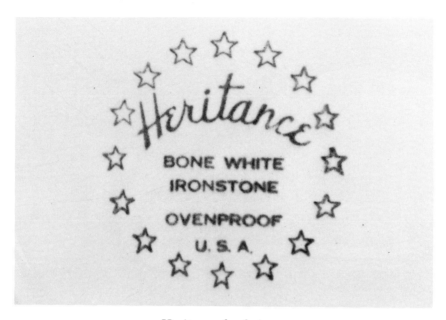

Heritance backstamp.

HARKER CHINA COMPANY. "Heritance" paneled white ironstone proved so popular that it has been brought out in several decorations as well. In white, a 69-piece service for 12 retails for $39.90.

Reprinted from *China, Glass & Tableware*, Clifton, New Jersey.

RAWHIDE

Stoneware shape and body. Large salad bowl and salt & pepper set. Rawhide may be found in a variety of pieces. 1960's.

Harker backstamps.

Row 1: Sun-Glo on Olympic shape (circa 1955) "Leaf and Flower" made for Sears, Harmony House backstamp.

Row 2: Laurelton made in green and beige (shown). Harker stoneware available in blue, pink, yellow, and white on pewter grey stoneware body. Sold in solid and mixed colors.

Row 3: Provincial Wreath on white stoneware, "Bouquet" and Pine Cone plates.

ROCKINGHAM-BROWN
DRIP GLAZE-IRONSTONE WARE

•

Oven-Dishwasher Proof

Complete Dinnerware Line, with
Specialty Pieces (34 items)

genuine
Quaker Maid
COOK
WARE
HARKER CHINA CO.
East Liverpool,
Ohio, USA

TRADEMARK

HARKER CHINA CO.

East Liverpool, Ohio   Established 1840

BLUE DANE

Harker backstamps.

Harker backstamps.

ROCKINGHAM WARE 1960's

These Rockingham Ware pieces were developed in the sixties for the Harker Pottery Company by Norman Clewlow, Harker modeller. The pieces were intended as inexpensive gift shop items and were fashioned after Rockingham pieces popular in the mid-1800's at many American potteries.

The 1960's versions of the early Rockingham pieces are soap dish, Toby pitcher and a hound-handled pitcher and tumblers. Daniel Greatbach is credited with creating a similar design in America as early as 1839. The design had been used earlier in England. Many potteries were making a similar Hound-handle pitcher in the mid-1800's, the most famous being made at Bennington, Vermont.

The Harker 1960's version of the hound-handled pitcher closely resembles the early version of the Harker-Taylor-Harker Rockingham pitcher.

This type ware (Rockingham Ware) is often erroneously referred to as Bennington. Bennington is a town in Vermont - a site of early American potteries. Rockingham Ware was named after the Duke of Rockingham whose potteries in England, it is said, first produced the ware.

Authentic Reproductions

First Rockingham Houndhandled 2-qt. Jug (8¼" high) produced in 1848. Matching 18 oz. Houndhandled Mug (5¾" high). Collectors' Gift — Individually Gift Packed.

HARKER CHINA CO.

Oldest in America

Established 1840   East Liverpool, Ohio

A 1965 ad for Rockingham ware.

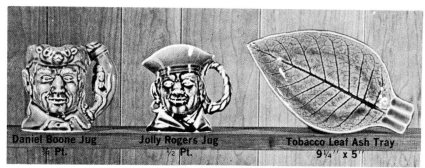

Daniel Boone Jug
¾ Pt.

Jolly Rogers Jug
½ Pt.

Tobacco Leaf Ash Tray
9¼" x 5"

Reproductions of early Harker Rockingham ware. These pieces are generally marked "reproduction" and were made for the 1964 gift trade.

2   FOREST FLOWER

4   FOREVER YOURS

Shellridge China was made for you. American design and craftsmanship bring you quality at these reasonable prices. Made to be enjoyed every day, Shellridge is genuine translucent china. Graceful and sophisticated in the contemporary manner, with styling that makes it adaptable to any decor. Every piece is ovenproof and fully guaranteed against chipping, crazing or breaking for one full year. See manufacturer's liberal warranty certificate.

GARDEN TRAIL

1   Rich with the scent of mingled garden colors. Its graceful elegance makes it something special every day — every meal.

FOREST FLOWER

2   The breath of an enchanted forest glen brings a look of treasured beauty to your table. Subtle tones of warm light brown and yellow sparkle as the mist of spring.

LEAF SWIRL

3   Timeless grace and enduring beauty combine with the modern simplicity of this contemporary pattern. Its charm is highlighted by combined hues of greys, beige and browns that make it something special for every occasion.

FOREVER YOURS

4   A garland of Rosebuds with enduring beauty creates color loveliness for your sense of good taste. A pattern to be loved forever.

Reprint of a Harker brochure.

Harker backstamps.

ASSORTED PATTERNS ON SHELLRIDGE SHAPE, VITREOUS CASUAL CHINA, EARLY SIXTIES

Row 1: Enchantment creamer and sugar, "Heritage" covered sugar, plain cup, no decal.

Row 2: Enchantment plate, Enchantment plate, Leaf Swirl bowl.

Row 3: Leaf Swirl Coffee server, covered casserole with warmer base, no decoration.

**VINTAGE PATTERN ON ROYAL GADROON SHAPE. A
SEMI-VITREOUS PATTERN MADE FROM 1947-1949.**

Row 1: Old Vintage, covered sugar, cup and saucer set, creamer.

Row 2: 10″ dinner, 13½″ platter.

Row 3: 8″ flat soup, sauce dish, 8″ round vegetable bowl.

From the collection of Betty's Glass Shop, Betty and Jim Cooper.

Row 1: "Colonial Lady" covered cookie jar or utility jar, bowl and cover, batter set and tray.

Row 2: Rolling pin, set of three bowls.

Row 3: Cup/saucer set, teapot Modern age, individual baker or casserole, creamer, tab handle bowl.

Row 4: Table shakers, range set with "Drips" jar, creamer and covered sugar.

HULL POTTERY CO.

The A. E. Hull Pottery Co. was founded in 1905 and its main production was in the kitchenware field until 1918, at which time art ware was also added.

In 1950 the factory was completely destroyed by fire. It was rebuilt and in one year and a half was back in business. At this point the name was changed to Hull Pottery Co.

The most important line now in the factory is the House 'n Garden Serving Ware Line, originally conceived to be used primarily out-of-doors. However, within months of its introduction it was in the dining rooms of many, many homes.

House and Garden Serving Ware

Crestone

Another OVENPROOF CREATION by Hull

Crestone, the newest casual serving-ware is saleable on sight! *Crestone's* refreshing Turquoise color and cascading white underglaze trim offers unusual eye-appeal. It's beautiful, it's ovenproof and sturdy and it's packed with special features. You'll love the uniquely designed deep-well saucers for cups and gravy boats, the comfortable platform handles, the easy-grip knobs that top interchangeable covers which invert and double for trivets. Over thirty sensibly-designed items such as *Crestone's* carafe are offered . . . and, at prices comparable to Hull's ever-popular Mirror Brown *House 'n Garden* line. Write for your *Crestone* and *House 'n Garden* folders today.

HULL POTTERY COMPANY

Crooksville, Ohio

Reprinted from *China, Glass & Tableware*, Clifton, New Jersey.

ILLINOIS CHINA COMPANY

Early information about Illinois China Company is sketchy. The best information we have been able to piece together is as follows:

The Illinois China Company was first located in Whitehall or Roodhouse, Illinois. (They are just a few miles apart.) Illinois China was moved to Lincoln, Illinois, by a group of Lincoln businessmen - James Shaw, William Coogan and David Hart - in approximately 1919.

The first listing for the Illinois China Company in the Lincoln, Illinois, Directory was 1920. The 1920 Directory lists D. H. Harts, President, Will Houser, Vice-President, J. H. Smith, Secretary-Treasurer.

The entire plant was destroyed by fire in 1922. A new plant was built with insurance funds. A gas-fired kiln replaced the coal-fired kilns in 1935. 2½-million dollars spent on the plant and equipment after the 1946 Stetson purchase.

See Stetson history for example of early Illinois ware.

Illinois China backstamp.

JACKSON CHINA COMPANY

The Jackson China Company can be traced back to 1910 through the deed books at Brookville, Pennsylvania. It was first known as the Bohemian Pottery Company at Falls Creek, and the Bohemian Company specialized in crocks and flower pots - until 1917 when the plant was bought by Harry Jackson.

The original investors and members of the original board were Mr. E. A. Fischel, Mr. H. W. Jackson, Mr. W. H. Cannon, Mr. J. Pifer, Mr. Frank Hahne, Sr. and Mr. Charles Dietz.

In the mid-1920's, an unnamed, disgruntled creditor of the original Bohemian Arts Pottery hid in the bushes adjacent to the railroad tracks and shot and killed Mr. Jackson and Mr. Darden. The assailant then turned the gun on himself and committed suicide. Mr. Fischel had been delayed out of town on a business trip or he too would have been killed. Local interests continued the operation of the company and the bank in DuBois was very involved due to loans they had made. The plant was owned by Emanuel A. Fischer and was known by Jackson China Company from 1923 - 1946.

In 1946 all shares of stock were purchased by Philip R. Distillator. Mr. Distillator doubled the floor space in the manufacturing area, added modern equipment in both forming and decorating. The work force more than doubled during the period of time. A decorating plant was also operated in New York but was destroyed by fire in 1967.

The company made dinnerware for home use and marketed it under the name of Royal Jackson. Competition from foreign countries forced the company out of this (dinnerware) business.

In September 1976, Mr. Andrew Greystake, a British attorney and investment banking consultant, purchased the company.

Jackson China, Incorporated, as it is now known, produces institutional china for restaurants and hotels.

Jackson China, Inc., currently employs 375 people and provides a local payroll of $4,000,000.

The Jackson China, Incorporated, of Falls Creek, Pennsylvania, was recently acquired by Newman Industries of Bristol, England. Newman Industries is a large multi-national company involved in ceramics, engineering and electric motors.

Jackson Vitrified China Co.
9 E. 55th St., N. Y.

Jackson China backstamps.

EDWIN M. KNOWLES

The Edwin M. Knowles Company was established in Chester, West Virginia, but moved to Newell, West Virginia, in 1900. The Knowles Company in later years was managed by a nephew, Fred B. Lawrence, Sr. Efforts to find a buyer for the plant in 1962 proved futile. In 1963, Robert Boyce and a Mr. Tuck, area businessman, bought the Knowles real estate.

Edwin M. Knowles backstamps.

Above: Early pitcher and bowl set made by Edwin M. Knowles Company.

Below: All "Fruits" utility plate, covered batter pitcher, covered syrup, shaker and cake lifter/pie server.

Row 1: Creamer and sugar "Pink Pastel", "Border Rim" plate, "Wildflower" plate.

Row 2: "Fruits" shaker, covered jug Knowles Utility Ware, "Fruits" plates.

Row 3: "Tuliptime" meat platter, Vegetable bowl, plate.

Row 4: Knowles utility ware "Tulip" cookie jar, "Tulip" pie baker, "Tuliptime" saucer dish, plate.

From the collection of John Moses and BA Wellman.

SEQUOIA—OVENWARE ATTRACTIVE AS YOUR MOST COLORFUL DINNERWARE—YET OVEN-PROOF AND ACID-PROOF

A NEW kind of Ovenware—light-weight American Semi-Porcelain — brilliant design combining Yellow, Blue, Green and Tangerine with bright Red trimming in colorful gaiety on the Ivory White background. Attractive enough to grace the proudest table. Wards prices are 20 to 33 per cent lower than elsewhere and *Wards will replace any piece that cracks or crazes in the course of baking.* Save time, save dishwashing—bake, serve and store in the same dishes.

(A) 3-Piece Bowl Set $149
$1.95 Value! Hold 1, 2⅜, 4 qts.
586 C 6991—Wt. 9 lbs.$1.49

(B) 3-Piece Range Set 79c
Salt and peppers. 4 in. high.
Covered jar 4 by 3 in. high.
586 C 6984—Wt. 3 lbs...79c

(C) Utility Pitchers 49c 18-oz.
586 C 6988-18-oz. 4¾ in. high.
Ship. wt. 1 lb. 4 oz......49c
586 C 6987—42-oz. 6 in. high.
Shipping weight
2 pounds 8
ounces.....69c

594 CBA

(D) Casserole and Tray $100 1½-qt.
Usual $1.49 Value!—Save 49c.
Covered Casserole and matching 10-in. serving tray.
586 C 6980—1½-Qt. Casserole, 7⅜-in. diam., and Tray.Ship.wt.61bs.8 oz.$1.00
586 C 6981—2-Qt. Casserole, 8⅜-in. diam., and Tray. Ship. wt. 7 lbs. 8 oz...$1.19

(E) Custard Cups 12c ea.
So handy—you'll find dozens of uses for them. Capacity each, 5 oz. 3½-in. diam. Ship. wt. ea. 12 oz.; six, 4 lbs. 8 oz.
586 C 6989—Six.69c; Ea.12c

(F) Beverage Pitcher 89c
New shape with ice lip for easy pouring. Large—70 oz. (2⅛ qts.) 7 in. high.
586 C 6985—Wt. 3 lbs...89c

(G) Refrigerator Set $119
Space saver—3 handy Jars each with cover. 4, 5 and 6-in. diams. Ship. wt. 5 lbs. 8 oz.
586 C 6992—Set.....$1.19

(H) Refrigerator Ice Lip Jug 98c
Convenient—shaped to fit in refrigerator. 54-oz. ice-lip Jug with cover. 7½ in. high.
586 C 6986—Wt. 3 lbs...98c

(J) Covered Butter Dish 79c
Keep butter covered and fresh. Tray 8½ by 4¾ in.
586 C 6990—Wt. 3 lbs...79c

(K) 3-Piece Salad Set 98c
$1.39 Value—Save 41c at Wards. Big salad bowl, 9-in. diam. Matching fork and spoon.
586 C 6983—Wt. 4 lbs...98c

(L) 3-Piece Waffle Set $198
Usual $2.49 Value! 42-oz. covered Batter Pitcher. 16-oz. covered Syrup Pitcher. Large attractive 11-in. serving Tray.
586 C 6993—Wt. 7 lbs.$1.98

11-Piece Set $209
$2.98 Value
Includes: 1½ qt. Covered Casserole and Plate; (D) Pie Plate and Server; (N) 6 Custard Cups; (E). Ship. wt. 18 lbs.
586 C 6995—11-Pc...$2.09

(M) Cookie Jar $119
$1.69 Value
Big 4-qt. size. Snug inset cover keeps cookies fresh. Good size for baking beans. 7½ in. high.
586 C 6994—Wt.4 lbs.8 oz.$1.19

(N) Heat-Proof Pie Plate 29c Pie Plate
39c Value. Deep, even-heating. 9½-in. Pie Plate. Matching Server listed below. Ship. wt. 3 lbs.
586 C 6982—Pie Plate....29c
586 C 6996—Server.
Ship. wt. 12 oz..........19c

Sequoia ovenware from a late 1930's Wards Catalogue. The pitchers making up the batter set are also sold separately as utility pitchers. See item number C.

Yorktown was made in solid colors and decalware. In keeping with the "concentric deco" pattern, there are no oval shape pieces. Even serving pieces are round.

Row 1: "Yorktown" white coaster, Shaker Cobalt blue, covered teapot Mango red, Shaker yellow, chop plate 10-¾".

Row 2: Penthouse round sauce or gravy boat, Penthouse shaker and covered casserole. Saucers in green, terra-cotta and pink.

Row 3: 1939 World's Fair chop plate 10-¾", AD cup "Picket Fence" tea cup, dinner plate 10".

The "Yorktown" pieces shown are from the collection of John Moses.

E. M. Knowles "Deanna" shape solid colors, stripes, plaids and decal ware.

Row 1: Dinner plate blue 10″, lug soup yellow, coffee server green, creamer red, sugar and cover pastel blue.

Row 2: "Rose" plate 9″, Shaker plaid, "Stripes" coffee server, "Mini Flowers" shaker, Wheat plate 10″.

Row 3: "Yellow Trim Poppy" plate 8″, "Daisies" platter, "Poppy" plate 7″.

Row 1: Tia Juana Flat Soup 8″, TJ shaker and cup, "Bench" platter 12″ and "Bench" round vegetable bowl 9″.

Row 2: "Sleeping Mexican" plate 6″, Sleeping Mexican shaker and AD cup, Knowles utility ware Tia Juana covered jar, Tia Juana II deeper ivory background gourds removed.

Knowles used at least three Mexican motifs on their Deanna shape, the most common being Tia Juana showing the Mexican sitting in a doorway. There are two versions of Tia Juana.

Row 1: "Leaf Spray" sugar, "Wildflower" creamer, saucer, 8″ plate.

Row 2: Golden Wheat meat platter, Golden Wheat on Yorktown.

Row 3: Utility Ware, refrigerator bowls, Tia Juana covered jugs, Tia Juana plate.

Row 4: Knowles utility ware serving tray, large mixing/utility bowl.

Golden Wheat $3.59 32-Pc.
USUAL $5.95 VALUE

A typically American pattern. Sprays of Golden Wheat in natural colors on charming modern shapes. Triple-selected first quality Ivory-White American Semi-Porcelain. Platters are round to harmonize with the other pieces. In the 95-Piece Set there are 2 round open vegetable dishes. Matching teapot and salt and peppers listed at right.

For Glassware and Cutlery, see Pages 320-324. Table linen on Pages 312-315. 95-Pc. set shipped in 2 packages. *All sets Mailable.* See Page 319 for composition of sets.

486 B 6251—32-Piece Set. Service for Six.
Shipping weight 23 pounds............................**$3.59**

586 B 6255—Creamer and Sugar. Wt. 3 lbs........**$1.18**

486 B 6252—53-Piece Set. Service for Eight.
Shipping weight 42 pounds..................................**$7.49**

386 B 6254—95-Piece Set. Service for Twelve. Shipping weight 76 pounds............**$14.95**

586 B 6255—Extra Pieces—*State Article.* 6 (5 oz.) Cup Teapot. Shipping weight 3 pounds. 8 ounces............**98c**
Salt and Peppers. Shipping weight 1 lb. 8 oz.....Pr. **49c**

586 B 6255—Open Stock on all but oval open vegetable dish. *State pattern and articles wanted*—see Page 319 for list of pieces and prices.

Golden Wheat from a 1939 Wards. Green Wheat by Knowles was introduced in 1936. "Inspired by, and complementing the Golden Wheat line, Green Wheat should prove a worthy companion." *1936 Crockery and Glass Journal.*

A Knowles backstamp.

KNOWLES, TAYLOR AND KNOWLES

Knowles, Taylor and Knowles can be traced to an 1853 beginning as Knowles and Harvey. Their plant number 1 was on the corner of 6th and Walnut in East Liverpool. Isaac Knowles is listed as sole owner in 1867 in the same location. Knowles, Taylor and Knowles are listed from 1872 to 1929 when they became part of the American Chinaware Corporation. All K. T. & K. plants are shown as being closed in 1931. (American Ceramic Society, 1945)

Knowles, Taylor and Knowles contributed much to the ceramic industry. Knowles, Laughlin and Harker were competing for the introduction of whiteware. Most sources credit Knowles with being the first to make whiteware. All ware prior to that time made in the area had been yelloware or Rockingham ware. Knowles also made the beautiful Lotus ware for a brief period of time.

Knowles, Taylor and Knowles backstamp.

THE HOMER LAUGHLIN CHINA COMPANY

The Homer Laughlin China Company owes its origin to a two-kiln pottery in East Liverpool, Ohio, built in 1871 by Homer Laughlin and his brother Shakespeare Laughlin. The brother withdrew in 1879 and from that year until 1896 Homer Laughlin carried on the business as an individual enterprise. The Laughlin Pottery was one of the first whiteware plants in the country. As early as 1876 Laughlin ware received the highest award at the Centennial Exposition held in Philadelphia in that year.

In 1889 William Edwin Wells came to East Liverpool to work with Homer Laughlin. Homer Laughlin incorporated his business at the end of 1896 and shortly thereafter sold his entire holdings to Mr. Wells and a Pittsburg group headed by Mr. Marcus Aaron.

The new management, with Mr. Aaron as President and Mr. Wells as Secretary-Treasurer and General Manager, soon abandoned the small River Road plant and expanded with two new and much larger plants at Laughlin Station, Ohio, three miles east of East Liverpool. They also purchased a third plant located close to the new ones and which had formerly been operated by another company. All of these plants were in operation by 1903. Very soon even these three plants were inadequate and in 1906 the first of the present factories, Homer Laughlin Plant 4 was built in Newell, West Virginia, just across the Ohio River from East Liverpool. In 1907 Plant 4 began operation. In 1913 Plant 5 was added.

The first revolutionary change in production methods came in 1923 when Plant 6 was built. The plant was equipped with continuous tunnel kilns instead of the old wasteful periodic kilns which had so long been the distinguishing landmark of potteries everywhere. The new type of plant was so successful that by 1929 two further tunnel kiln plants, Plant 7 (1927) and Plant 8 (1929), had been added. In 1929 the old East Liverpool factories fired their last ware and were withdrawn from production; meanwhile, in the years 1926 to 1934, the old kilns in Plant 4 and Plant 5 were replaced with modern tunnel kilns. Equally noteworthy with the change in firing methods has been the rapid mechanization of the potteries in more recent years. Spray glazing on high speed conveyors replaced many an old fashioned dipping tub. Conveyors moving at a slower speed reduced the wasted motion of men and materials. Even in the fashioning of the ware itself, mechanical jiggering came to substitute in large part for the traditional hand operation.

Quite as marked as the change in the production methods has been the change in the character of the ware produced.

In January 1930, after more than forty years of magnificent work in the development and expansion of the business from a small riverside pottery in Ohio to the five great factories in West Virginia, and to a position of unquestioned leadership in its field, W. E. Wells retired from active director of the business and was succeeded by his son, Joseph Mahan Wells. Mr. Aaron became Chairman of the Board and his son, M. L. Aaron, succeeded him as President. Under the leadership of the younger Mr. Aaron and Mr. Wells, the company continued the manufacture of its previous successful wares and turned in addition to the creation of a series of new developments which have radically altered the type of domestic dinnerware in the American home.

First of these developments was the Wells Art Glaze line - Matt Green, Peach, and Rust, and later Melon Yellow. Then followed the exquisite smooth texture, deep ivory glaze, known as Vellum, equally effective in undecorated ware and as a base for decorative treatments. The next outstanding step was in the field of cooking ware for table use — Ovenserve and Kitchen Kraft. From these most successful utilitarian wares, Homer Laughlin proceeded next to the creation of the most outstanding colored glaze lines of modern times, and in that field produced Fiesta, Harlequin and Rhythm — wares which have become almost synonymous for colored glazes and have brought new cheer and warmth and joy to millions of Americans. A correlative development in the field of decorated ware resulted in the Homer Laughlin Eggshell Line — thin, light and graceful as no previous earthenware had been — ware of distinction and enduring quality. In 1959, the company started production of fine translucent table china, as well as a vitreous line for hotel and institutions.

Joseph M. Wells became Chairman of the Board and his son, Joseph M. Sells, Jr., assumed the position of Executive Vice-President on January 1, 1960.

From the original two-kiln plant, employing about sixty people and producing about five hundred dozen pieces of dinnerware per day, the company grew to the employment of 2,500 people, the use of 1,500,000 square feet of production area, and the production of thirty thousand dozen pieces of dinnerware per day.

In 1976 approximately 1,200 employees produced over 46 million pieces of dinnerware with modern methods and equipment.

DATING HOMER LAUGHLIN CHINA

The original trademark merely identifying the product as Laughlin Brothers appeared from the beginning in 1871 until around 1890. Unfortunately, reproductions are unavailable. The second trademark featuring the American Eagle astride the prostrate British Lion, signifying the end of the domination of the British in the dinnerware field in this country, was in use until around 1900. The third trademark merely featuring the initials HLC with slight variations has appeared on all dinnerware manufactured since that time and continues today.

In 1900 the trademark featured a single numeral identifying the month, a second single numeral identifying the year and a numeral 1, 2, or 3 designating the point of manufacture as East Liverpool, Ohio.

In the period 1910 - 1920, the first figure indicated the month of the year, the next two numbers indicated the year, and the third figure designated the plant. Number 4 was "N", Number 5 was "N5", and the East End plant was "L".

A change was made for the period of 1921 - 1930. The first letter was used to indicate the month of the year such as "A" for January, "B" for February, "C" for March. The next single digit number was used to indicate the year and the last figure for the plant.

For the period 1931 - 1940, the month was expressed as a letter, but the year was indicated with two digits. Plant No. 4 was "N", No. 5 was "R", No. 6 and 7 were "C", and No. 8 was listed as "P". During the period E-44R5 would indicate May of 1944 and manufactured by Plant No. 5. The current trademark has been in use for approximately 70 years, and the numbers are the only indication of the year that items were produced.

The Homer Laughlin Company is one of the largest producers of restaurant ware and dinnerware in existence. It would be an impossible task to picture all the ware turned out by Homer Laughlin in their many years of production. The Homer Laughlin Company is best known with collectors for their now famous Fiesta and Harlequin lines. Harlequin was reissued in 1978 and the plates are marked Homer Laughlin 1978. (See marks) For more information, be sure to see *The Collectors Encyclopedia of Fiesta* by Sharon and Bob Huxford.

At left a 1933 backstamp. At top are early Homer Laughlin backstamps. At bottom is a 1980 Homer Laughlin backstamp.

Harlequin

ironstone dinnerware

Harlequin was introduced to the public in 1938 and lasted until the late fifties according to Sharon and Bob Huxford, authors of *Collector's Encyclopedia of Fiesta*.

Solid colors on a lighter weight body, Harlequin was sold through the Woolworth stores.

Homer Laughlin backstamps.

FIESTA—*in gay new colors*

Fiesta Table Service Unit, illustrated above, consists of nine charming pieces: Turquoise coffee pot, Yellow platter 12 inches across, Red open vegetable bowl 8½ inches wide, Blue creamer and sugar, Red pepper and Green salt shaker.
A65104 Table Service Unit. **$7.50**

New! Smart!! Different!!! 7 Piece Juice Set in genuine Fiesta. This colorful set includes a 30 ounce Yellow pitcher and six tumblers—one each, Turquoise, Red, Blue, Green, Ivory and Yellow.
A65105 7-Piece Juice Set.............**$1.95**

Originating in California, inspired by the colorful festivals of Mexico, Fiesta dinnerware has flashed across the country in a gay blaze of color. Its beautiful rainbow shades have captivated the hearts of housewives, bringing cheer and gaiety into the home, adding festive charm to al fresco dining. Fiesta deserves a wide acclaim, for, in addition to its brilliant assorted colors, genuine Fiesta is a supreme quality glazed semi-porcelain, modernly shaped and beautifully formed. There's a unique thrill in setting a table with Fiesta's color spectrum; an endless variety of mixing, blending, matching or contrasting the individual place settings. New arrangements every day . . . eye appeal that transforms eating from a humdrum routine to the zest of a gay party. Please order by number.

PRICES OF FIESTA SETS

A65100	24-Pc. Service for 4	**$11.00**
A65101	36-Pc. Service for 6	16.00
A65102	48-Pc. Service for 8	22.00
A65103	72-Pc. Service for 12	32.00

The Homer Laughlin Company will long be remembered for their famous Fiesta colored ware introduced at a 1936 trade show. Fifty-four different items in four colors made up the original assortment. Different color assortment and items were added or dropped over the years.

AMBERSTONE

Row 1: Quarter lb. butter, sauce boat, salt and pepper set, cup

Row 2: Saucer, small dessert dish, platter or liner for sauce boat, 6″ dessert plate

Row 3: Platter, coffee server, dinner plate

Row 4: Large soup bowl, Handled tray

A 1967 Sheffield Amberstone order blank lists the following pieces: dinner plate, dessert dish, bread and butter plate, coffee cup, saucer, vegetable bowl, covered sugar, creamer, 13 platter, large soup plate, ash tray, salt & pepper, salad plate, soup/cereal bowl, covered casserole, sauce boat, relish tray, coffee server, tea server, covered butter, round serving platter, jumbo salad bowl, covered jam jar, serving pitcher, jumbo mug, and pie plate. Only pieces large enough to accommodate the design carry it, other pieces, are plain. Some of the hollow ware pieces are marked Fiesta.

1930-31 Wards catalog

FOR THE MODERN HOSTESS

$10 25 New Art China — Flight of the Swallows

We have been very fortunate in securing this beautiful new shape and decoration for exclusive mail order presentation. No other Mail Order House will show it during the season of this catalogue. The newest idea in shape and unusually artistic in design, it was created this year. One of the finest department stores in New York City had a pre-showing, the first time it was offered to the public—in March.

Note the narrow edge of the plates; the new design handled vegetable dish—without lip—which makes washing as easy as an ordinary plate—and the delightful **square salad plates**.

The body of this semi-porcelain is creamy ivory, fine smooth glaze. The outer edges of plates are unusual because of narrow green band separated from main body by narrow black line. Foliage spray has orange and green leaves. The flight of the swallows is in natural colors. Except through our catalogue these dishes will probably not reach the smaller cities of America before 1931. Write for our Free Dinnerware Booklet. See Easy Payment Budget Plan, Page 457.

Set consists of 36 Pieces as follows: **6 Teacups and Saucers, 6 Dinner Plates, 6 Square Salad Plates, 6 Sauce Dishes, 1 Sugar Bowl (2 pieces), 1 Creamer, 1 Platter, 1 Open Vegetable Dish, 1 Gravy Boat.**

450 G 3531—We Pay Postage $10.25

$8 29 New Art China—Solid Colors — Deep Rose—Light Green

A most unusual glaze has been developed by some of the finest chemists in the ceramic field for these two sets. The secret formula gives to these beautiful dishes a finish that has **created an instant demand for them wherever they are shown.**

Soft mellow texture like the delicate surface of a bird's egg. The inner and outer edge of the rim has a faint high light. The body color shows creamy through the dark and rich rose or green coloring. Best quality semi-porcelain body. Note interior of handled vegetable dish.

Looks—for all the World—like old china imported by our forefathers. Nothing like it sold in America before 1930, it is now achieving tremendous popularity in New York and Chicago. Ward's have been successful—and certainly fortunate—in arranging for the exclusive mail order showing of these beautiful sets. We Pay Postage.

Set consists of 36 Pieces as follows: **6 Teacups and Saucers, 6 Dinner Plates, 6 Bread and Butter Dishes, 6 Sauce Dishes, 1 Sugar Bowl (2 pieces), 1 Creamer, 1 Platter, 1 Open Vegetable Dish, 1 Gravy Boat.**

450 G 3532—Green.....$8.29   450 G 3533—Rose..$8.29

Easy Payments
See BUDGET PLAN, Page 457

$9 98 New Art China — Flowers of the Dell

Another of the modern new shapes with a narrow band edge and the new design handled vegetable dish that is without an inside lip to catch and retain food. As easy to wash as a bowl. The two sprays of dell flowers, green, brown, blue and violet almost touch across the center of the plates. And what delightful plates—edged with green, creamy ivory background. The fine smooth glaze which is so apparent will last the life of the set—for this dinnerware represents not only beauty—but quality.

So new and modern! This particular pattern and shape was produced after April of this year. At the present time it is enjoying tremendous sales in New York City.

This set is identical in composition and shape as the "Flight of the Swallows"—Differs only in the decoration. Write for our Free Dinnerware Booklet.

Set consists of 36 Pieces as follows: **6 Teacups and Saucers, 6 Dinner Plates, 6 Square Salad Plates, 6 Fruits (Sauce Dishes), 1 Sugar Bowl (2 pieces), 1 Creamer, 1 Platter, 1 Open Vegetable Dish and 1 Gravy Boat.**

450 G 3530—We Pay Postage $9.98

Homer Laughlin backstamp.

Row 1: Ivory sugar and cover with red, butter dish, Green art glaze platter, Ivory creamer with red trim.

Row 2: Tab handled green nappy, coffee server ivory with Hollyhock decal, covered green syrup.

Row 3: Green Art glaze cup, rose teapot, rust demi-cup and saucer, flat soup bowl "Palm Tree."

ITEMS AVAILABLE

1 Tea Cup	8 Coupe Soup 8"	15 Sauceboat	22 Water Jug
2 Tea Saucer	9 Cereal Soup	16 Casserole Cov'd	POPULAR SETS—ADDITIONAL ITEMS OBTAINABLE FROM OPEN STOCK
3 Plate 10"	10 Fruit 5½"	17 Sugar Cov'd	
4 Plate 9"	11 Nappie 9"	18 Cream	20 Pc. B SERVICE FOR 4 WITH 9" PLATES
5 Plate 8"	12 Platter 11½"	19 Salt Shaker	20 Pc. AT SERVICE FOR 4 WITH 10" PLATES
6 Plate 7"	13 Platter 13½"	20 Pepper Shaker	32 Pc. D SERVICE FOR 6 WITH 9" PLATES
7 Plate 6"	14 Pickle	21 Tea Pot Cov'd	53 Pc. C SERVICE FOR 8 WITH 10" PLATES

THE HOMER LAUGHLIN CHINA COMPANY, NEWELL, WEST VIRGINIA

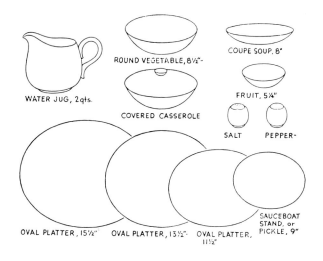

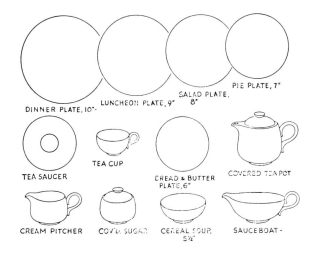

RHYTHM SHAPE

Row 1: All Rhythm, covered sugar, creamers, covered teapot, cup/saucer set

Row 2: Dinner plate 10″, sauce or gravy boat, cereal/soup dish 5½″, Fruit or sauce dish 5¼″

Row 3: Salt and Pepper set, Provincial 7″ plate, decaled covered teapot, creamer not Rhythm but Cavalier Shape

A 1926 wholesale catalogue shows "the popular new octagonal shape" in the Raymond pattern. A variety of treatments and decals were used on the Yellowstone octagonal shape over a period of many years. A colorful peacock is found on some pieces of Homer Laughlin ware. The Art glazes are marked Wells Art Glazes.

At right: Yellowstone shape, assorted decals.

A 1926 wholesale catalog reprint showing Rosetta pattern.

Homer Laughlin backstamps.

Yellowstone octagonal shape with assorted decals from the collection of John Moses.

Row 1: Republic, Georgian N-1577, Georgian G-3468, Republic
Row 2: Possibly Liberty, Nautilus, Nautilus N-1577 Ferndale, Nautilus N — 1594 Tulip
Row 3: KK 436 Pie Plate, Nautilus Regular, Liberty L 613
Row 4: Georgian G-3370, Georgian, Georgian G-3499

Homer Laughlin backstamps.

A variety of marks used over a period of years by The Homer Laughlin Company, Newell, West Virginia

All Oven-serve pieces from the 1935-45 period with assorted decals. Homer Laughlin's KitchenKraft was another popular oven-to-table line.

Priscilla teapot

PRISCILLA

Row 1: Priscilla covered sugar, saucer, creamer.

Row 2: Cake plate, 9″ plate, 8″ plate.

Row 3: Covered casserole, mixing bowl.

Row 4: Priscilla coffee server, larger mixing bowl.

Nautilus Eggshell and Oven-Serve from the 1940's.

Priscilla on eggshell. This lovely pattern is attracting quite a bit of attention from collectors of American dinnerware.

Homer Laughlin Priscilla backstamp.

English Garden decal on square
Century shape as offered in a
1933 Sears catalogue.

Assorted decals on Homer Laughlin's Century Shape

The Virginia Rose blank is estimated by Mr. Ed Carson of The Homer Laughlin Company to have been made from 1935 to 1959 with as many as 150 different decals used on this blank. This pattern is the pattern most collectors refer to as Virginia Rose. Many other serving and dinnerware pieces are available in Virginia Rose, already a favorite with collectors.

VIRGINIA ROSE BLANK
THE HOMER LAUGHLIN COMPANY

Row 1: Virginia Rose gravy boat, salt & pepper shaker sets, egg cup, creamer, covered sugar

Row 2: Virginia Rose covered butter (century shape) pitcher, covered vegetable

Row 3: Virginia Rose dinner plate, cup and saucer set, flat soup, pie baker

Row 4: Virginia Rose 3 pc- mixing bowl set, pickle dish or gravy boat liner, platter or meat dish

CHATEAU   APRIL   MARGARET ROSE   ARISTOCRAT

LEXINGTON   CASHMERE   RAMBLER ROSE   NASSAU

Lightweight "Eggshell" Semi-Porcelain

Virginia Rose blank, assorted decals

Epicure

Homer Laughlin's newest and smartest dinnerware for casual dining!
Its superb styling with textured glazes in charming colors of Dawn Pink,
Snow White, Charcoal Gray and Turquoise Blue creates an incomparable table setting. Sturdy . . . Multi-purpose . . . Ovenproof . . .
Meeting America's demand for function and beauty at modest prices.

Full color National advertising starting in May issues of leading consumer magazines will bring pre-sold customers to your store.

Plan now to meet the demand with EPICURE — The most salesworthy
dinnerware 1955 will see.

The Homer Laughlin China Co.
NEWELL, WEST VIRGINIA

Skytone blank (except creamer in upper right-hand corner is Kraft-blue). The decal is Stardust and was a very popular pattern in the 1940's and 1950's.

Homer Laughlin Skytone backstamp.

BRIAR ROSE...

Deep Ivory Vellum Glaze

*Has Wild Rose Sprays
and Platinum Edges*

95 Piece Set $24⁹⁵

Now Greater Value Than Ever

WE'VE lowered the price on our best seller! Our enormous sales told us that this pattern, this quality was *right*. So, armed with a huge order, and cash to pay for it, we went direct to the Wells' Pottery, exclusive makers of this new ware. We specified first quality sets and named a low price. The makers agreed! And you get the *full* benefit of this saving.

The Vellum glaze on this semi-porcelain ware has a satiny luster, a glowing, deep-ivory tint with the richness of parchment. Fragile-looking wild-roses in delicate pink that shades almost to ivory, soft color gray-green leaves and thorny brown twigs fall in a naturalistic spray over this rich background. Bright, polished platinum line-edges. Smartly modern in its new square shape and rounded, scalloped corners. It's already a favorite with hundreds because it's new, beautiful, fine quality and the best value anywhere. For pieces in sets, see Page 268. Two largest sets have two-handled soup-cups. **All Sets Shipped Not Prepaid. 95-Piece set Not Mailable.** See this set in actual colors—send for our free Dinnerware Circular. *Sold in sets only.*

32-Pc. Set: Service for 6
450 VF 4276
$5⁹⁸

53-Pc. Set: Service for 8
450 VF 4277
$12⁹⁵

95-Pc. Set: Service for 12
150 F 4279
$24⁹⁵

FROM A 1933 SEARS CATALOGUE

Briar Rose is only one of the many decorations found on Homer Laughlin's Century shape. Riviera (colored glazes) was introduced in 1938 and Sharon and Bob Huxford in their *Collector's Encyclopedia of Fiesta* tells us it was a limited line and sold exclusively by the Murphy Company. Riviera colors are blue, light green, red, yellow and ivory.

Century Shape colored glazes, Riviera

Homer Laughlin's Organandy Pastel After-Dinner set

Organdy Pastels

SET SEASON'S SMARTEST TABLES

$2⁷⁹

20 Pieces

Lovely pastel borders on eggshell semi-porcelain create a table service that every woman will want. Exquisitely tinted . . . definitely flattering to your table. Cool Lime Green, pale Maize Yellow, soft Sky Blue or Icing Pink, rims each piece of hollow ware, circles each plate. Handles are green. Styled in Swing shape. Thinner and lighter than ordinary American semi-porcelain—yet just as strong. Every set is assorted in four colors. Open stock on opposite page. For composition of sets, see Page 441 . . . Buy also the Matching Tumblers banded in the same beautiful pastel shades, listed below. *For Easy Terms, see Page 5.*

35 L 4404—Give catalog number and state size of set you want.

20-Pc. Set. Service for 4. Shpg. wt., 13 lbs... **$2.79**	**32-Pc. Set.** Service for 6. Shpg. wt., 15 lbs.... **$4.89**	**53-Pc. Set.** Service for 8. Large Dinner Plates. Shpg. wt., 28 lbs..... **$9.29**
Sugar and Creamer. Shipping weight, 3 lbs.. **1.04**	**Set of 8 Tumblers.** 4 Water or Ice Tea glasses 12 oz; 4 Fruit Juice glasses 5 oz. **35 L 244**—Shipping weight, 4 pounds....................... **75c**	

NAUTILUS EGGSHELL SHAPE

circa 1935-1955
Apple Blossom (N-1627 decal number)

The Homer Laughlin China Company is one of the largest producers of American-made restaurant and dinner ware. It would not be possible to picture all of the ware this gigantic company has produced over the years.

Homer Laughlin Eggshell backstamps.

Row 1: All Brittany shape variations
Row 2: Brittany W538, Brittany W-538 Blue Brittany cup/saucer
Row 3: Nautilus shape, Brittany B-1420 Green, May be Debutante shape
Row 4: Brittany Sample, May be Cavalier shape, Brittany sample

Clive

For everyday meals ... for formal dining—impressive *Clive* dinnerware fits every occasion! Deep maroon panels and floral sprays are brilliantly accented with rich Gold trim for added elegance. 95-piece sets have large round platters instead of oval.

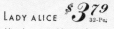

LADY ALICE $3.79 32-Pc.

Lady Alice has warm Maroon border with soft-colored Bluebells and Roses. Lovely for formal and informal occasions. Open Stock and 94-Pc. Set have new 13-in.-Round platter instead of 15-in. oval platter. Oval Vegetable dish not available. For pieces in Sets, see Page 486.

P486 C 6306—32-Piece Set. Service for 6. Shipping weight 20 lbs........$3.79
P486 C 6307—53-Piece Set. Service for 8. Shipping weight 38 lbs.......$7.49
P386 C 6309—94-Pc. Set. Service for 12. Same as 95-Pc. without Oval Vegetable Dish. Ship. wt. 68 lbs. Cash...$14.95
$2 Dn. $2 Mo. on Time—See Inside Back Cover.
586 C 6310—Open Stock. See Page 482.

Catalog reprints showing Homer Laughlin dinnerware.

Homer Laughlin backstamp.

Various Homer Laughlin shapes and decals.

LEIGH–CRESCENT

A listing for The Crescent Pottery first appeared in the Alliance, Ohio, City Directory in 1921-22 with Charles L. Sebring as president. Crescent was still listed in the 1927-28 directory with the name of Frank Sebring. Crescent was still listed in 1929-30 with the name of Leigh Potters, Inc. in parenthesis. The pottery was listed as Leigh Potters, Inc. with Frank Sebring, Chairman, Charles Sebring, President, Frank Sebring, Jr., Vice President, Charles Baker, Secretary, and George Stanford, General Manager. The last listing for the pottery was 1938.

Frank Sebring had retained the molds from The Tritt China Plant in Niles, Ohio. (See Universal Pottery) Strangely enough, when the Tritt operation was reopened, the Niles Tritt plant was also named Crescent. Their backstamp was also the half-moon shape. So, for at least a short period of time, there were two Crescent plants - one in Niles, Ohio, and Alliance, Ohio. There are some remembrances about an infringement suit involving the Crescent name. At any rate, The Crescent Company in Niles changed its name in 1923 to Atlas China Company. (See Universal Pottery)

The Leigh Pottery building was sold to Alliance Manufacturing.

A 1940 article from the Alliance Review reports that Charles Leigh Sebring was leaving Sebring to be the design manager of Edwin M. Knowles China Company, then the third largest in the United States. Charles L. Sebring was also associated with Limoges and Salem China Companies and at that time (1940) was chairman of the United States Potters Association.

A catalog advertisement for Housetops.

The Sienna ware Crescent was a trademark of ware made at Alliance, Ohio.
The Crescent China Company at Niles also used the half-moon mark at least for a short period of time.

1930's ads for Leigh dinnerware.

Leigh Ware was named after the owner of Leigh Potteries of Alliance, Ohio. In a 1929 article on Leigh Ware by Alden Welles in *The Crockery and Glass Journal.* C. L. Sebring is said to be "one of the most progressive forces in the business today." (1929) The color of Leigh Ware is achieved by the umbertone body and not the glaze. A unique innovation indeed! At the time of the 1929 article, it was pointed out that Leigh Ware had not long been on the market. Gale Turnbull is credited with designing the ware under the direction of technical supervision, Joseph Palin Thorley. The dinner service is described as conservative with the details of bundles, decorative knobs and the "setback" form of handles.

The "novel treatment of the patterns" on the creamy tan background are what sets the Leigh Ware apart from all other dinnerware of its time. Pastel borders of two or more pastel colors, "artful placing" of decoration and a silver trim (actually platinum and white gold) around the edges were the three types of decorations used.

Leigh (according to the same article) had produced an art ware line comprised of "lamp bases, vases, flower bowls and fruit bowls, wall pockets, book ends, etc."

Leigh backstamps.

Be sure to read Universal's early history dating back to the early twenties in Niles, Ohio. It is possible that two plants called Crescent were in operation at the same time, if but briefly. (Circa 1922-23) The same backstamp (half-moon) was used both at Niles and Alliance.

Row 1: Marked Crescent Tulip liner plate, covered sugar, cup and saucer set.

Row 2: Hot plate in Farberware frame "Basket", Mayfair cup, "Indian Tree" hot plate.

Row 3: Leigh Petit Point covered casserole, ice bucket with metal handle.

Row 4: Both marked Leigh, Mayfair, Green Wheat.

Row 1: "Tulip" cup/saucer, Tulip plate, candy dish in Farberware frame and handle.

Row 2: "Tulip" bowl with metal frame, "Tulip" plate in metal frame with hot water.

Row 3: "Tulip" serving plate with metal frame, Round "Tulip" plate with metal frame and handle.

LEIGH

Row 1: "Fuchsia" oval 13″ platter, tea-pot, gravy boat

Row 2: "Iris Bouquet" 9″ plate, 7″ plate, 5″ sauce dish, cream soup

Row 3: "Manhattan" demitasse cup/saucer set, one pound butter, creamer and covered sugar

THE LIMOGES CHINA COMPANY

The Limoges China Company was located in Sebring, Ohio, and was one of the many potteries owned by the Sebring family. They are credited with founding two towns - Sebring, Ohio, for the purpose of opening potteries and Sebring, Florida, probably for the purpose of rest and recreation - all done on $7,000 and all borrowed money.

The Limoges China Company was opened in approximately 1901 by F. A. Sebring, one of the Sebring brothers. Mr. Sebring's plans for Limoges China Company was to produce "thin porcelain products" like European ware. Highly trained help was brought from Europe and materials were imported from Europe.

The third year of business for Limoges was a disastrous one, as a fire destroyed equipment and is said to indirectly be the cause of the untimely death of the European ceramic expert.

Limoges China Company was completely renovated and shut down only briefly. The reopening was under the supervision of one of the younger Sebring brothers and semi-porcelain/earthenware was produced. Limoges also claimed the first of the tunnel kilns and decals are said to have made their debut at Limoges. Limoges also claimed the first "industrial ceramic laboratories" with graduate ceramic engineers. Limoges also claims to be one of the first to have a full-time artist and designer. Quite an impressive list of claims of "firsts."

In 1946, there was a campaign to sell retail Limoges ware only through stores bearing the name "House of American Limoges." This was probably to overcome the charges made by the Haviland people of Limoges, France. For this reason, "American" became a part of Limoges' advertising.

Limoges backstamps.

MT. CLEMENS

Row 1: All Mt. Clemens yellow glaze, Old Mexico on Alara shape plate, soup bowl, cup, vegetable bowl.

Row 2: Stetson decorated Alara shape "posies" creamer, item 2-4 are old Mexico line from Mt. Clemens, #3 Stetson decorated "Posies" sugar, #5 Stetson decorated sugar

Row 3: Marked "Stetson", Petit Point Rose decal plate, sugar, creamer, cup, bowl is "Springtime"

The Mt. Clemens Pottery had been owned by the S. S. Kresge Company since 1920. S. S. Kresge (now K-Mart) decided to sell the operation in 1965 and apply proceeds to their rapidly expanding operations. Mr. David Chase of Hartford, Connecticut, was the buyer and Mr. Sam Sabin became associated in a sales capacity. Mr. Sabin retained ownership of the Sabin China Company in McKeesport, Pennsylvania. The Sabin-McKeesport operation was destroyed by fire in 1979 and Mr. Sabin and his son David transferred their operation to Mt. Clemens where they have a partnership arrangement with Mr. Chase. They now decorate their ware in the old Mt. Clemens facilities and consider the possibility of actually manufacturing dinnerware.

Row 1: Poppy creamer, gravy boat, sugar

Row 2: Poppy salad plate 7″, covered vegetable, plate 9″

Row 3: Poppy small serving dish or platter, large platter

All California Poppy on Mt. Clemens Toulon shape

PADEN CITY POTTERY COMPANY

Red cooking ware fired in one upright kiln was the first ware made at the Paden City Pottery in Paden City, West Virginia. The Paden City Pottery was founded in 1907 by George Lasell.

Vases, teapots and bulb bowls were new items at the 1922 Ft. Pitt Hotel Show. The mahogany finish was reported as being a late development of Paden City Pottery. Tea sets in jet and mahogany were also offered in 1922 as was kitchenware. By December 1923 Paden City's plain white semi-porcelain dinnerware in the Ransom shape was ready for delivery.

Paden City Pottery is credited with originating the underglaze decal and the Caliente colored glaze. By 1949 Paden City Pottery had six tunnel kilns and personnel totaling 800. Paden City Pottery closed in the 1950's.

Row 1: Several pieces with this shape have been found marked Regina P.C.P.C. We can only assume that this is the shape name and of course P.C.P.C. stands for Paden City Pottery Company. "Springblossom" plate, cup, "Orange Blossom" casserole in Manning Bowman frame. "Touch of Black" plate and cup

Row 2: Regina Jonquil plate, serving plate American Beauty on Minion shape, American Beauty A.D. cup and saucer.

Row 3: Series of novelty cartoon plates - cartoons by Peter Arno, cobalt Caliente on Regina shape, Tangerine or Mango 6″ Caliente plate

Triple Guaranteed

When you buy your Dinnerware at Wards—you are protected by Wards Triple Guarantee!

1—Wards guarantee Open Stock on all dinnerware, and we will obtain replacements as long as pattern is made by the pottery.

2—Wards guarantee prices 20 to 35% lower than most prices on comparable dinnerware.

3—Wards guarantee safe delivery—and complete satisfaction.

AND—Wards offer a NEW service—make up your own set—include just the pieces you want at an additional saving—See Page 319.

NEW! CALIENTE RAINBOW
Dinner Set in Mixed Colors

$3.79
22-Pc. Set

A new idea for informal dining! In the 22-pc. set (service for 4) there is a complete set of one solid color service for each person—Tangerine, Yellow, Blue and Green. Put a complete outfit in front of each person, or mix up the colors—put the blue cup on tangerine, yellow or green saucer, put the yellow bread and butter plate with blue dinner plate, etc. The 32-pc. set (service for 6) includes 2 blue outfits, 2 yellow outfits, one tangerine outfit, one green outfit. 53-pc. set includes 2 outfits of each color. With all sets, vegetable bowl is green, platter yellow. First Quality American Semi-Porcelain. *Mailable.*
486 A 6173—22-Pc. Set. Ship. wt. 18 lbs..$3.79
586 A 6175—Creamer, Sugar. Ship. wt. 4 lbs.1.00
486 A 6171—32-Pc. Set. Ship. wt. 23 lbs.. 4.79
486 A 6172—53-Pc. Set. Ship. wt. 42 lbs.. 9.98
586 A 6175—*Open Stock on Next Page. When ordering from open stock be sure to state colors wanted . . . Tangerine, Yellow, Blue or Green.*

$2⁴⁹ 20-Pc.   *Colorful Gay Caliente Ware*   **$4⁴⁹** 32-Pc.
NOW FULLY OVEN-PROOF

Caliente—so popular for informal dining—so gay and colorful for Spring and Summer meals! Wards prices are 20% to 30% less than elsewhere. *Approved by Good Housekeeping as oven-proof.* Comes in Tangerine, Yellow, Blue or Green. Put a complete service of one color at each place—or mix up the colors. First quality Triple-Selected American Semi-Porcelain. Colors are applied in the glaze—they can't wear off. See Page 319 for composition of sets.

When ordering Open Stock and Extra Pieces—Be sure to State Color: Tangerine, Blue, Yellow or Green.

486 B 6169—**20-Piece Service for 4.** One service of each color for 4 persons. Shipping weight 14 pounds..................**$2.49**
486 B 6171—**32-Piece Service for 6.** 2 Blue, 2 Yellow, 1 Tangerine, 1 Green Service, Green Vegetable Bowl, Yellow Platter. Shipping weight 23 pounds **$4.49**
(G) 586 B 6175—**Creamer and Sugar.** *State color.* Shipping weight 3 pounds **$1.18**
486 B 6172—**53-Piece Service for 8.** Two services of each color; Blue Sugar and Creamer, Green Vegetable Bowl and Yellow Platter. Shipping weight 42 pounds **$8.98**
586 B 6175—**Open Stock.** *State pattern, articles wanted and color:* Tangerine, Yellow, Blue or Green. See Page 319.

Matching Tumblers with Safe-Edge Rim
586 B 6645—9½-oz. Wt. 5 lbs. Set of 8 .....39c
586 B 6598—5-oz. Wt. 3 lbs. Set of 8 .....37c

586 B 6175—**Extra Pieces.** *State article and color:* Tangerine, Yellow, Blue or Green. Shipping weights: 2 lbs., 1 lb., 3 lbs., 8 oz., 2 lbs.
(B) Salt and Pepper Shakers.................43c
(E) Candlesticks. Pair.................79c
(F) Ice Lip Jug, 64-oz 89c
(H) 6-(5-oz.) cup Teapot.................$1.29

Matching Oven-Proof Cooking Ware
(A) 586 B 6943—Casserole with 7-in. pie plate cover. 1½-qt. capacity. Ship. wt. 5 lbs. *State Tangerine, Blue, Green or Yellow* 95c
(C) 586 B 6940—Modern 1½-Qt. Casserole. Yellow only. Chromium plated base. Black Bakelite handles. Shipping weight 7 lbs. $1.59
(D) 586 B 6942—Large 10-in. Salad Bowl. Shipping weight 4 pounds. *State color:* Tangerine, Blue, Green or Yellow $1.19
586 B 6945—**3-Piece Bowl Set** (not shown). 7½-in.—Tangerine; 8¼-in.—Yellow; and 9⅜-in.—Green. Shipping weight 5 pounds.......98c

Our Finest Casserole
Colorful Modern! Ovenproof Semi-Porcelain Casserole (7½-in. diam. holds about 2 qts.). Bake in the oven—serve on the table in the detachable Chromium-plated frame. Wt. ea. 5 lbs.
586 C7682—Red Casserole, Yellow cover, Brown bakelite handles on frame..**$1.89**
586 C7683—Blue Casserole, Yellow cover, White handles on frame......**$1.89**

Reprints from 1930's and 1940's catalogues

CALIENTE

Row 1: Covered sugar, shaker, covered teapot, saucer, creamer

Row 2: Dinner plate, dessert plate, dinner plate

Row 3: Cream soup, covered casserole, candleholder, cup and saucer set

From the collection of John Moses

Marks found on Paden City Pottery Company's ware. You will find other marks. Shell-Krest is also found as Shell-Crest. I believe this Papoco mark to be a Paden City Pottery Company mark but I have not been able to verify this information.

An advertisement for Paden City Patio.

Row 1: Patio decal platter on Shell-Crest shape, oval bowl

Row 2: Patio plate, small bowl, large plate

Row 3: Nasturtium decal on Shell-Crest shape covered sugar/creamer, "Far East" on Shell-Crest shape plate, Shaker with rose decal. (This rose decal is called Vermillion Rose by another company), Nasturtium creamer or gravy boat.

Row 1: All Shenandoah Ware, Strawberry 8″ plate, Jonquil 9″ plate, Poppy 7″ plate.

Row 2: All Shenandoah Ware, Morning Glory covered sugar and creamer, teapot, 7″ plate. Wartime.

Row 3: "Floral" covered casserole, "Flaming Rose" bowl, Patio decal on covered casserole.

Row 4: "Bluebell", Early bowl with gold trim, "Red Rose" plates

Nasturtium
$3⁹⁸
32 pieces

• Rich 22K Gold stippling on every piece.
• Three clusters of Nasturtiums on each plate.
• Modern shape—dinner plates have large eating surfaces.

Dinnerware decorated with 22K Gold is a bargain at this price. Especially with its unusually life-like floral sprays and popular shape. Gay glowing nasturtiums on ivory glazed American semi-porcelain, four times selected. All sets have large 9-inch dinner plates.

35 L 04444—State size of set. Mailable.
32-pc. set. Serves 6. Shipping weight, 20 lbs......$3.98
Sugar and Creamer. Shipping weight, 3 lbs......1.17
53-pc. set. Serves 8. Shipping weight, 40 lbs......7.98

A 1940's ad for Paden City tableware.

Row 1: Modern Orchid on round shapes, Modern Orchid may also be found on Trend shape.

Row 2: "Yellow Rose" on Minion Shape. Minion Shape was introduced in August 1952.

Row 3: Duchess on Paden City's Ivory Tu-Tone shoulder, 1942, Ivy.

Row 4: Paden Rose platter, 7″ plate, 6″ plate, cup and saucer.

Paden Bak-Serv Autumn Leaf

Row 1: Jonquil sugar and creamer, "Posies" cup/saucer, plate.

Row 2: Grandiose meat platter, Grandiose was used on coupe shape with Greenbrier holloware, 1952. More "Posies" on coupe shape.

Row 3: "Wild Rose" on Princess line 9″ plate, 7″ plate, individual custard and teapot both marked Northern Products, Chicago. I can only assume at this time that these two pieces are Paden City.

Row 4: Shenandoah Ware in Farberware frame, Corn is Green designed exclusively for Paden City Pottery by Anton Refergier. Other patterns designed by Anton Refergier for Paden City Pottery were His Arabian Night, Design 44, The Rite of Spring and Sea Shell.

Row 1: Shellcrest shape, "Far East" creamer, sugar, "Acacia Flowers" cream and sugar.

Row 2: "Far East" on Shell-Crest, 9″ plate and 6″ plate, "Blossoms" meat platter on Shellcrest.

Row 3: Nasturtium on Shell-Crest, also found on Shenandoah Ware. Patio on Shellcrest.

Row 4: "Rust Tulip" on Shellcrest, "Tulip" may be American Tu-Tone shape, Tulip on service plate with wide cobalt band with gold filigree.

An advertisement for Shenandoah ware.

PFALTZGRAFF POTTERY

The present-day Pfaltzgraff Co. traces its original roots back to the early 1800's and, with its predecessor companies, is one of the oldest manufacturers of pottery in the United States. The Pfaltzgraff family has been continuously involved in the manufacture of stoneware and related products since that time. The current president is Louis J. Appell, Jr. whose mother is a direct descendant of the first member of the family to conduct pottery manufacturing in this country. Today's company is the outgrowth of a number of small pottery-making plants which over the last century and a half existed in several localities in York County, Pennsylvania.

The Pfaltzgraff name originated in the Pfalz area of the German Rhineland where the picturesque castle bearing the family name still stands. This famous landmark, seen by thousands of tourists each year, is reflected in the company's castle trademark.

One of the main concerns of life in the new United States in the early 1800's was the preservation of food for use in winter. To answer this need, the early products of The Pfaltzgraff Co. were storage crocks of stoneware with gray salt glaze and blue decoration which were used for pickles, sauerkraut, apple. butter and salted meat; jugs for vinegar, hard and soft cider, and molasses — all the good foods that added variety to the hearty fare of the German and Scotch-Irish settlers. Any of these early Pfaltzgraff crocks or jugs that have survived bring a high price at antique shows today.

Serving the needs of the community has always been one of the company's major goals. Like many contemporaries of early America, a Pfaltzgraff pottery was one of the community's most popular gathering spots, particularly during cold Pennsylvania winters. Because of its warmth, the pottery was the scene of dances and other events. Advertisements in local papers offered facilities for baking beans with slow-simmered cooking while the kiln was being heated up to the high temperature necessary for the proper firing of stoneware.

As technical and sociological changes in living came, one by one the early potter's main products fell into disuse. Glass jars with sealed lids were invented which introduced a whole new way of preserving food. An ice-making machine made refrigeration more widespread. Tin vessels which were lighter and more durable than stoneware were cheap and readily available. Changes in smoking habits led to the disappearance of clay pipes. Glass replaced stoneware patent medicine bottles. A new tariff bill brought American potters in competition with lower-paid European workers, and in the 1920's the Prohibition Amendment ended a good market in stoneware whiskey jugs.

Thus, to stay in business, potters had to change with the times. To supplement its dwindling household stoneware business, Pfaltzgraff for many years produced animal and poultry feeders. In the early days of this century red clay flower pots also became an important product line. As these products too began to yield to competition from other materials, Pfaltzgraff designers turned increasingly in the 1940's and 50's to other forms of household products and to giftwares. Brightly colored mixing bowls, custard cups, planters, cookie jars, ashtrays, and similar products became the staples of the line. These early examples of the company's current products found a ready market in gift and variety stores.

Soon an even stronger demand was triggered for new Pfaltzgraff dinnerware and serving pieces. These stoneware products were beautiful enough to be used for special occasions yet functional and sturdy enough to be used every day. Over the past twenty-five years Pfaltzgraff has introduced four extremely successful dinnerware lines — Gourmet, Heritage, Yorktowne, and Village, all still available with a wide range of accessories. To complement these wares the company manufactures tin, copper, and decorates glassware from other manufacturers.

Last year the company created new excitement in the retail world by introducing a different concept in dinnerware called "Compatibles." It is a colorful collection which can be mixed, matched, stacked, nested with new shapes to appeal to contemporary casual living.

In recent years Pfaltzgraff has expanded dramatically to meet consumer demand. Additional manufacturing facilities have been built in York and in nearby Adams County, including the largest pottery constructed in the United States since World War II. While time and technology have changed the original character of Pfaltzgraff products, the Pfaltzgraff reputation for high quality at a reasonable price has not changed. The company continues to produce useful and attractive products with the same integrity and pride that have been a Pfaltzgraff tradition since the early days of the 19th Century.

Even though the Pfaltzgraff Company's history dates back to 1805, the company as we know it today is a relative newcomer to dinnerware, as Pfaltzgraff made their first dinnerware in 1940.

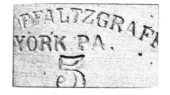

Photo #1 Top Left: Yorktowne

Photo #2 Top right: Heritage

Photo #3 Village

Photo #4 Gourmet

234

POPE GOSSER CHINA COMPANY

The Pope Gosser China Company was located in Coshocton, Ohio. They were members of the ill-fated American Chinaware Corporation until its demise in 1932. Their early ware does not have the appearance of quality ware. Pope Gosser did make some lovely ware in the forties as evidenced by the Florence pattern (Shown). Pope Gosser also made Rose Point and later sold the molds to Steubenville. You will find Rose Point made by both companies. The Canonsburg Pottery eventually wound up with the Rose Point molds and they, too, marketed Rose Point.

Pope Gosser
dinnerware and backstamps.

Florence

POTTERY GUILD

The Pottery Guild marked pieces have, until recently, been one of the big mysteries of dinnerware research. The Pottery Guild was a sales organization formed in 1937 by Mr. J. Block, founder of The Block China Company. Pottery Guild was granted a certificate of incorporation, August 10, 1937, in New York County and was dissolved by proclamation, March 8, 1946. Mr. Jay Block has remembrances of his father buying Pottery Guild ware from The Cronin Company, Minerva, Ohio. Pottery Guild, Hostess Ware pieces were widely distributed through wholesale houses and catalogue stores.

Pottery Guild backstamp, and below, a reprint from 1939 Wards catalog.

CALICO FRUIT OVENWARE—GUARANTEED OVEN-PROOF AND ACID-PROOF

Wards Will Replace Any Piece that Cracks or Crazes in Course of Baking

Every Piece guaranteed oven-proof and acid-proof. A new kind of Ovenware. Light-weight American Semi-Porcelain—as attractive as your china dinnerware—heat-proof to bake in—beautiful to serve in. Smart "Calico Fruit" design in rich Blue, Green, Orange and Red over dainty Ivory background. Bake, serve and store in the same pretty dishes—save time —save dishwashing.

3-Piece Bowl Set $1¹⁹
J Holds 1½, 2¼ and 4½ pints. 6, 7 and 9-in. diams. Large bowl not recommended for oven use. Ship. wt., set 9 lbs.
586 B 6877—Set.....$1.19

Custard Cups 12ᶜ Each
K For custards, cupcakes, clover leaf rolls, muffins, etc. Cap. ea. 5 oz. 3½-in. diam. Heat-proof. Shipping weight each 12 oz.
586 B 6878—Six........69c
Each...................12c

482 WARDS K

Pitchers in 3 Sizes 44ᶜ 16-oz.
Heat-proof pitchers—for cream, milk, iced and hot drinks, etc.
L 586 B 6888—45-Oz. 5½ in. high. Ship. wt. 3 lbs....74c
M 586 B 6887—30-Oz. 4⅝ in. high. Ship. wt. 2 lbs....59c
N 586 B 6886—16-Oz. 3¾ in. high. Ship. wt. 1 lb. 4 oz.44c

Range Set 89ᶜ
P Saves steps at the stove. Pair of salt and pepper shakers, 2⅝-in. tall. Covered jar for drippings, 5 in. by 4½ in. high. Heat-proof.
586 B 6880—Wt. 2 lbs. 4 oz.89c

11-Piece Set $2²⁹
$2.94 Value! Includes: Covered Casserole and Plate, 9-in. Pie Plate, Server and 6 Custard Cups described separately. Ship. wt. 18 lbs.
586 B 6891—11-Pc. Set..$2.29

Beverage Pitcher 98ᶜ
R Large—holds 5 pints. New shape with ice lip for easy pouring. 6½ in. high.
586B6885—Wt. 3 lbs. 8 oz.98c

3-Way Casserole $1¹⁹
S 3-Way! Use the 8-inch 1½-qt. Casserole covered or open —use the pie plate cover separately. Matching 9-inch plate included. Ship. wt. 8 lbs.
586 B 6870—Complete...$1.19

3-Piece Salad Set 98ᶜ
T Big salad bowl, 9-in. diam. by 2⅝ in. deep. Matching fork and spoon included.Wt. 4 lbs. 4 oz.
586 B 6875—3-Pc. Set.....98c

32ᶜ
9-in. Pie Plate

Cookie Jar $1¹⁹ $1.49 Value
U Big 7½-pt. size! Snug inse[...] in. high, 8-in. diam.—good siz[...] for baking beans too. Heat-proof Shipping weight 5 pounds.
586 B 6881.............$1.1[...]

3-Piece Waffle Set $1⁹⁸
V 3½-pt. covered Batter pitch[...] er, 6 in. high; 1-pint covere[...] Syrup Pitcher, 5 in. high, 11¾ b[...] 8¼-in. Tray with Red band.
586 B 6882—Shipping weigh[...] 11 pounds ....$1.9[...]

Heat-Proof Pie Plates 32ᶜ 9-in.
W Deep even-heating Pie Plate[...] Bake, serve, store in them Heat-proof. Matching server be[...] low.
586 B 6873—9 inches. Shippin[...] weight 2 pounds. 12 ounces...32[...]
586 B 6874—9⅝ inches. Ship ping weight 3 pounds........37[...]
586 B 6879—Pie Server. Ship. wt. 12 oz...........21[...]

Row 1: "Calico Flower" syrup jug, "Sombrero" syrup jug.

Row 2: Holland jug "Tulips", Jiffyware jug "Apples", ball jug "Pear".

Row 3: Calico Fruit, covered cookie jar, Calico Fruit serving plate.

Row 4: "Peach" salad bowl, "Calico" teapot covered casserole.

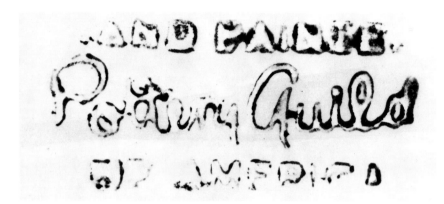

Pottery Guild backstamp.

15 PIECES—HEAT AND COLD RESISTANT—STUNNING PATTERN IN 5 COLORS, PLATINUM STRIPES

- Handled Cake Plate (12 inch) and Server
- Ball Beverage Jug — 2½ quarts
- Holland Beverage Jug — 2½ quarts
- Salad Bowl — 11 inch
- Casserole with Pie Cover—1½ quarts
- Handled Pie Plate (10 inch) and Server
- Range Set (4 Pieces)

A new and beautiful set of genuine Pottery Guild, oven-proof Hostessware. It's the latest type of baking and tableware, a light-weight, oven-proof pottery that is as attractive as china dinnerware, yet is unconditionally guaranteed heat-proof. With this practical set you can prepare, bake, serve, and store—without changing dishes! That means fewer dishes to wash! You'll enjoy preparing foods in this handsome Hostessware. You can bake in it, then serve in it—even use it for storing in your refrigerator, for it is positively guaranteed against breakage from either heat or cold. The set of fifteen pieces pictured above is a beautiful ensemble of Ivory with a china-like finish. Each piece is decorated with a lovely Peach pattern that is a blend of brilliant, fade-proof colors. An outstanding value!

Shipping weight 50 lbs.

A70110 Complete Set..................... **$12⁵⁰**

PURINTON POTTERY

The Purinton Pottery was opened in 1936 in Wellsville, Ohio, by Bernard Purinton. Purinton continued to operate at that location until 1941 when the pottery was relocated in Shippenville, Pennsylvania. Ground-breaking for the Shippenville-Purinton plant was in 1941 and open house for the new 300′X100′ plant was November 21, 1941. The first ware was drawn on Pearl Harbor Day, December 7, 1941. Officers were President, Bernard S. Purinton, Sales Manager, J. M. Hammer, Secretary/Treasurer, William J. Bower. The Shippenville Chamber of Commerce was instrumental in getting Purinton's move to Shippenville.

The Purinton Pottery did only hand-painting, using no decals. Purinton employed 100 workers from the area and provided an annual income of $140,000. William H. Blair and Dorothy Purinton were chief designers for Purinton Pottery. Harry Blair Purinton tells us that their Apple pattern was their first and best pattern.

A newspaper account from *The Derrick* tells of the plant's closing on May 30, 1958. Plans were pending to bring in outside management and sales help to reorganize and reopen the plant. On further investigation, we determined that "outside help" to be the Taylor-Smith-Taylor Company of Chester, West Virginia.

Final closing of the Purinton Pottery of Shippenville, Pennsylvania, is believed to be 1959. The end of a 61-year pottery association for the family, dating back to 1898 when Bernard Purinton's father, John, helped form the United States Pottery Company of Wellsville, Ohio.

Purinton made a line of solid color shapes for Rubel, a New York sales organization. These pieces were marketed under the name of Rubel.

ALL APPLE PATTERN

Row 1: 12 oz. tumbler, 6 oz. juice, salt & pepper shaker (part of range set), cup and saucer set

Row 2: Sugar jar, 6 ¾″ salad plate, cookie jar

Row 3: Dutch 2 pt. jug, drippings jar, 1 pt. small jug

Purinton **SLIP WARE**

Rubel & Company

Purinton Pottery Co.

Famous for FREE BRUSH *Purinton Slip Ware*. Tableware: Individual and distinctive pieces.

Purinton backstamps.

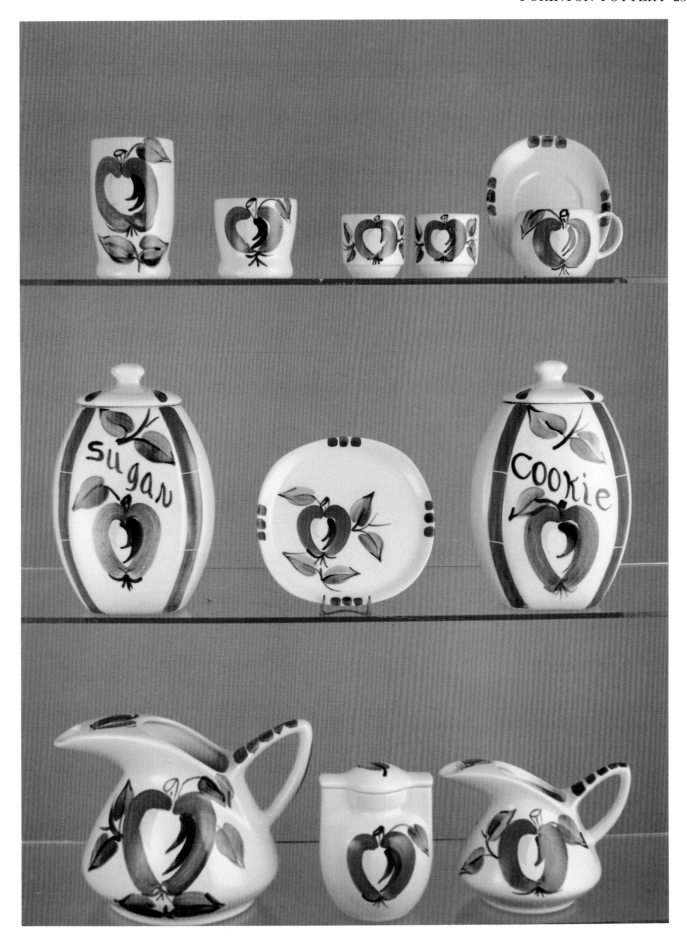

RED WING

Red Wing Pottery was founded in Red Wing, Minnesota, in 1878. Red Wing produced crocks, stoneware, and jugs until changing times in the 1920's caused a lack of interest in these products. Red Wing changed their trend in the twenties with a line of art pottery and more importantly added a colored dinnerware line, "Gypsy Trail," in the thirties.

Red Wing added a hand-painted dinnerware line in the forties and by the fifties had captured the dinnerware market with their Bob White pattern. An anniversary group was introduced in 1953, the 75th anniversary of Red Wing. "Capistrana" and "Country Gardens" were patterns from the anniversary group. Both patterns were on Red Wing's Tweed Tex surface texture.

A strike hit the company June 1, 1967. Liquidation began in August, 1967, and was completed in 1969. Red Wing dinnerware was sold at Red Wing several years after the manufacturing was discontinued.

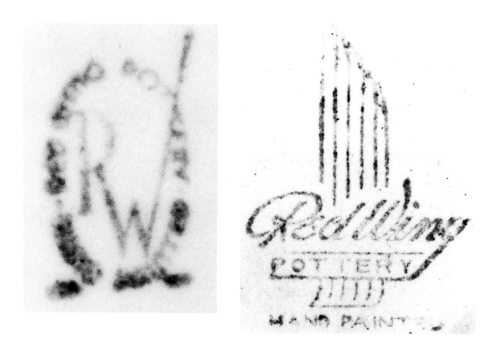

Red Wing backstamps.

LEXINGTON ROSE

Row 1: Tea pot, cup/saucer set, dinner plate.

Row 2: Creamer, covered sugar, gravy boat with liner

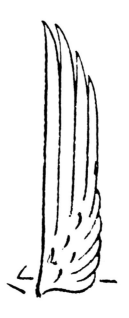

Red Wing backstamps.

Bob White

Hand Painted - Color Fast - Oven Proof
Detergent Safe

Bob White
BY RED WING

Coffee cup 1.45
Saucer 1.00

Plates, dinner 2.00
salad, 1.50, bread and butter, 1.00

Sauce or fruit 1.00   Cereal, salad 1.50   Rim soup 1.85

SETS

● **16 Piece Starter Set** Service for 4 .. 17.95
includes four each salad plate, dinner plate, cup and saucer.

● **45 Piece Set** Service for 8 .... 59.95
includes eight each salad plate, dinner plate, cup, saucer, cereal bowl. One each vegetable dish, 13" platter, sugar and cover, creamer.

RED WING POTTERIES, inc.
RED WING, MINNESOTA

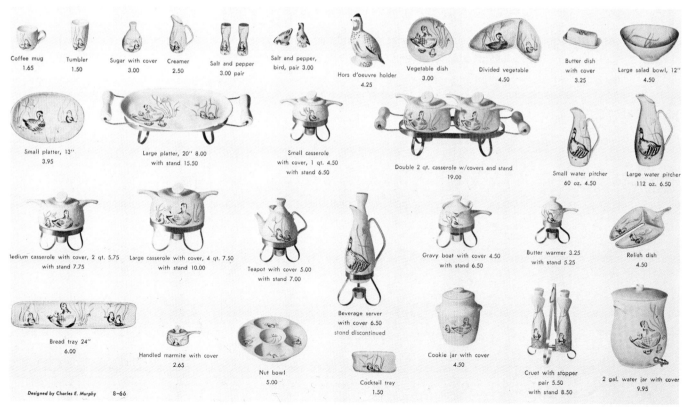

| Coffee mug 1.65 | Tumbler 1.50 | Sugar with cover 3.00 | Creamer 2.50 | Salt and pepper 3.00 pair | Salt and pepper, bird, pair 3.00 | Hors d'oeuvre holder 4.25 | Vegetable dish 3.00 | Divided vegetable 4.50 | Butter dish with cover 3.25 | Large salad bowl, 12" 4.50 |

Small platter, 13" 3.95

Large platter, 20" 8.00 with stand 15.50

Small casserole with cover, 1 qt. 4.50 with stand 6.50

Double 2 qt. casserole w/covers and stand 19.00

Small water pitcher 60 oz. 4.50

Large water pitcher 112 oz. 6.50

Medium casserole with cover, 2 qt. 5.75 with stand 7.75

Large casserole with cover, 4 qt. 7.50 with stand 10.00

Teapot with cover 5.00 with stand 7.00

Beverage server with cover 6.50 stand discontinued

Gravy boat with cover 4.50 with stand 6.50

Butter warmer 3.25 with stand 5.25

Relish dish 4.50

Bread tray 24" 6.00

Handled marmite with cover 2.65

Nut bowl 5.00

Cocktail tray 1.50

Cookie jar with cover 4.50

Cruet with stopper pair 5.50 with stand 8.50

2 gal. water jar with cover 9.95

Designed by Charles E. Murphy   8-66

Red Wing's Bob White dinnerware has been declared by some as the most popular pattern of the 1950's. Bob White was designed by Charles Murphy who later went to work for the Stetson Company, Lincoln, Illinois

*...a new look
for your table*

It's fiesta time every time you dine on this exciting new **RED WING** dinnerware, handpainted in rich browns, greens, and vivacious melon accents, lightly flecked with brown overall. Tampico . . . a pattern to pep up that 3-times-a-day routine . . . to make all your entertaining colorful and different.

. . . the life of   party!

If dinnerware could dance,   ampico would surely outstep them all! Set your   table with this vivacious dinnerware, and . . . *suddenly it's a party!* . . . whether you're serving 'burgers backyard style or snacking on TV tables.

Like all **RED WING** dinnerware, Tampico is oven proof and color fast . . . the delightful design sealed under the glaze to stay like new through years of festive dining.

RED WING'S *Tampico*

different! festive! colorful!
. . . the new "South of the Border" look in dinnerware

Tampico DINNER WARE

hand painted—color fast—oven proof

JANUARY 1965

	Each
Plate, 6½", B and B.	$ 1.15
Plate, 8½", Salad.	1.65
Plate, 10½", Dinner.	2.25
Coffee Cup.	1.55
Coffee Mug.	1.75
Saucer.	1.10
Sauce or Fruit.	1.15
Cereal.	1.65
Rim Soup.	1.90
Sugar and cover.	2.75
Creamer.	2.25
Salt and Pepper—Pair.	2.25
Nappy.	3.00
Divided Vegetable.	4.95
Large Salad Bowl, 12".	5.95
Butter Dish and Cover.	3.50
Small Platter, 13".	4.95
Large Platter, 15".	6.25
Casserole and cover.	6.50
Small Water Pitcher, 1 qt.	3.50
Large Water Pitcher, 2 qt.	5.95
Teapot and cover.	5.25
Beverage Server and cover.	6.50
Gravy Boat and tray.	4.75
Relish Dish.	3.50
5 Comp. Nut Dish.	5.00
2 gal. water cooler & cover & stand.	13.95

SETS
16 Piece Set: Service for 4. . . . . $17.95
Four each 8½" plate, 10½" plate, cup, saucer.
45 Piece Set: Service for 8. . . . . $59.95
Eight each 8½" plate, 10½" plate, cup, saucer, cereal. One each sugar and cover, creamer, nappy, small platter.

 RED WING POTTERIES inc.
RED WING, MINNESOTA

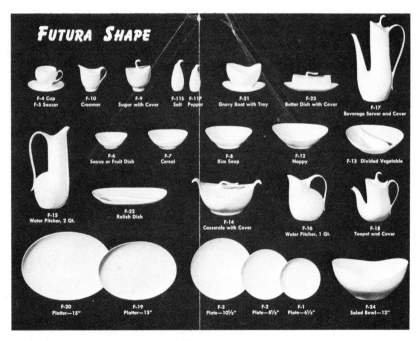

NEW *FUTURA SHAPE*

RED WING's new shape is modified oval, designed for practicality as well as interest and grace. Plates, bowls and cups are easy to handle, easy to stack, and require minimum table space—ideal for outdoor and buffet service. Cups feature a slightly narrowed "non-splash" lip. Beverage servers, salts and peppers, handles on bowls and covers are in "different" shapes to lend zest to your service.

Tampico on the futura shape - 1950's

DINNERWARE BY RED WING
Hand Painted - Color Fast - Oven Proof
Detergent Safe

APRIL, 1963

	Each
Plate 6", B&B	$1.50
Plate, 7", Salad	2.00
Plate, 10", Dinner	2.50
Cup	2.00
Saucer	1.25
A. D. Cup	1.75
A. D. Saucer	1.10
Sauce or Fruit	1.50
Cereal Salad Soup	2.00
Sugar with Cover	3.50
Creamer	2.50
Salt and Pepper	3.00
Vegetable Dish	3.75
Divided Vegetable	6.95
Salad Bowl, Medium, 10"	7.95
Butter Dish with Cover	4.50
Platter, 13" Small	4.95
Platter, 15" Large	5.95
Casserole with Cover, 2½ qt.	7.95
Water Pitcher, 1½ qt.	7.95
Teapot with Cover	7.50
Beverage Server with Cover	8.95
Gravy Boat with Cover	7.50
Divided Relish	4.50
Celery Dish	3.95
Bread Tray, 24"	8.50
Bean Pot with Cover, 1½ qt.	7.95
Ash Tray	1.00
16 Piece Set	19.95
45 Piece Set	69.95

Set Compositions:

16 Piece Starter Set—4 each 7" plates, 10" plates, cups, saucers.

45 Piece Set—8 each 7" plates, 10" plates, cups, saucers, cereals, 1 sugar with cover, 1 creamer, 1 vegetable dish, 1 small platter.

RED WING POTTERIES, inc.
RED WING, MINNESOTA

Pépe

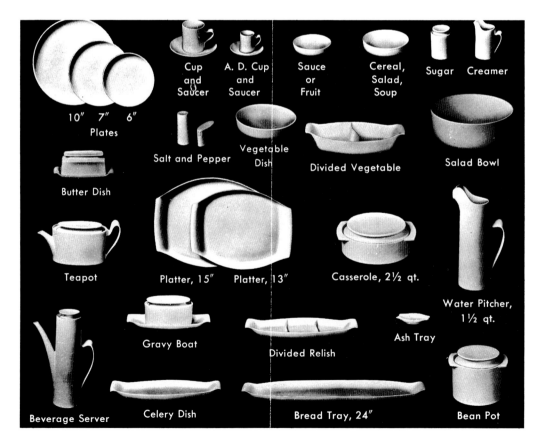

Pepe is already a favorite of collectors. The 1963 brochure describes Pepe as "a dramatic Spanish motif of the modern school." Flecked beige undertones are highlighted with sunburst of bittersweet and deep mauve.

VILLAGE GREEN
Color Fast - Oven Proof
Detergent Safe

Large Bean Pot, 4 qt.
$5.00

Small Bean Pot, 2 qt.
$3.50

Warmer
$3.00

**VILLAGE BROWN
DISCONTINUED**
No longer available

- **16 Piece Starter Set** Service for 4 includes four each bread and butter plate, dinner plate, cup, saucer. $9.95
- **45 Piece Set** Service for 8 includes eight each bread and butter plate, dinner plate, cup, saucer, sauce or fruit. One each vegetable dish, 13″ platter, sugar and cover, creamer. $29.95

RED WING POTTERIES, inc.
RED WING, MINNESOTA

*Village Green
and
Village Brown*

6″ Bread & Butter Plate $.90
8″ Salad Plate $1.00
10″ Dinner Plate $1.25

Cup $1.00
Saucer $.90

Coffee Mug $1.40

Beverage Mug - $1.50

Sugar $2.25

Creamer $1.75

Small Salad Bowl $1.15

Cereal $1.00

Sauce or Fruit $.90

Rim Soup $1.25

6″ Baking Dish $1.25

12″ Baking Dish With Cover $3.50

12″ Baking Dish $2.00

Chop Plate, 14″ $4.00

Large Platter, 15″ $4.00

Small Platter, 13″ $2.75

Vegetable Dish $2.50

Divided Vegetable $3.00

Gravy With Tray $3.75

Butter Dish $2.75

Handled Marmite $1.75

Marmite $1.50

Salt & Pepper $3.00, pair

Large Salad Bowl, 12″ $4.00

Medium Salad Bowl, 9″ $2.50

Casserole, 4 qt. $5.50 Stand $2.50

Medium Casserole, 2 qt., $4.00 Stand $2.00

Casserole, 1 qt. $2.50 Stand $1.50

Syrup Jug $1.50

Teapot, 6 Cup $4.00

Beverage Server, 8 Cup $4.00

Pitcher, 4 Cup $2.00

Pitcher, 10 Cup $4.00

2 Gallon Water Jar $9.00

Village Green and Village Brown

Village Green is another popular collectible Red Wing pattern. Heavy and substantial, Village Green is second in popularity only to Red Wing's Bob White. Mid 1950's

ROYAL CHINA COMPANY

Royal China Company is located in Sebring, Ohio. The Royal China Company was formerly the old E. H. Sebring plant. Everyone that I have talked to credits the success of Royal to Beatrice Miller. The Royal plant expanded and eventually became part of the Jeanette operation. Royalton was Royal's tradename for their plastic dinnerware line.

Royal China, Inc.
15th St. & California Ave.,
Sebring, Ohio

Royal China backstamps.

Gold lace salt and pepper, creamer.

Advertisements from the late 1940's and early 1950's for Royal China.

CAVALIER iron stone

Genuine American Ironstone by Royal China

Quality CAVALIER Ironstone is produced by skilled craftsmen in America's most modern pottery. With the addition of eight new patterns, Royal is more exciting, more sales appealing than ever.

BETTER STYLING . . . MORE VERSATILITY
Genuine American Ironstone by Royal China . . . seventeen distinctive patterns that make their statement quietly but effectively. Accentuated with today's fashion colors, Royal's superbly styled casual dinnerware is at home on a buffet table or at a formal dinner party. Royal . . . the most versatile, most desirable line of medium-priced dinnerware in the industry.

Brentwood

Triple Treat

Clear Day

Overture

Casablanca

Currier & Ives

A Royal China brochure.

Sunny Day

Night Song

Dynasty

Hidden Valley

Casa del Sol

Medici

Blue Willow

Middlebury

SALEM CHINA COMPANY

Biddam Smith, John McNichol and Dan Cronin are credited with the founding of the Salem China Company in 1898 in Salem, Ohio. They had been with the Standard Pottery operation in East Liverpool, Ohio. They had been pessimistic about the future of the pottery growth in East Liverpool. There was little activity in the new operation and by 1918 the business needed a considerable amount of capital to continue.

F. A. Sebring was given an option on the Salem plant in 1918. F. A. was looking for a spot for his son returning from the war. Floyd McKee was asked to rejoin the Sebrings and to manage the Salem operation until Frank Jr. (Tode) was discharged.

Possession was taken August, 1918. McKee retired in 1950 and became chairman of the Board. At that time J. Harrison Keller became president and general manager. The Salem China Company is still operating but no longer as a manufacturer.

A variety of marks was used on Salem pieces over the years. Some of those marks are shown here.

Row 1: 6″ plate "Basket", 8″ plate "Basket", "Colonial" ashtray with Farberware frame

Row 2: "Yellowridge" 9″ plate, 6″ "Bluebird" plate, 9″ "Maple Leaf" plate.

Row 3: "Goldtrim" 6″ plate, butter pat "Goldtrim", "June" 7″ and 9″ plate. All of row 3 is on "Briar Rose" shape.

Row 1: "Streamline" shape "Tulip" covered sugar, creamer, cup and saucer set, Sailing plate on "Tricorne" shape.

Row 2: "Mandarin Red" covered sugar, creamer, cup, "Sailing" on "Tricorne" shape.

Row 3: "Rust Tulip" on "Victory" shape platter, "Rust Tulip" 6″, 7″ and 6″ plates.

Row 4: "Petit Point Basket" 9″ plate, 7″ plate on "Victory" shape, 9″ Bryn-Mawr on Symphony shape.

Salem backstamps.

SALEM CHINAWARE FOR QUALITY and LASTING BEAUTY

Carolyn Service Plates

They add that extra touch of color and decoration to any table setting. Striking floral design with heavy embellished border accent their beauty. Colored rims are overlaid with a beautiful filigree of 23K. gold. Wide gold line adorns the edge. Center design shows full blown rose in a nest of blue and green leaves, surrounded by dainty pink and yellow flower. **Carolyn Service Plates** are available in a choice of colored rims: Maroon, Pink, Blue or Green. **State color rim desired.** Packed 6 of a color to a carton.

Shipping weight, 11 pounds.
1290E585. Per set of 6...................................... **$9.50**

Godey Prints Service Plates

Nothing could be lovelier than this modern dinner table setting, based on the old-time themes of Grandmother's day, of vivid colors and lavender and lace. Three different Godey Prints are featured throughout the Service Plate set, each authentically reproduced in warmth of color, quaintness of style and clearness of detail. Wide heavy border comes in maroon, pink, blue or green with delicate gold filigree over the color and shoulder of the plate. The edge is banded in 23-kt. gold. Truly a delightful pattern for anyone who cherishes the beauty and loveliness of things old fashioned, brought down to us from days gone by. Packed 6 of color to carton. Shipping weight, 11 pounds.

State color rim desired.
1289E625. Per set of 6....................

$10.00

Features of Salem China.—American china (semi-porcelain) body. Flawless, permanent, underglaze decoration. Patented process develops light weight. Bodies are exceptionally non-brittle. Shapes developed by famous stylists. Open stock.

COMPOSITION OF SALEM SETS

35-Piece Set	53-Piece Set
(Ship. wgt. 25 lbs.)	(Ship. wgt. 38 lbs.)
6—Cups	8—Cups
6—Saucers	8—Saucers
6—Dinner Plates 9 in.	8—Dinner Plates 9 in.
6—B & B Plates 6 in.	8—B & B Plates 6 in.
6—Fruits	8—Coupe Soups 7 in.
1—Meat Platter 11 in.	8—Fruits
1—Open Veg. Dish 8 in.	1—Cov. Sugar (2 Pcs.)
1—Cov. Sugar Bowl (2 Pcs.)	1—Cream Pitcher
1—Cream Pitcher	1—Meat Platter 11 in.
	1—Open Veg. Dish 8 in.

100-Piece Set
(Shipping weight, 80 lbs.)

12—Cups	1—Open Veg. Dish 8 in.
12—Saucers	1—Gravy Bowl 1 pt.
12—Dinner Plates 9 in.	1—Meat Platter 11 in.
12—Pie Plates 7 in.	1—Meat Platter 13 in.
12—B & B Plates 6 in.	1—Cream Pitcher
12—Coupe Soups 7 in.	1—Cov. Sugar (2 Pcs.)
12—Fruit Dishes	1—Cov. Veg. Dish (2-Pc.)
6—Oatmeals	
1—Open Butter Dish	

Commodore Pattern

Always in good taste and harmonizes with any table setting. 23K. gold of unusual beauty and appeal. Delicately traced border and classic medallions of gold.

Nation wide acceptance among all types of stores and buyers has proven the continued popularity for this type of pattern. Featured on the plain Symphony Shape with wide rims and creamy white surface, making a perfect background for a pattern of this kind.

1286E965. 35-Pc. set	**$17.50**
1287E1395. 53-Pc. set	**$26.00**
1288E2650. 100-Pc. set	**$50.00**

BRYN-MAWR PATTERN

Gay, charming floral sprays in soft, dual-tone colors of brown, lavender and gray with an edge line of platinum gold on an ivory white translucent semi-porcelain body. New, gracefully shaped handles and feet add that extra appearance that brings forth praise. You get years of pleasure and service from every piece.

8676E975. 35-Pc. Set... **$18.50**	**8677E1450.** 53-Pc. Set... **$28.50**	**8679E2750.** 100-Pc. Set... **$55.00**

INDIAN TREE

Originally created by the celebrated English designer, Thomas Minton, in the 18th Century, this design has been popular ever since. This pattern gives you a combination of a beautiful legend, plus a lovely decoration. This pattern is rich in gay flowers, featuring deep pinks, blues, and yellows supported by colorful foliage. It has real eye-appeal and is meeting with splendid acceptance on the part of discriminating buyers.

7537E825. 35-Pc. Set... **$16.50**	**7538E1225.** 53-Pc. Set... **$24.50**	**7540E2650.** 100-Pc. Set... **$52.50**

Dinner Sets

Prices Subject to Catalog Discount
See Page 1A

"Basket of Tulips"

EX5041— 32 Pc. Set _ _ _ $10.90
EX5042— 53 Pc. Set _ _ _ 21.40
EX5043—100 Pc. Set _ _ _ 41.20

The various colored Spring Tulips on our Bonjour shape makes this a friendly pleasing pattern; finished with a wide Platinum band. This set reflects quaint charm and dignity.

"Standard"

EX5044— 32 Pc. Set _ _ _ $12.60
EX5045— 53 Pc. Set _ _ _ 24.60
EX5046—100 Pc. Set _ _ _ 47.50

For those who do not want an extreme modernistic shape — the white beauty of the ware and the four narrow floral sprays of buds combined, make this an attractive and desirable number. Its beauty is enhanced by a blue edge line.

"Tulip"

EX5047— 32 Pc. Set _ _ _ $9.80
EX5048— 53 Pc. Set _ _ _ 19.20
EX5049—100 Pc. Set _ _ _ 37.00

The most outstanding feature of this pattern is the vividly blended colors of the Tulip. The decorations set on the side of the plate is most unusual and attractive.

"Formal"

EX5050— 32 Pc. Set _ _ _ $13.10
EX5051— 53 Pc. Set _ _ _ 25.70
EX5052—100 Pc. Set _ _ _ 49.60

Colors which are a "natural!" This pattern is decorated with a ¼" Rust and Gold outer border, and a 1", 22 carat Gold design on the inside border. Any hostess will appreciate the pleasing variation this pattern offers.

"Cadet Series"

EX5053— 32 Pc. Set _ _ _ $12.60
EX5054— 53 Pc. Set _ _ _ 24.60
EX5055—100 Pc. Set _ _ _ 47.50

Sophistication is predominant. This set will make a smart inviting dinner table. It is a delightful expression of modern decoration.

COMPOSITION OF SETS (For composition of smaller sets see opposite page)

100 Pc. Set *(Shipping Weight 80 lbs.)*

Popular Sized Sets			
12 Cups	12 Coupe Soups 7"	1 Gravy Boat	1 Covd. Sugar (2 Pcs.)
12 Saucers	12 Fruits	1 Cheese Plate	1 Covd. Veg. Dish (2 Pcs.)
12 Dinner Plates 9"	1 Ob. Open Veg. Dish 9"	1 Meat Platter 11"	1 Jelly Bowl
12 B and B Plates 6"	1 Rd. Open Veg. Dish 8"	1 Meat Platter 13"	
12 Pie Plates 7"	1 Pickle Dish	1 Cream Pitcher	1 Covd. Butter (3 Pcs.)

Cambridge Crystal Glassware Pages 226 and 227

Dinnerware

List Prices Subject to Catalog Discount

• • COLORFUL, new and smart patterns styled to thrill the modern housewife.

"Dutch Petit Point"

EX5019—32 Pc. Set _ $ 9.90
EX5020—53 Pc. Set _ 19.40
EX5021—100 Pc. Set _ 37.50

Very colorful is this **Petit Point** design of a **Dutch Boy and Girl**, worked in red, blue and warm light brown on a cream background and red and blue bands on the border. An interpretation of an authentic Dutch masterpiece, done in Petit Point needlework design. Bonjour shape.

For Composition

of Sets

See PP. 224-225

"Sailing"

EX5018½—32 Pc. Set _ _ _ _ _ _ $10.40
EX5018—53 Pc. Set _ _ _ _ _ _ 20.40

Unusually smart, this streamlined design is a reproduction of a well-known artist's version of a ship motif. The **coral and black sailboats** with their guiding stars are reminiscent of the bright sails of an old-world fishing fleet. Set off by coral and platinum lined edges.

"Summer Day"

EX5022—32 Pc. Set—$10.40
EX5023—53 Pc. Set— 20.40
EX5024—100 Pc. Set— 39.40

Lovely harmony of color and balance are reflected in this pattern of a smart blue and white flower pot, in which sprays of red, black and green flowers are artistically placed. The Bonjour shape is lovely to look at and practical to use.

All Priced

F. O. B. New York

or Factory at Salem, Ohio.

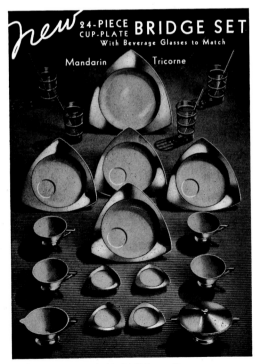

"Mandarin Tricorne"

EX5025—24 Pc. Cup-Plate Bridge Set _ _ _ $10.70

The outstanding bridge set of the year with its unusual Tricorne shape and new cup-plate feature. Plates have solid gay red borders, with white interiors. Cups—solid red exterior, white interior. Glasses have gay red stripes. Set consists of 4 cup-plates; 4 cups; 4 beverage glasses; 4 sippers; 4 nut dishes; 1 creamer; 1 sugar and cover (2 pcs.); 1 sandwich tray. This novel set solves the hostess' serving problem and its gay colors add a festive note to any Bridge or Buffet Luncheon or Afternoon Tea.

American Dinnerware

"Monogram"

EX5015— 35 Pc. Set _ _ _ _ _ _ _ _ _ _ _ _ _ $14.90
EX5016— 53 Pc. Set _ _ _ _ _ _ _ _ _ _ _ _ _ 23.10
EX5017—100 Pc. Set _ _ _ _ _ _ _ _ _ _ _ _ _ 48.10

The essence of "smartness" is reflected in a dinner table set with monogrammed silver, glassware and dishes. This lovely streamlined pattern is beautifully decorated in 23 karat gold; available with any desired initial. **(Monogrammed Dinnerware is made to order and requires a few extra days for shipping.)**

Dinnerware Sets

Prices Subject to Catalog Discount
See Page 1A

"Rose-Marie"

EX5026— 32 Pc. Set _ _ _ _ $12.60
EX5027— 53 Pc. Set _ _ _ _ 24.60
EX5028—100 Pc. Set _ _ _ _ 47.50

The entire center of the plate is covered by a cluster of Rose Buds of various soft pastels. A touch of Platinum on the edge produces a stimulating effect and adds a note of elegance.

"Aristocrat"

EX5029— 32 Pc. Set _ _ _ _ $16.40
EX5030— 53 Pc. Set _ _ _ _ 32.10
EX5031—100 Pc. Set _ _ _ _ 62.10

The established popular Century Shape with a smart new decoration. The entire border is finished in Delphinium Blue with four narrow black lines superimposed on the inner edge. Bordering this is an inner Platinum band. The hollow ware of this set is allover Delphinium Blue with black lines and Platinum bands and white interiors.

"Fruit Basket"

EX5032— 32 Pc. Set _ _ _ _ $12.60
EX5033— 53 Pc. Set _ _ _ _ 24.60
EX5034—100 Pc. Set _ _ _ _ 47.50

A distinctive pattern in both shape and decoration. Delightful little Fruit Baskets form the border of rich colors. All offset by an unusual narrow Checkerboard band in black and yellow on the edge. This dinner set will look well on any table and will reflect the good taste of the hostess.

"Jeanette"

EX5035— 32 Pc. Set _ _ _ _ $9.80
EX5036— 53 Pc. Set _ _ _ _ 19.20
EX5037—100 Pc. Set _ _ _ _ 37.00

A somewhat conventional pattern on our New Yorker Shape—the lightly embossed edge and the tinted ware blend beautifully with the new flower pot decoration. The colors are a harmonious blend of soft blues, yellows and orange.

"Victory"

EX5038— 32 Pc. Set _ _ _ _ $8.70
EX5039— 53 Pc. Set _ _ _ _ 17.00
EX5040—100 Pc. Set _ _ _ _ 32.80

The graceful lines and perfect symmetry that characterizes this handsome set make it unusually smart and popular. The border deviates from the standard floral embossing by being fluted. The handles on the hollow pieces are convenient and attractive. Although undecorated, this pattern has a stateliness hard to surpass.

COMPOSITION OF SETS (For composition of larger set see opposite page)

Composition of 53 Pc. Set

6 Cups	6 Fruits
6 Saucers	1 Meat Platter
6 Dinner Plates 9"	1 Open Vegetable Dish
6 B & B Plates 6"	

(Shipping Weight about 22 lbs.)

Guaranteed
Safe
Delivery

Composition of 32 Pc. Set

8 Cups	8 Fruits
8 Saucers	1 Vegetable Dish 8"
8 Dinner Plates 10"	1 Meat Platter 13"
8 B & B Plates 6"	1 Creamer
8 Coupe Soups 7"	1 Covd. Sugar Bowl (2 Pcs.)

(Shipping Weight about 39 lbs.)

MODERN DINNERWARE
Introducing the New VICTORY SHAPE
with decorations to enhance its natural beauty.

DINNER SETS SHOWN ON THIS PAGE ARE MADE UP OF THE FOLLOWING PIECES

32-Pc. Set:	53-Pc. Set:	100-Pc. Set	
6—Cups	8—Dinner Plates 9″	12—Cups	1—Meat Platter 11″
6—Saucers	8—Bread & Butter Plates 6″	12—Saucers	1—Meat Platter 13″
6—Dinner Plates 9″	8—Coupe Soups 6″	12—Dinner Plates 9″	1—Jelly Bowl
6—Bread & Butter Plates 6″	8—Fruits	12—Pie Plates 7″	1—Cov. Butter (3-pcs.)
6—Fruits	8—Cups	12—B & B Plates 6″	1—Cheese Plate 6″
1—Meat Platter 11″	8—Saucers	12—Coupe Soups 6″	1—Gravy Boat
1—Open Vegetable Dish 8″	1—Covered Sugar (2-pcs.)	12—Fruits	1—Cov. Sugar (2-pcs.)
	1—Creamer	1—Ob. Open Veg. Dish 9″	1—Cream Pitcher
	1—Platter 11″	1—Rd. Open Veg. Dish 8″	1—Covd. Veg. Dish (2-pcs.)
	1—Open Vegetable Dish 8″	1—Pickle Dish	

Doily Petit Point

This "Doily Petit Point" pattern on the new Victory shape is an outstanding contribution to modern designing. This very beautiful pattern embodies all the dignity and grace of rare old lace. The design features a beautiful rose center with a floral border, all worked out in the new Petit Point or cross-stitch design. The handles are all treated with a wide gold bar giving added attractiveness to this decoration. A fawn background adds the final touch to this lovely pattern.

The shape is the new "Victory," designed by a noted ceramic designer of the Cleveland Art School. Surely if you are interested in fine furnishings for that home of yours this beautifully shaped chinaware so smartly decorated will appeal to you. You will find listed below three different size sets, one to meet the requirements of any size family.

NO. 22K10
32 PC. SET
$9.25

NO. 22K11
53 PC. SET
$15.70

NO. 22K12
100 PC. SET
$32.00

"Jane Adams" Pattern

Bright gay flowers feature this decoration, with yellows and greens predominating. Dainty orchid buds also enhance the attractiveness of this lovely design. It is a two spray design. The handles are treated in appropriate colors.

This "Jane Adams" pattern is as attractive as a refreshing summer floral spray. It sets off the modern dining table to such great advantage that knowing hostesses are unusually enthusiastic about it. You, too, can be sure that what it does for other tables it most assuredly can do for yours. The new "Victory" shape forms a perfect background for the smartness of its modern pattern. You will be interested in knowing that this shape was designed by a noted ceramic designer of the Cleveland Art School. This is truly a lovely shape.

NO. 22K13
32 PC. SET
$9.25

NO. 22K14
53 PC. SET
$15.70

NO. 22K15
100 PC. SET
$32.00

**A SMART, MODERN SHAPE SET OFF BY
ATTRACTIVE DESIGNING**

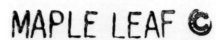

Salem China Co.
Box 277, Salem, Ohio

Salem backstamps.

THE SCIO POTTERY COMPANY

The Scio Pottery Company was founded by Lew Reese in 1932. The plant had been built in Scio in 1920 as an additional production plant by Albright of Carrollton, Ohio. The operation was closed in 1927.

Lew Reese visited Scio in 1932 and looked over the abandoned plant. The property was purchased by Reese at a sheriff's sale for $8,000 on a time payment plan. He immediately started repairs on the plant, living in a corner of the plant.

By February, 1933, the Scio-Ohio Pottery Company lacked funds for a payroll, raw materials and orders. The story goes that a clay salesman got his company to advance clay and Reese himself went to Chicago and persuaded a large firm to take the first carload of cups. When the first payroll fell due, Lew Reese had a cash balance of 11 cents. Twenty townspeople put up $100 a piece and Scio began a history that has spanned nearly a half-century.

Scio's Ranson shape with Hazel pattern.

Currier & Ives coupe shape.

Dorset Platinum trim.

SEBRING POTTERIES

George A. Sebring had five sons: Oliver, George E., Ellsworth H., Frank A. and Joseph Sebring. The father had worked around in the potteries and seemed to be content in doing just that.

In 1887 in East Liverpool, Ohio, a pottery was formed by George Ashbaugh, Samson Turnbull and the Sebring brothers. Frank A. soon became the leader of the brothers.

The Sebring brothers,* Ashbaugh and Turnbull were able to take over the Agner Fautts Pottery for $12,500.00. They all did what was necessary and reopened the plant with $7,000.00. Soon after the plant was opened, Ashbaugh and Turnbull pulled out, the Sebrings buying their share for $11,000.00.

The Sebrings leased the East Palestine Pottery Plant in 1893. They were offered a bonus to build a plant in East Palestine (Ohio China Co.). In 1899, the Sebrings bought a large plot of land in Mahoning County, Ohio, just four miles from Alliance. They sold their interest and concentrated on Sebring, Ohio, and some of their plants included Sebring, Oliver, French China and Limoges China. Around the 1920's or late-teen's, Sebrings purchased the Salem China works.

The Sebrings are a study within themselves. They were involved with many potteries and change of names of potteries over the years. They also founded Sebring, Florida, but it was not a pottery location.

Heirloom Corinthian Shape-Sebring Pottery- Sebring, Ohio

Row 1: Cup/Saucer set, Small bowl ?, 7″ plate

Row 2: 9″ plate, covered vegetable bowl

Row 3: Teapot, gravy boat, 8″ plate

Row 4: platters or meat dishes

Sebring backstamps.

* One source credits Ashbaugh and Turnbull as early Sebring partners and yet another source reports the early partners to be S. J. Cripps and Ashbaugh. Rarely will you find positive information concerning the early history of the pottery people.

SHAWNEE POTTERY

A chance finding of an Indian arrowhead by Malcolm Schweiker created the interest to research what tribes had lived along the Muskingum. Mr. Schweiker discovered that Shawnee settlements had once been in the area and he named his new pottery - Shawnee.

The new Shawnee Pottery was housed in the former American Encaustic Tiling Company in Zanesville, Ohio. The date was 1937. Addis E. Hull, Jr. resigned from the A. E. Hull Pottery of Crooksville to manage the newly-formed Shawnee Pottery.

The hostilities toward other countries was beginning to build in the late 1930's and buyers were looking for American-made ware. Shawnee was able to get several accounts and, in 1938, George Rum Rill of Rum Rill Pottery suggested working with Shawnee. Rum Rill was not a manufacturer but a jobber or sales organization.

Many changes took place during the war years but operation resumed in 1946. Malcolm Schweiker sold his interest and Addis Hull resigned. By 1954, like many American potteries, Shawnee was suffering from an operating loss. Also in 1954, John Bonistall came to Shawnee to serve as vice-president and general manager.

Bonistall is credited with breathing new life into the dying pottery. He made many changes, introduced new ideas. Shawnee's dinnerware, Corn Queen and Corn King, have long been popular with collectors. Shawnee also made lobster sets under the Kenwood division of Shawnee.

Shawnee Corn pattern.

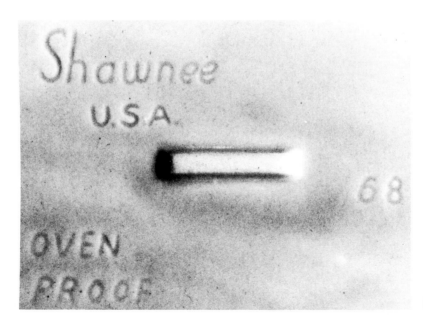

Shawnee backstamp.

SOUTHERN POTTERIES

Southern Potteries was established in 1918 in the hope that the Carolina, Clinchfield and Ohio Railroad would further encourage industries to the area. The pottery was built by Ted Owens of Minerva, Ohio. Difficulty in keeping experienced potters and the training of local people caused a couple of reorganizations of the pottery.

The hand-painting on the bisque and cheap wages paid the local help contributed to the success of the pottery. Literally thousands of pieces were sold for theatre premiums in the 1940's. Also the ability to discard one pattern and start another, with little or no expense, was another contributing factor to Southern's success.

The Southern Potteries was liquidated in the 1950's and was sold to the National Casket Company, thus ending another American pottery story. Southern Potteries started in business as Clinchfield Ware, became Southern Potteries, and later was better known as Blue Ridge China Company.

Many decorating companies made matching or co-ordinating designs to go with the hand painting being done at the Southern Pottery plant.

Boxed sets of Blue Ridge China are relatively easy to come by. Children's feeding dishes were made by Southern Potteries as they were by many other American dinnerware companies.

Former decorators of the Southern Potteries identified the pieces shown for us. Many patterns and variations of those patterns are hand painted on a smaller variety of blanks, making for an almost limitless array of handpainted patterns.

Wild Rose is the pattern shown on the Colonial blank as identified by workers.

Row 1: Crabapple on Colonial blank, Tiger Lilly on Skyline blank, Variation of Crabapple on Colonial.

Row 2: Fruit on Colonial, Cosomi on Skyline, Farmhouse on Woodcrest.

Row 3: Poppy on Candlewick, Mixed Fruit on Colonial, Spring Garden on Candlewick.

Row 4: Plaid Fruit on Skyline, Spring Flowers on Colonial, Cosmos on Skyline blank.

Southern Pottery backstamps.

Southern Potteries Breakfast Set.

A variety of marks used over the years
on Southern Pottery pieces.

STANGL POTTERY

The Stangl Pottery had its beginning as early as 1805 as the Fulper Pottery. Another larger plant was built in 1928 in Trenton, New Jersey. J. M. Stangl was president for many years and the dinnerware line is marked "Stangl."

Stangl was purchased in 1978 by the Pfaltzgraff Company. One of the Stangl dinnerware patterns, "Indian Tree", is now being made by Hartstone Potteries.

One of the most unusual patterns to come from Stangl is the "Cactus and Cowboys" hand-painted and artist-signed pieces. Each piece is slightly different. Three different artists sign the various "Cactus and Cowboys" dinnerware.

"Cactus and Cowboys" dinnerware is from the collection of Greg Ciccolo and printed with exclusive, one-time-only permission rights. Photography is by Gregory Ciccolo.

China, Glass & Tablewares   Mar 1963

Orchard Song

Bittersweet

Country Garden

Fruit

Thistle

Fruit & Flowers

Sculptured Fruit - 1967

China, Glass & Tablewares   Mar 1963

Magnolia

Most Stangl pieces are marked Stangl and many will have the pattern name included, quite a break for the collector.

Stangl backstamps

STETSON CHINA COMPANY

Also known as Stetson Pottery Company

Louis Stetson was an immigrant from Poland who worked for his uncle in a clothing store on Chicago's Maxwell Street. Louis heard there was money to be made buying whiteware, decorating the whiteware and then reselling the ware. Louis visited the Mt. Clemens Pottery with this in mind. Mt. Clemens' production was increasing at this time and they let Mr. Stetson have whiteware as a starter. The arrangement really amounted to Mt. Clemens financing Stetson's venture - a venture that proved to be a successful one for both parties. Stetson eventually took all of Mt. Clemens off-selection merchandise.

Mr. Louis Stetson brought his nephew Joe from Poland to work for him and it is said he was an even better operator than Louis. Louis passed away and Joe eventually became the owner of the Stetson operation. Stetson had been decorating the whiteware he purchased from Mt. Clemens in Chicago and the Illinois China Company in Lincoln, Illinois. In 1946 he bought the Illinois China Company. Stetson bought odd lots of decals, making his operation an even more profitable one.

Soon after buying the Illinois China Company, Stetson discontinued the use of decals and used hand painting. We know he brought in decorators from both Red Wing and Southern Potteries. Some sources say the hand painting only lasted 2 - 3 years and Stetson went back to decals.

Nearly all of Stetson's later ware was sold to a Chicago brokerage firm who in turn sold the ware to grocery and furniture stores to be used as premiums. Golden Empress was one of these lines and has a wide 22-karat gold border with various decaled centers.

At one time, Stetson was the second largest employer in Lincoln. Stetson also had a plastics plant and it was at some time sold to Allied Chemical.

The Stetson China Company went out of business in 1965. The Stetson family ran a Stetson - Fostoria outlet in Lincoln, Illinois, on North Kickapoo Street. The outlet store opened in 1959 and was the brain child of Joe Stetson and his son-in-law, Burt Chudacoff. The Lincoln Courier, July 18, 1979, reported the final closing sale of the Stetson - Fostoria outlet store.

A November 1965 article in *China, Glass and Tablewares* announced that Lincoln China Company would be closed down within a year. The plant had formerly been The Stetson operation and Stetson had sold its melamine equipment and other equipment to Allied Chemical. Allied then operated the business as Stetson Products, Plastic Division. "Several top Stetson executives" went with Allied and the name change to Lincoln China Company was part of the sales package deal. The Stetson name could no longer be used.

Stetson backstamps.

Stetson backstamps.

Row 1: Illinois China Company small plates, variety of decals. First two are Mt. Clemens.

Row 2: Stetson decorated Mt. Clemens ware.

Row 3: Stetson hand painted "Ionic" shape "Cynthia" (all row 3 and 4)

Stetson Duncan Hines backstamp.

MT. CLEMENS

This photograph is a classic example of my experiences this past year. When these pieces were photographed, I assumed they were all made by Stetson except the two on the top right row. They are both marked Illinois China Company.

Now we know that Row 1 "Steps" and "Suzanne" are Mt. Clemens' Alara blank. It is believed that both these pieces were decorated by Stetson in his Chicago location. Row 2 - Platter is marked Stetson Mexicalis and again is decorated by Stetson on blank purchased from Mt. Clemens. The sugar and plate are from Mt. Clemens' Old Mexico line. Row 3 - Stetson's hand-decorated line. This one is called Cynthia, at least when it appeared in Sears' Spring and Summer 1949 catalogue. It's a dead ringer for one of Blue Ridge China Company's patterns. Stetson's Cynthia has a ruffled edge. The shape name is Ionic.

STEUBENVILLE POTTERY

The Steubenville Pottery was organized in 1879 in Steubenville, Ohio. By 1881, the business had grown and the pottery was incorporated. Progress continued under the direction of W. B. Donaldson.

By 1910, The Steubenville Pottery had continued to grow and H. D. Wintringer became president of the board of directors. The Wintringer name continued to be an important name at the Steubenville operation.

The pottery closed its doors in 1959. The buildings were sold to a chemical company and the Canonsburg Pottery in Canonsburg, Pennsylvania, purchased the Steubenville molds. Some "Rose Point" and "Adam Antique" was made after 1959 or stock-on-hand was sold under the Steubenville label at Canonsburg, Pennsylvania. A line called "Partio" was also sold in 1965 under the Steubenville name. Woodfield and Russel Wright's "American Modern" line are Steubenville's most readily recognized patterns. "American Modern" molds were not included in the sale to Canonsburg.

In 1948, Steubenville had three divisions advertised: Monticello, Steubenville, and American Modern. Steubenville's Monticello Dinnerware was " an important new collection" that included "Pate sur Pate." "Pate sur Pate" was available in solid colors with contrasting colors. Other Monticello lines were decorated with decals.

Row 1: Russel Wright "American Modern" creamer Seafoam green, "Woodfield" Rust bowl, Shaker set, Rust and Tropic Green.

Row 2: Tropic green covered sugar, Rust teapot, Creamer Golden Fawn.

Row 3: "American Modern" after-dinner cups and saucers, "Woodfield" tea and toast set.

Row 4: More plates showing a variety of colors, Salmon, Rust, and Golden Fawn.

Woodfield

Gay and unusual is this smart leaf pattern by Steubenville. The distinctive shape of *Woodfield* will add an exciting new beauty to your tables . . . the unique pieces will add a new joy to dining. Mix them or match them in five wonderful, wonderful colors: Golden Fawn, Salmon Pink, Tropic, Rust and Dove Gray.

A DINNERWARE MASTERPIECE BY THE STEUBENVILLE POTTERY CO., STEUBENVILLE, OHIO

Steubenville backstamps.

Backstamps

Trade publication reprint.

TAYLOR, SMITH & TAYLOR

The Taylor, Smith & Taylor Pottery was founded in 1899 by C. A. Smith and Colonel John N. Taylor, using the facilities of the Taylor, Smith & Lee Pottery which had ceased operations three years earlier.

In 1903 the company was reorganized and the Taylor interests were purchased by W. L. Smith and his son, W. L. Smith, Jr. The firm remained under the ownership and management of the Smith Family until early 1973 when the plant was purchased by Anchor Hocking Corporation to become the foundation of its Pottery Division.

TS&T began operations as a nine-kiln pottery employing approximately 50 persons. In those early days, only local clays were used. Today, TS&T buys clay from Kentucky, Georgia, Tennessee, North Carolina, and Florida. For many years both earthenware and fine china bodies were used. The china body was discontinued in the early 1970's.

Today's plant is one of the largest and most automated in the United States. More than 50,000 dozen pieces per week are produced by the firm's 500 employees.

All of the ware produced by TS&T today is made of an ironstone body and is ovenproof and dishwasher safe. It is regularly tested by independent laboratories to guarantee that it passes the Federal Drug Administration's lead and cadmium tests.

TS&T dinnerware is marketed world-wide by Anchor Hocking Corporation's Tableware Division.

Taylor Smith & Taylor closed in 1981.

Taylor, Smith, and
Taylor backstamp.

DOGWOOD

Reprinted from a 1942 TST pricing book

A famous T.S. & T underglaze pattern that has been a firm favorite in the past decade. It is made in plain colors of red, blue, green or brown, or is hand painted with many colors.

T.S.&T. underglaze prints such as Dogwood, Castle and Spring Bouquet are printed direct from original copper engravings made exclusively for the pottery by the distinguished ceramic artist, J. Palin Thorley. Protected under the glaze of every piece of ware is an etching so fine one can see each thread-like pen stroke.

LU RAY PASTELS

Lu Ray pastels was one of Taylor, Smith and Taylor's most popular lines. Lu Ray enjoyed a long run from the late 1930's until the early fifties. Five pastel colors make for an interesting mix or match set. Of these five colors, Windsor Blue, Persian Cream, Sharon Pink, Surf Green, and Chatham Gray. Chatham Gray is the most difficult color to find.

A 1940's Ward's catalogue shows Lu Ray Sharon Pink pitcher and Lu Ray Empire shape salt & pepper shakers with a pastel set called "Rainbow." TS&T officials tell us "mixing with another shape has always been a common practice and the Rainbow name was used with several shapes over the years." Catalogues and advanced collectors have been most helpful with Lu Ray pastels information.

Lu Ray Pastels from the collection of John Moses

Row 1: Windsor Blue footed pitcher, Surf Green water tumbler, Sharon Pink juice pitcher, Persian Cream juice tumbler, Sharon Pink cake plate (also sold with wicker handle and metal handle).

Row 2: Chatham Gray 7″ plate, Sharon Pink gravy boat, Surf Green muffin cover and 8″ underplate, Sharon Pink ¼ lb. covered butterdish, Sharon Pink egg cup.

Row 3: Windsor Blue covered teapot, Persian Cream after-dinner cup and saucer, Windsor Blue covered A.D. coffee pot, Sharon Pink A.D. creamer and Windsor Blue A.D. covered sugar.

T.S. & T. backstamps.

Row 1: Lu Ray dinnerware; tab handled soup, after dinner sugar, after dinner pot and creamer, cream soup. plate.

Row 2: Lu Ray dinnerware; two sizes of plates, 1959 calendar plate and tab handled serving plate.

Row 1: "Leaf" creamer Lu Ray shape, backstamped Coral Craft, "Leaf" cup, "Sweet Pea" Empire shape shaker, "Petit Point Bouquet" Delphian shape, late twenties.

Row 2: "Leaf" Lu Ray plate 9″, "Leaf" cream soup, "Leaf" Empire shape sauce-boat.

Row 3: Handled Ramequin, originally in "Chateau Buffet" line - late 50's, sold as a special item to Quaker Oats. Center cup and standing pieces are "Design 69." The bowl at right is Taylor bowl shape still in use.

Row 4: "Green Dots" probably Avona shape, early thirties, "Floral Bouquet" probably Fairway shape, early thirties, "Morningside" probably Delphian shape, late twenties.

Row 1: Silhouette Laurel shape sugar (lid missing) and creamer, Autumn Harvest Versatile shape covered ¼ lb. butter, Daisy Sugar unhandled, Versatile shape.

Row 2: "Roses" "Bokay" plate, AD cup and coffee server, same shape as Lu Ray, Daisy, Versatile shape plate 9″.

Row 3: "Touch of Brown" plate, "Tulips" plate, "Bridal Flower" and "Bokay" plate. No information could be found about these patterns.

Row 4: 1960 calendar plate Laurel shape (sold to theaters and retail stores), used as gifts. Silhouette, Laurel shape 9″, Autumn Harvest, Versatile, shape Ever-Yours collection, late 50's - 60's. Large volume supermarket promotional pattern.

T.S. & T. backstamps.

John Gilkes, design director for Taylor, Smith and Taylor, tells us the shape or blank name for the Pink Castle pattern is Garland. Mr. Gilkes joined T.S.&T in 1953 and the Garland shape was phased out in 1953. Mr. Gilkes said, "the Garland shape had an English look which was beginning to lose favor." The Versatile line replaced the Garland shape.

The premier backstamp is believed to be a long-time slogan of T.S.&T. Mr. Conley recalls that "Premier Potters of America" was used on their cartons and dates back to the thirties.

Taylor, Smith & Taylor's response to Fiesta is thought to be Vistosa. Pie crust edges in nearly the same colors as Homer Laughlin's Fiesta. Vistosa came in mango red, cobalt blue, light green and deep yellow. Important Vistosa pieces known to exist, but not pictured, are a 12″ footed salad bowl and sauceboat.

VISTOSA (1938 - EARLY 40'S)

Row 1: Vistosa, cobalt blue 9″ plate, chop plate yellow 11″, teacup and saucer yellow.

Row 2: Vistosa, mango red creamer, covered sugar bowl, AD cup and saucer cobalt, egg - cup green.

Row 3: Vistosa ball jug yellow, shaker cobalt blue, 6-cup mango red teapot, shaker mango red.

Vistosa from the collection of John Moses

UNIVERSAL POTTERY

The first known pottery in Niles, Ohio, was the Bradshaw Pottery. It was in business from 1902 - 1910. Frank Sebring purchased the Bradshaw plant and incorporated it under the name of Tritt in 1912. Tritt was a brother-in-law and the business never quite came up to Mr. Sebring's expectations. He sold the Tritt operation about 1921, keeping the molds.

In 1921, Mr. Ahrendts, Stevens and Gilmer purchased the property with Mr. Chester Wardeska, secretary of the newly-formed Crescent China Company. About 1923 it was necessary to change the name of the Crescent China Company to The Atlas China Company due to an infringement claim based on prior registration.

The Atlas China Company remained in business until a fire. The Atlas plant in Niles was rebuilt and modernized following the 1925 fire. It continued to operate until nearly 1928. At that time, it was decided to consolidate all operations in the Cambridge factory and that plant was enlarged.

The Oxford Pottery was formed and financed by a group of Cambridge people in 1913. It was spearheaded by several former employees of the Guernseyware Company. Their product was a line of brown kitchenware, such as teapots, beanpots, custards, etc., made chiefly from crude red clay mined from the land surrounding the plant and owned by the company. The venture was successful from the start, but the business never expanded and after the loss of one of the chief executives and a year not up to standard, some of the stockholders were vulnerable to an offer for their stock by Mr. Ahrendts and he succeeded in acquiring control.

The Globe China Company was organized in 1925 with the same three men who started the Crescent Company in 1921. The Atlas Company decided to consolidate all its operations, thus the name Atlas-Globe. Atlas-Globe never filed for bankruptcy but, in the 1930's, worked out a creditor's agreement for the orderly liquidation of the assets with the Oxford Company acting as agent. At the same time, Oxford amended its charter changing the name to Universal, increasing the capital structure and purchasing the Atlas-Globe properties.

The original Oxford plant facilities were used in the production of ovenware in the early years of Universal and it was not unusual to identify their ware as Oxford ware. When this plant was converted to ceramic tile in 1956, the trademark for Oxford was adopted.

Plant number 2 was converted into a Wall Tile Manufacturing Company in 1956, Plant #3 ceased operations in 1957, and Plant #1 closed in 1960, ending the dinnerware industry in Cambridge, Ohio.

Universal Potteries, Incorporated, Cambridge, Ohio, was formed in 1934 through the acquisition of the old Atlas-Globe plant properties by The Oxford Pottery Company. The Oxford organization was a local organization that amended its charter to provide for the increased investment and property expansion.

The resulting company consisted of three manufacturing plants, one located at Niles, Ohio, and subsequently dismantled. The other two remaining plants were enlarged and improved and were known as Plant 1 and Plant 2 of Universal Potteries, Inc. During 1947 the plant embarked on an expansion program that included a brand new facility completed in 1948 and known as Plant 3.

Universal's "Ballerina" and "Ballerina Mist" color glazes, both plain and decorated, have best distinguished the company. Universal used a detergent-resistant decal called permacel.

Universal also added distinction to its line by the versatility of its products as evidenced by the complete assortment of cooking ware and "guaranteed ovenproof" refrigerator items.

Universal Potteries, Incorporated, had 200 employees in 1934 and 650 in 1956. Without exception, managers and supervisors of Universal Potteries, Incorporated, came up through the ranks of the factory force.

Universal Potteries, Incorporated, closed its doors in 1960.

Some of the backstamps used on Universal shapes
over the years.

CAT-TAIL

Cat-tail is already a very popular pattern with collectors. A Universal executive tells us that the Cat-tail decal was made up for an East Liverpool pottery. The name of the pottery is not known but they did not use the decal.

Universal used the Cat-tail design on their Camwood shape, their Old Holland shape and Laurella shape (possibly other shapes). Please keep in mind "exclusive" meant only exclusive shapes with a particular decal to be sold only to one buyer.

One of the interesting facets of Cat-tail is the variety of pieces to be found aside from the different shapes mentioned above. Glass, linens, tinware and even a kitchen table make up the extensive pieces available for the Cat-tail collector.

The ad from the Needlecraft magazine shown on the opposite page is from a 1934 "Needlecraft" and the maker is unknown at this time.

A Cat-tail jug with reamer has created quite a stir, both with dinnerware collectors and reamer collectors. Watch for it!

Universal backstamps

This Cattail is not Universal's. Reprinted from a 1930's *Needlecraft* Magazine.

Row 1: Cat-tail saucer on Universal's Old Holland shape marked "Wheelock". Wheelock was a department store in Peoria, Illinois. Shakers, 6″ plate on Old Holland.

Row 2: Teapot (lid may not be correct), Batter jug-part of set, creamer on Laurella

Row 3: Pie or cake server, glass pitcher, ice tea tumbler, salad set, tablecloth

Row 4: Cat-tail plate on Laurella, Early serving plate marked Universal Potteries - Oven Proof, Cambridge, Ohio

Wheelock mark on saucer and 6″ plate, Row 1.

Universal Potteries mark on server, Row 4 - Item 2.

A hard to find Cat-tail tumbler marked Universal.

Bake and Serve in "Cat Tail" Oven Proof Kitchenware

COMPLETE 9-PC. REFRIGERATOR SET

From Your Oven to Your Table with Cat-tail Kitchenware—Guaranteed Ovenproof

New flavor for your meals . . . new zest to your cooking . . . with ensembled dinner and kitchenware! Perky Red and Black cat-tails decorate oven-proof kitchenware—matching Cat-Tail dinnerware (35 E 04414) on Page 533.

Finest quality American semi-porcelain with Ivory color glaze. All pieces brush trimmed in red. *Each piece fully guaranteed oven-proof and acid-proof* . . . will be replaced if it crazes in baking. Tested in Sears own laboratories.

(A) 9-Pc. Refrigerator Set $2.79
Equip your refrigerator with this set. Consists of: **Canteen Jug** with stopper; cap., 1 qt. 7 oz.—only 7½-in. high to fit refrigerator. **Covered Jars**, 4, 5 and 6-in. diam. are 3, 3¹³⁄₁₆ and 4¹³⁄₁₆ in. high; **Covered Casserole**, 8¼ in. diam., 4¼ in. high. Cap. 61 oz.
35 E 05042M—Shpg. wt., 12 lbs.

(B) Canteen Jug   85c
Only 7½-n. high. Cap., 1 qt. 7 oz.
35 E 5041M—Shpg. wt., 2 lbs. 8 oz.

(C) 3-Pc. Bowl Set $1.29
Consists of: generously sized bowls, 6, 7 and 8½-in. diam.; 28, 40 and 60-ounce capacity.
35 E 5032M—Shpg. wt., 6 lbs. 4 oz.

SEARS PAGE 536 ◇

(D) 3-Pc. Casserole Set $1.19
8¼-in. diam., 4¼ in. high. Plate, 9 in. diam.
35 E 5034M—Shpg. wt., 6 lbs.

(E) 2-Pc. Casserole $1.09
8½-in. diam., holds 1½-qts. Pie-dish cover, 7½-in. diam., 1½ in. dp.
35 E 5037M—Shpg. wt., 4 lbs. 8 o⁻.

(F) Handy Pitcher   55c
5½ in. high. Two-pint capacity.
35 E 5040M—Shpg. wt., 1 lb. 8 oz.

(G) 6-Pc. Ice-Box Set $1.29
4, 5 and 6-in. diam. covered jars. 3, 3¹³⁄₁₆ and 4¹³⁄₁₆ in. high.
35 E 5033M—Shpg. wt., 5 lbs. 8 oz.

(H) 2-Pc. Pie Set   59c
Deep pie plate, 10-in. diam. with server.
35 E 5036M—Shpg. wt., 2 lbs. 12 oz.

(J) 3-Pc. Salad Set   98c
Consists of: Bowl, 9½-in. diam., 3½ in. high. Matching fork and spoon, each about 10 inches long.
35 E 5035M—Shpg. wt., 3 lbs. 8 oz.

(K) 4-Pc. Range Set   85c
Salt and peppers 4⅛-in. ht. Covered jar, 3 in. high. 4¼-in. diam.
35 E 5031M—Shpg. wt., 3 lbs.

(L) Set of 6 Custard Cups   69c
Generous 5-oz. cap. 3¼-in. diam.
35 E 5039M—Shpg. wt., 2 lbs. 12 oz.

(M) Ice-Lipped Pitcher   95c
Large, ball-shaped tilt jug. Holds two quarts. Ice-lip assures easy dripless pouring. Excellent for cool iced drinks; for steaming hot chocolate. And just the right size!
35 E 5038M—Shpg. wt., 2 lbs. 12 oz.

1940

1940 Sears catalogue reprint.

H 89c
J 39c
K 65c
L $1.19
M 69c
P $1.79

Matched economy Pantryware—bright cattail design

The pantryware for the thrifty buyer. Not equal to our finest Maid of Honor Pantryware above, yet it is well made of steel with a smooth white lithographed outside finish and a protective rust-resistant inside finish.

[H] **Step-on Can.** 10-quart capacity. About 13 inches high. Painted inset.
11 J 2803M—Shipping weight 4 lbs. 3 oz. . . 89c

[J] **Oval Wastebasket.** Bright white with red inside. 12⅝ inches high. Straight sides.
11 J 2805M—Shipping weight 2 lbs. 2 oz. . . 39c

[K] **Cake Cover and Tray.** 5¼ inches high, 10¼-inch diameter cover.
11 J 2804M—Shipping weight 2 lbs. 2 oz. 65c

[L] **Double Compartment Bread Box.** 2 doors. 11¾ inches high. Lower shelf about 12x12⅝ in.
11 J 02801M—Shipping weight 6 pounds. $1.19

[M] **Single Compartment Bread Box.** 13⅝x9 9/16x6 in.
11 J 2802M—Shipping weight 3 pounds. 69c

[N] **4-piece Canister Set.** Sizes 4 15/16 in. high by 4 3/16-in. diam.; 5⅝x5 in., 6⅜x6 in., 7⅜x7 1/16 in.
11 J 2800M—Shipping weight 2 lbs. 9 oz. . . . . . Set 65c

Maid of Honor Kitchen Scale

[P] The neatest, most attractive kitchen scale we have ever seen at this low price. Very handy, too, for weighing articles up to 24 pounds. Convenient for weighing packages to be mailed. Useful on farms, in hotels and in city homes. (Not legal for use in trade.) Made of heavy gauge steel painted white, with attractive cattail design. Clear plastic dial face. Figures are stamped legibly on revolving white dial. Easy adjustment makes constant accuracy possible. Height 6¾ inches. Weighing surface 6x6 inches; base 6¼x6¼ inches. A good buy at this low price.
11 J 7851M—Shipping weight 4 pounds. . . . . .

Cat-Tail Kitchenware . . . Guaranteed Oven and Craze Proof
9-Piece Refrigerator Set (A, B, and C)
A
B
C
D
E
F
G
H
J
K

- Created by skilled designers for kitchen beauty and space efficiency.
- Perky red and black cat-tails and red lines decorate every piece.
- Finest quality American semi-porcelain with ivory color glaze.
- Guaranteed against crazing—every piece is ovenproof . . . acid resistant.
- Tested by Sears and independent laboratories . . . to give tops in wear.
- Priced for real savings. See Page 666 for Matching Cat-tail Dinnerware.

9-Piece Refrigerator Set
$2.79 Set. Set of: (A) 3 Covered Jars, 4, 5, 6 in. diam.; 3, 3¾, 4¾ in. high. (B) Covered Casserole, 8¼ in. diam.; 4⅝ in. high. 2 qt. cap. (C) Canteen Jug with stopper. Cap. 1 qt. 7 oz. Ht., 7½ in. to fit refrigerators. Shpg. wt., 12 lbs.
35 H 5152M—9-Pc. Set. $2.79

(A) 6-Pc. Ice Box Jar Set
$1.19 Set. Store food in covered jars! Set of 3 covered jars, 4, 5, 6 in. diam., 3, 3¾, 4¾ in. high. Genuine space savers. Stack conveniently for storing in refrigerator or pantry. Shpg. wt., 5 lbs. 8 oz.
35 H 5145M—Set. $1.19

(C) Canteen Jug
Only 85c. Keep juices and water fresh and cool! 7½ in. high to fit refrigerator. 1-qt. 7 oz. cap. Cork stopper. Shipping weight, 2 lbs. 8 oz.
35 H 5041M. 85c

(D) Handy Pitcher
55c. It'll come to the table every day with milk, water, or even waffle batter. 1 qt. 5 oz. cap. 6 in. high. Shpg. wt., 1 lb. 8 oz.
35 H 5151M. 55c

(E) Ice-Lipped Pitcher
95c. Just what you want for iced drinks! Ice-lip assures drip-less pouring. 5⅞-in. high; 2-qt. 10-oz. cap. Wt., 2 lbs. 12 oz.
35 H 5149M. 95c

(F) Giant Cooky Jar
$1.35. Even the heartiest cookie-eating family finds this jar plenty big! Full one-gallon capacity. 9 in. high. Shpg. wt., 9 lbs.
35 H 5153M. $1.35

(G) 2-Pc. Pie Set
57c. Bake and serve your pie in the same dish. Deep pie plate. 10-in. diam. with easy-out server. Shpg. wt., 2 lbs. 12 oz.
35 H 5036M. 57c

(H) 6 Custard Cups
69c Set. Bake custards, mold salad or serve pudding in them! Large 6-oz. cap. 3⅜ in. diam. Shpg. wt., 2 lbs. 12 oz.
35 H 5150M—Six for. . . 69c

(K) Covered Casserole
$1.09. Serve food piping hot! Snug cover with knob. 8¼-in. diam.; 4½ in. high. 1¾-qt. cap. Shipping weight, 4 lbs. 8 oz.
35 H 5148M. $1.09

(J) 4-Pc. Range Set
85c. Keep your pepper and salt on the stove! Large salt and pepper shakers, 4 in. high. Covered lard jar. 3 in. high.
35H5143M—Shpg.wt., 3 lbs. . 85c

46-piece matching Breakfast Set

- 46 pieces with matched black and vermilion cat-tail decorations
- 5-Pc. solid oak Breakfast Set
- 32-Pc. set of semi-porcelain dishes
- Gay 9-pc. cotton luncheon set

$23.89 Cash. 46-Pc. Set. $3 Down

Extension Table top, 42x30 inches; opens to 52x30 inches. Legs bolt on. **Chair** seats, 15x14 inches. Height of back from seat, 17½ inches. Pearl white or fawn tan. **State finish.** Shipped from near Louisville, Ky.
1 LM 8637F—**Complete 46-piece Breakfast Outfit.** Shipping weight, 120 pounds. $23.89
1 LM 2527F—**5 Pcs.** Table, 4 chairs. Shpg. wt., 100 lbs. 18.98
Chair only. Shipping weight, 13 pounds. Each. . 2.85

Inexpensive pantryware pieces advertised in a 1940's Sears Catalogue include 10 qt. 3″ high Cattail step-on garbage can, oval wastebasket 12-5/8″ high, cake cover, double breadbox, single breadbox, 4-piece round canister set, kitchen scales. In the 1941 Sears Catalogue a breakfast set, choice of enameled white hardwood or solid oak Fawn Tan finished. The table and seats of the chairs are decorated with black and Vermillion cat-tail. Included in the "breakfast outfit" was 32-piece set of Cat-tail dinnerware and a nine-piece cotton luncheon set. All 46 pieces for $19.98 cash. In 1942 the 9-piece cotton luncheon set did not have the cat-tails. It appears to have a stripe around the edge.

Accessory pieces shown are from a 1940's Sears Catalogue

Row 1: Glass shaker set in red metal rack, Sugar (lid missing), shaker set.

Row 2: Jug, side handle jug with cork stopper, utility or milk pitcher

Row 3: Canteen jug, yet another style shaker, part of 3 piece set (lids missing), cookie jar (lid not correct)

Row 4: Platter, dessert or salad plate, covered 1 lb. butter, kitchen scales

Row 1: Hollyhocks salad bowl, Rose bowl made for Sears, Blair "Criss Cross" bowl

Row 2: Holland Rose on Old Holland plate and small bowl, Rose on Laurella Item. No. 3 on Row 1 is marked "Made especially for Blair". Neither the Blairs nor the Universal people were able to recall the circumstances. At least one other piece with yet another decal has turned up marked the same way.

RAMBLER ROSE OR IRIS

Row 1: Rambler Rose plate, utility shaker, gravy boat.

Row 2: Rambler Rose utility or milk pitcher, flat bowl, plate 9″.

Row 3: Iris or Fleur de Lis Iris jug, covered stack set, covered casserole.

Row 4: Iris pie baker, canteen refrigerator jug, dinner plate.

Both of these patterns were made for S. B. Davis Company. You may expect to find a large variety of pieces in Rambler Rose and Iris. 1940's.

Row 1: Largo sugar (lid missing), salt & pepper set, creamer, small utility bowls.

Row 2: Largo luncheon plate, dessert plate 6″, and pie baker 10″.

Row 3: Red Poppy utility plate 11½″, small plates.

Row 4: Windmill covered utility bowl, shaker, Fruit and Flowers utility tray or plate.

The Largo pattern was made for the S. B. Davis Company and comes in a wide variety of pieces. Red Poppy was sold to department stores and catalogue stores. Both patterns are from the forties.

Row 1: Woodvine gravy boat, salt & pepper set, sugar & creamer.

Row 2: Woodvine covered utility jar, gravy liner or relish dish, plate 6″.

Row 3: Woodvine plate 9″, oval vegetable bowl, luncheon plate.

Row 4: Woodvine cup and saucer, flat soup bowl, utility tray.

Woodvine was Universal Potteries' most popular "booster" line. A "booster" line was a dinnerware line used as a premium line for grocery stores on a coupon basis to stimulate business. Many of Universal's patterns were "boosters" in the 30's and 40's.

Universal backstamp.

Row 1: Blue and white refrigerator ware made for Montgomery Ward in the 1940's. While the blue and white ware was made for Wards it is unknown if the "God Bless America Piece" was made for Wards.

Row 2: Blue and white canteen jug, covered cookie/cracker jar, coffee server

Row 3: Cat-tail teapot coffee base (ochre colored cattails) Woodvine decalled jug, Teapot (same as item #1)

Row 4: Canteen refrigerator jugs with a variety of decals, you will find many other decals on these covered jugs.

Several American potteries made plates and bowls to fit chrome and aluminum frames. This "Grecian Urn" decal is on Universal's Laurella shape and in a Farberware frame. A *House Beautiful* ad from summer of 1940 shows the same plate in a different style frame. You will find all kinds of dinnerware items in a variety of frames.

CALICO FRUIT

Row 1: Calico Fruit plate 6″, utility shakers, saucer.

Row 2: Utility plate 11½″, plate 7″, breakfast plate 9″.

Row 3: Custard cup 5 oz. capacity, 3-jar refrigerator set 4″, 5″, 6″ diameters.

Row 4: Covered refrigerator jug 3 qt. capacity, soup bowl, serving bowl, utility pitcher.

Calico Fruit is already a popular pattern with collectors and was sold in the forties in department and catalogue stores. It is difficult to find table pieces such as saucers, plates with good bright decals. Calico Fruit had matching tinware and glass condiment sets as shown in 1946-47 Ward's catalogue.

Semi-porcelain Dinnerware...C

A to L CALICO FRUIT OVENWARE. Semi-Porcelain guaranteed absolutely heatproof, cold-proof and acid-resisting. Matches Calico Fruit Dinnerware described below.

(A) 86 C 7720L—RANGE SET. 4-in. Jar, 4-in. Salt and Pepper. Ship. wt. 4 lbs........... 98c
(B) 86 C 7728L—COVERED REFRIGERATOR JUG. 3-pt. capacity. Ship. wt. 3 lbs........... $1.15
(C) 86 C 7729L—3-COMPARTMENT PLATE. 10-in. diameter. Ship. wt. 2 lbs.................59c
(D) 86 C 7718L—3-JAR REFRIGERATOR SET. 4-in., 5-in., 6-in. diameters. Ship. wt. 6 lbs.... $1.39
(E) 86 C 7717L—3-PC. MIXING BOWL SET. 6¼-in., 7½-in., 9-in. diameters. Ship. wt. 9 lbs. 1.39

M to Y WHITE ROSE (proof and ac background. The colo oven to table, they are

(M) 86 C 7681L—3-PC.
(N) 86 C 7687L—COVE
(P) 86 C 9190L—CAKE
(R) 86 C 7682L—3-JAR

From Universal — these new, fast-selling *Ballerina* Specialty Sets!

16-Pc. Barbecue Set. *8 French Casseroles, 8 Coffee Mugs. Forest Green, Chartreuse, Dove Grey, Burgundy Colored Glazes; also in decorated patterns. Retail $14.39*

17-Pc. Beverage Set. *1 Ice Lip Jug, 8 Tumblers, 8 Coasters. Forest Green, Chartreuse, Dove Grey, Burgundy Colored Glazes; also in decorated patterns. Retail $9.95*

18-Pc. After Dinner Coffee Service. *1 A.D. Coffee Server, 8 A.D. Cups, 8 A.D. Saucers. Forest Green, Chartreuse, Dove Grey, Burgundy Colored Glazes; also in decorated patterns. Retail $8.49*

18-Pc. Tea Set. *1 Teapot, 8 Tea Cups, 8 Tea Saucers. Forest Green, Chartreuse, Dove Grey, Burgundy Colored Glazes; also in decorated patterns. Retail $8.95*

Smart, practical — moderately priced! These are the come-ons that make Ballerina colored glaze specialty sets hot sellers from the moment you put them on display. And they're *packaged for resale*, solid-color or assorted — ideal gifts for brides, Mother's Day and other gift occasions. See them at the Pittsburgh show ... you'll want *all four for your store!*

Universal Potteries, Inc.

Three Modern Plants • Cambridge, Ohio

Representatives

Paul Goldwyn, Room 308-310
225 Fifth Ave., New York City
C. B. Jacoby, P. O. Box 14022, Houston 21, Texas
A. E. Miller, 1581-B Merchandise Mart, Chicago, Illinois
L. E. Heiser, Box 236, Tiffin, Ohio
Robert Snyder, RD 4, Salem, Ohio
F. W. Kasper, Gate 14, Lakewood, Crystal Lake, Ill.
Mrs. H. W. Becker, 515 Kinloch Building
St. Louis, Missouri
J. A. Wentz, Space 284 Western Merchandise Mart
1355 Market St., San Francisco, California
Russell M. Stoakes, 94 So. Greer
Memphis 11, Tennessee
Perry Karasek, 1528 42nd St.
Belview Heights, Birmingham, Ala.

Canadian Representative

Sidney Druckman, 79 Wellington St., Toronto, Ontario

UNIVERSAL'S BALLERINA SHAPE — COLORED GLAZES

Ballerina was one of Universal's most popular shapes. It was made in solid color glazes and a variety of decals on an ivory glaze.

The four original colors were Periwinkle Blue, Jade Green, Jonquil Yellow and Dove Grey. Chartreuse and Forest Green were added in 1949. In 1950, Charles Cobelle, designer, created five exclusive new patterns for Universal's Ballerina shape. Advertised as "Modern designs with a touch of the abstract", the five new patterns were Painted Desert, Mermaid, Passy, Gloucester Fisherman, and The Fountain.

A 1951 ad lists five colored glazes on Ballerina. Forest Green, Jonquil Yellow, Chartreuse, Dove Grey. In 1955, Pink and Charcoal were added to the Ballerina line. Pink and Charcoal were "high-fashion" colors for 1955. Also in 1955 a big promotion was announced for Moss Rose on Ballerina but the ad does not state that Moss Rose is a new item. Another 1955 Ballerina ad lists Forest Green, Chartreuse, Burgundy, Dove Grey, Pink and Charcoal as basic colored glazes. Ballerina was also available in other "decorated motifs" including the ever popular Moss Rose pattern.

Ballerina Mist was another popular line for universal. The body of the ware is a "wispy blue-green" and with decals.

Row 1: Red and White Kitchenware from the collection of Greg Ciccolo. Bean pot, syrup pitcher, teapot 6-cup, shaker, Ball Jug.

Row 2: "Circus" Spoon, Shaker, Teapot 6-cup, utility jug 2-cup.

Row 3: "Broadway Rose" Atlas Globe mark, Blue Oxford Stoneware mug 8 oz., Green Water jug 2 qt., utility bowl, green individual bean pot.

WARWICK

Warwick demi-set, plate, teapot, sugar, creamer, cup/saucer. The Warwick China Company was founded in Wheeling, West Virginia in 1887. It was built in town and this made any expansion impossible. Some dinnerware was made but Warwick is most famous for its early art pieces. For more information about the Warwick China Company, be sure to read *Why Not Warwick,* by Don and Patricia Hoffman. The set shown is dated 1944.

WESTERN STONEWARE

The Western Stoneware was formed in April 1906, expressly for the manufacture of stoneware items. Stoneware is made from a natural clay that requires no other minerals. Real stoneware factories are by necessity located near the natural clay deposits. A high temperature is used in the firing (2290° F). Real stoneware is an excellent ware for baking and large pieces are excellent insulators, keeping food hot or cold for an indefinite period.

In 1954, Eva Zeisel developed for Monmouth Pottery a line of "nearly 50 new shapes" and 15 new patterns of highly vitrified stoneware. Three solid glaze colors, both mat and glossy finish, also came in hand-decorated pieces. Described by Walter Browder in an article in *Crockery and Glass Journal* as "a basic dinnerware line with basic serving pieces in classically quiet and simple shapes . . . but there is a surprise in a second serving line of humorous bird shapes."

Western Stoneware was also the maker of the now famous Mar-Crest line of stoneware made for the Mar-Crest Company. Mar-Crest was a premium or "booster" item for service stations, grocery stores and other businesses in the 1950's.

Marcrest

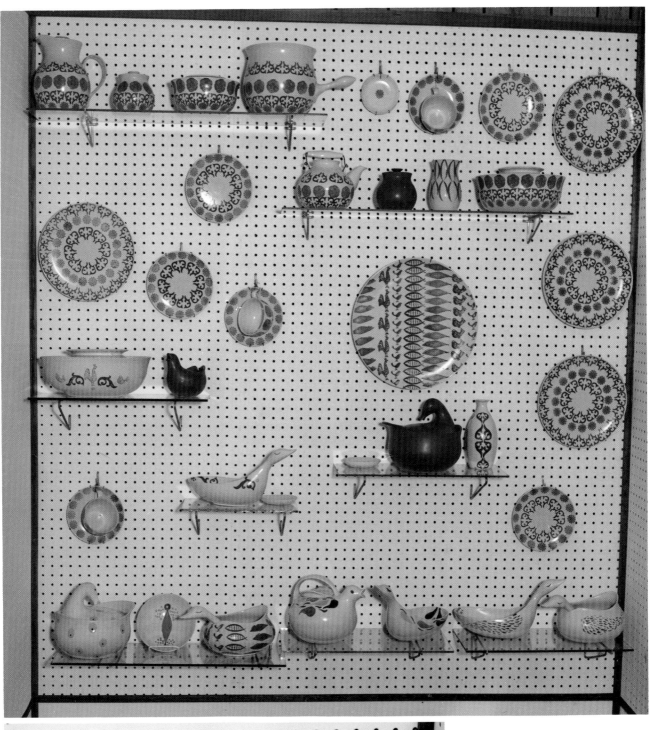

Designed by Eva Ziesel for
Western Stoneware

GLOSSARY

Acid Gold - a type of dinnerware decoration in which the design is acid-etched into the body, then painted with liquid gold which is fired on and burnished.

Baker - a vegetable or serving dish, open and often oval in shape.

Basaltware - unglazed stoneware, usually black, with a dull gloss.

Batch - the precise mixture of clay and other ingredients which, by heat processing, is transformed into hard clayware.

Bisque (or biscuit) - the porous clay after the first firing.

Bisque Fire - the first firing or baking, which hardens a dinnerware piece in its final shape.

Blank - an undecorated piece, usually one to be subjected to further processing.

Body - composite materials that make up clay.

Body and Paste - the composite materials from which potter's clay is made.

Bone China - a specific type of fine china manufactured primarily in England. The body contains a high proportion of bone ash to develop greater translucency, whiteness, and strength. Like fine china, it is made primarily for the retail trade.

Bright Gold - A liquid gold paint decoration which, when fired, comes out bright and therefore requires no burnishing, or polishing.

Burnished Gold - a more expensive gold dinnerware or glassware decoration that comes out of the kiln dull and must be rubbed up to a shine.

Casting - process where liquid clay is poured into a mold and allowed to set, forming a hollow piece.

Ceramics - all products made from clay.

China - a thin, translucent, vitrified body, which is generally developed in two firings: first, at a relatively high temperature to mature the purest of raw materials; and second, to develop the high gloss of the covering glaze.

China and Porcelain - are different names for the same thing.

Cooking Ware - a broad term applied to earthenware, porcelain and china where the shapes are designed for cooking or baking as well as serving. It has a smooth, glazed surface, is strong, and is resistant to thermal shock.

Compote (or Comport) - A footed or stemmed dish varying in height, size, and bowl shape, sometimes covered, used for serving candy, jelly, nuts, bon bons, etc.

Coupe Shaped - a plate curved upward at the edge lacking a shoulder.

Crackled ware - Clayware or glassware whose surface is marked by a network of tiny cracks deliberately induced for decorative effect by sudden cooling.

Craze - tiny cracks caused by the difference in contracting of the body and glaze.

Crockery - a term, often synonymous with earthenware, used to describe a porous opaque body for domestic use. Because of its permeability, it is normally glazed.

Cruet - Any stoppered bottle that can be used for oil, vinegar, or other liquid dressing.

Decalcomania (or Decal) - A special design-bearing sheet used in dinnerware decoration. The sheet is first applied to a piece of ware. The paper is then removed, resulting in the transfer of the decoration to the ware. Subsequent firing makes it permanent.

Dipping - process where china is dipped in liquid glaze, prior to second firing.

Dresden - A white china generally very heavily decorated, originally developed in Dresden, Germany.

Earthenware - a type of clayware fired at comparatively low temperatures, producing a heavy, porous body that is opaque, not as strong as china, and lacking that product's resonance. Because earthenware dinnerware is generally in the low and medium-price brackets and lends itself to a variety of decorative styles and methods, it is well suited for everyday use.

Embossing - a raised or molded decoration produced either in the mold or formed separately and applied before firing.

Engobe - a type of decoration in which white or colored slip, or liquid clay, is applied over the body of the ware.

Epergne - an ornamental table piece having two or more arms and designed to hold flowers, candles, and, in recent use, candies, nuts, and other tidbits.

Etching - A decoration on glassware or clayware eaten into the ware by acid. Either of two methods, needle etching or plate etching, may be used to apply the decoration.

Faience - Originally a type of French-made pottery, the term is used today to refer to a fine glazed earthenware usually bearing highly colorful decoration.

Firing - a baking process under carefully controlled temperatures to which all ceramic ware is subjected for hardening, strengthening, and fusing together its various ingredients.

Flatware - plates or platters of any size.

Flux - a material that aids the melting and fusion of ceramic ingredients under heat. The most commonly used fluxes in dinnerware manufacture are feldspar and bone ash.

Gadroon edge - a molded dinnerware border design which resembles braided rope.

Glaze - a glass layer covering a ceramic product and the article is baked until the coating becomes hard and permanent.

Glost Firing - dinnerware's second firing, the purpose of which is to harden and set the glaze. Temperatures are generally lower than those of the first, or bisque, firing.

Glost Kiln - oven for baking glazed pieces to harden the glaze.

Graffiato, Graviata, or Sraffiato - a design is scratched in the glaze to show background color. It is then reglazed and refired.

Green Ware - unfinished clay ware which has not been fired.

Ground-lay - An underglaze dinnerware decoration generally taking the form of wide borders of dark colors such as maroon, deep blue, etc. The process consists of dusting the powdered color onto an oil coating.

Holloware (or hollow ware) - are cups, bowls, pitchers, etc.

Hotelware - a heavy china dinnerware made specifically for use in hotels, institutions, and restaurants. It is stronger than china for home use but lacks the translucency and delicacy of the latter.

Intaglio - decoration in which the design is sunk beneath the surface of the piece. It is the opposite of embossing.

Ironstone - a historic term for durable English stoneware. The composition and properties are similar to porcelain, except that the body is not translucent and is off-white. In more recent times, this term has been used to describe a number of other products.

Jasper - a stoneware body, either white or colored, noteworthy for its fine, soft finish. This type of ware was first developed by Josiah Wedgwood and its best known form today is the popular blue-and-white ware by Wedgwood.

Jigger- machine on which plates are made.

Jolley - cup-making machine.

Kaolin - a pure, white, top-grade clay used in making fine china.

Kiln - the oven in which dinnerware is fired, or baked. Pottery men pronounce the word as if it were spelled without the "n".

Limoges - French porcelain produced in the vicinity of Limoges, France.

Lining - a dinnerware decoration, either machine or hand applied, consisting of one or several parallel lines running around the outer edge of a plate.

Lug soup - a soup plate with two projecting pieces on opposite sides of the rim by which the plate is carried.

Luster - A ceramic glaze coating, metallic in nature, which gives the finished piece an iridescent effect.

Majolica - a type of Italian pottery glazed with tin enamel and generally decorated in rich colors.

Mat finish - a flat glaze finish without gloss. The first word is usually misspelled "matte."

Mold - form used for shaping holloware pieces.

Mold marks - ridges on clayware or glassware indicating the points at which the mold that formed a piece was separated for removal of the ware.

Nappy - in dinnerware, a round vegetable dish. A glassware nappy, however, is any round or square dish from fruit size up, used for various serving purposes.

Open Stock - an approach to dinnerware retailing in which the ware is sold in individual pieces or small groups rather than in complete, predetermined composition or sets. Implied, also, is the fact that patterns offered in open stock will be available for an indefinite period following their introduction.

Ovenware - clayware that is able to withstand the heat of a kitchen oven without damage, thus permitting a homemaker to prepare oven-cooked food in it and then use it for table service. In styling, such ware is usually of casual design and features bright colors.

Overglaze decoration - design applied to clayware after it has been fired and glazed. Because they are not subjected to high temperatures, the colors in such decoration tend to be more vivid than those in underglaze designs.

Parian - a fine unglazed porcelain developed in England, so named because it is said to resemble marble from the Greek island of Paros.

Paste - the mixture from which dinnerware is made. The two basic types are soft paste, which includes a high percentage of powdered glass, and hard paste, which is a mixture of kaolin, flint, and feldspar.

Pate Sur Pate - ornamentation made by painting paste upon paste until the desired thickness is obtained.

Pin Marks - small depressions on the underside of a glazed piece left by the pins which support it in the kiln as it is fired. Although they are usually polished off, the marks cannot be completely eradicated.

Place setting - Usually five (although sometimes four or six) matched pieces of dinnerware for setting a single place at a table. Higher priced ware is generally offered in such a group to keep the price at a comparatively popular level.

Porcelain - a hard, translucent clayware body that differs from china only in the manufacturing process. In all other respects the two are so much alike that the terms are generally used interchangeably.

Potter's Wheel - a round platform, rotated either mechanically or manually, upon which the potter throws, or forms, a circular shape. The device originated in ancient times.

Pottery - as a generic name, pottery includes all fired clayware produced. As a specific name, pottery describes the low porous body ware which is generally colored. The term is properly applied to the clay products of primitive peoples, or to decorated art products made of unrefined clays and by unsophisticated methods.

Ceramic products acquire strength through the application of heat. The chemical composition of the materials used determines, with the heat applied, the strength, porosity, and vitrification of the fired product. Primitive pottery, often baked in the sun and composed of one or more unrefined clays, had little strength and was quite porous.

Quimper Ware - Colorful French-made pottery of a peasant character which takes its name from the town of Quimper.

Reject - a piece of ware withheld from shipment because of an imperfection that prevents it from meeting first-quality standards.

Restaurant China - a uniquely American blending of fine china and porcelain designed and engineered specifically for use in commercial operations. The body was developed to give great impact strength and durability, with the extremely low absorption that is required in public eating places. Decorations are applied between the body and the glaze, thereby protecting the decoration during commercial use.

Most of the ware is subject to a high temperature first firing, and lower temperature second firing. Some ware is fired, however, in a one-fire operation wherein the body and glaze mature at the same time. Like fine china, American restaurant china is vitrified.

Run of Kiln (or R. K.) - a grading term denoting dinnerware as it comes out of the kiln, not subjected to inspection or weeding out.

Saggers - fire-resistant containers for articles to be fired.

Salt Glaze - a semi-mat or half-glossy glaze obtained by injecting salt into the kiln during the glaze firing.

Screen Printing - a method of ceramic and glassware decorating in which stencil-like screens are used in applying colors to the ware.

Seam - a ridge on a piece of molded holloware caused by the tiny crack between two or more parts of the mold.

Seconds - in the vernacular of the consumer, ware with slight defects, frequently not even detectable, offered at prices below what they would ordinarily have to pay for so-called perfect ware.

Selection - the weeding out of imperfect ware, a process to which dinnerware is subjected at various stages in its manufacture.

Selects - near-perfect dinnerware pieces as determined by careful inspection and removal from the group of imperfect pieces.

Semi-vitrified (or Semi-porcelain) - a type of dinnerware about halfway between china and earthenware in appearance and durability.

Sgraffito - a type of ceramic decoration produced by coating a piece with a layer of colored slip, or liquid clay, then incising a design in that layer to let the original body color show through.

Shoulder - the raised rim of the traditionally shaped plate.

Silica - one of the earth's most abundant minerals and a vital ingredient in ceramic manufacture. It is the basic component of glass as well as of ceramic glazes and high-quality clayware bodies.

Slip - clay mixed with water to a creamy consistency.

Slip coating - a layer of slip applied to a clayware body for decorative effect.

Stoneware - a non-porous ceramic body made of unprocessed clays, or of clay and flux additives, fired at elevated temperatures. It is quite durable but lacks the translucence and whiteness of china. It is resistant to chipping and rings clearly when struck. It differs from porcelain chiefly in that it is colored other than white, which results from iron or other impurities in the clay.

Tank - a furnace used in the glass manufacturing process, the walls of which are of refractory brick that serves to retain the heat and hold the molten glass.

Terra Cotta - a hard, unglazed earthenware used most frequently for vases, architectural decoration, etc.

Texture Glaze - a colored glaze in which dripping, running, eruption, or some other controlled disturbance is introduced to heighten the decorative effect.

Toby Jug - a small jug or mug in the form of a stout old man wearing a three-cornered hat that serves as the mouth of the vessel.

Torte plate - a glass serving plate for sandwiches, cake, or cold meat. Comparable to a chop plate in dinnerware, it ranges in size from about 12 to 20 inches.

Transfer Printing - a decorating method similar to the one in which decalcomania is used but permitting only one color at a time to be applied.

Translucence - that quality of fine china or plastic dinnerware that makes it semi-transparent. It may be demonstrated by placing the hand across the back of a piece and holding it up to the light. A silhouette of the hand will be visible through the body of the piece.

Tunnel Kiln - a long, tunnel-like oven in which dinnerware is fired as it moves through on slow-moving flat cars.

Underglaze Decoration - a ceramic decoration that is applied directly to the biscuit, or unglazed body, and then covered with a protective glaze coating that makes it highly resistant to wear.

The terms vitrified, vitreous and semivitreous describe the relative openness of the fired ceramic body. This openness is determined by immersing a piece of unglazed ware in water under specific conditions and determining the amount of water absorbed into the open pores of the body. By Federal Government standards, a body gaining less than 0.5%, by weight, is termed vitrified or vitreous; a body with more open pores is termed semivitreous. The terms adsorption and porosity are more or less synonomous, with the former referring to the relative volume of water added to the open pores and the latter referring to the relative volume of water added to the pores. Vitrification is brought about by the temperature and time of firing as well as by the amount and type of fluxing agents added to the composition.

Wasters - pieces marred in the kiln.

INDEX

PRICE GUIDE

Page 17

Old Crow punch bowl
     set, complete...........$225.00-250.00

Page 18

Mug $20.00-25.00

Page 19

Row 1:
   1. Cup $3.50-4.50
   2. Cup $3.50-4.50
   3. Ashtray.................. $20.00-25.00
   4. Ashtray.................. $4.00-6.00
   5. Ashtray.................. $4.00-6.00
Row 2:
   1. Child's plate $15.00-20.00
   2. Child's plate $15.00-20.00
   3. Child's plate $15.00-20.00
   4. Basket plate $12.00-15.00
Row 3:
   1. Plate....................... $22.00-25.00
   2. Mug........................ $20.00-25.00
   3. Mug........................ $18.00-22.00
   4. Deviled egg plate
      .... $18.00-22.00
Row 4:
   1. Plate....................... $20.00-25.00
   2. Plate....................... $20.00-25.00
   3. Plate....................... $10.00-12.00

Page 21

Row 1:
   1. Pencil holder $25.00-30.00
   2. Creamer.................. $20.00-25.00
   3. Cup $12.00-15.00
   4. Plate....................... $12.00-17.00
   5. Platter.................... $20.00-25.00
Row 2:
   1. Covered jug............. $75.00-80.00
   2. Rolling pin $120.00-130.00
   3. Stacked refrigerator
      set of 3 .... $35.00-45.00
   4. Covered bowl.......... $40.00-45.00

Row 3:
   1. Sanka mug (Hall).... $10.00-12.00
   2. Teapot.................... $35.00-40.00
   3. Sanka mug
      (made in Japan) ... $8.00-10.00
   4. Sit and sip, set $40.00-45.00
Row 4:
   1. Plate....................... $25.00-30.00
   2. Pitcher $45.00-50.00
   3. Plate....................... $20.00-25.00

Page 22

Advertising ashtrays..... $8.00-10.00

Page 23

Row 1:
   1. Plate....................... $22.00-25.00
   2. Cake lifter $20.00-25.00
   3. Plate....................... $25.00-30.00
Row 2:
   1. Plate....................... $20.00-25.00
   2. Jackson plate $27.00-32.00
   3. Plate....................... $25.00-30.00
   4. Ashtray.................. $35.00-40.00
   5. Ashtray.................. $25.00-30.00
Row 3:
   1. Plate....................... $22.00-27.00
   2. Ashtray.................. $32.00-37.00
   3. Plate....................... $20.00-25.00

Page 29

Row 1:
   1. Bowl....................... $10.00-12.00
   2. Covered soup.......... $20.00-22.00
   3. Cup & saucer set.... $10.00-12.00
   4. Covered sugar $15.00-17.00
Row 2:
   1. Plate....................... $6.00-8.00
   2. Coffee server
      (lid missing)......... $32.00-37.00
   3. Creamer................. $15.00-17.00
Row 3:
   1. Serving plate $25.00-30.00

Row 4:
   1. Plate....................... $12.00-14.00
   2. Rectangular plate.... $12.00-14.00

Page 31

Row 1:
   1. Cup & saucer set.... $10.00-12.00
   2. Covered sugar $14.00-17.00
   3. Salt & pepper set ... $12.00-14.00
   4. Closed handle cup
      and saucer set $15.00-17.00
Row 2:
   1. Mug........................ $15.00-18.00
   2. Creamer................. $14.00-16.00
   3. Pitcher $12.00-15.00
   4. Tumbler................. $12.00-14.00
Row 3:
   1. Serving bowl........... $14.00-16.00
   2. Water pitcher
      with ice lip $40.00-45.00
   3. Covered soup $18.00-20.00
Row 4:
   1. Dinner plate $12.00-14.00
   2. Bowl $8.00-10.00
   3. Casserole $20.00-25.00
      with cover $32.00-37.00

Page 33

Row 1:
   1. Nut dish................. $6.00-8.00
   2. Bowl....................... $10.00-12.00
   3. Cup $8.00-10.00
Row 2:
   1. Plate....................... $15.00-17.00
   2. Cruet..................... $25.00-30.00
   3. Salt & pepper set ... $14.00-16.00
   4. Saucer..................... $5.00-7.00
Row 3:
   1. Celery dish $20.00-25.00
   2. Dinner plate $14.00-16.00
Row 4:
   1. Divided vegetable... $30.00-35.00
   2. Square plate $15.00-20.00

Page 37

Row 1:
1. Cup & saucer set...... $17.00-20.00
2. Tumbler $15.00-20.00

Row 2:
1. Dinner plate $18.00-20.00
2. Utility bowl $20.00-25.00

Page 39

Row 1:
1. Sugar $15.00-17.00
2. Creamer................. $15.00-17.00
3. Plate..................... $4.00-6.00
4. Covered casserole... $35.00-40.00

Row 2:
1. Plate..................... $14.00-16.00
2. Ashtray................. $4.00-6.00
3. Plate..................... $12.00-14.00

Row 3:
1. Covered carafe....... $32.00-37.00
2. Bowl $22.00-27.00
3. Tumblers, each $15.00-18.00

Row 4:
1. Bowl $20.00-25.00
2. Plate..................... $15.00-18.00
3. Bowl $55.00-60.00

Page 40

Large plate.................. $50.00-60.00

Page 41

Row 1:
1. A.D. cup, saucer,
     set red $15.00-20.00
2. Creamer................. $12.00-14.00
3. Sugar $12.00-14.00
4. Cup & saucer set.... $15.00-20.00
5. Creamer................. $14.00-16.00

Row 2:
1. Pitcher $40.00-45.00
2. Salt & pepper set ... $15.00-20.00
3. Covered sugar $14.00-16.00
4. Creamer................. $14.00-16.00
5. Coffee server.......... $45.00-50.00

Row 3:
1. Gravy boat............. $15.00-20.00
2. Plate..................... $12.00-14.00
3. Covered butter $35.00-40.00
4. Plate..................... $4.50-6.50
5. Bowl $17.00-19.00

Row 4:
1. Divided plate $10.00-12.00
2. Cup & saucer set.... $12.00-14.00
3. Water set,
     pitcher.................. $40.00-45.00
   Tumblers, each....... $15.00-20.00

Page 43

Catalina fish plate......... $95.00-100.00

Page 44

Pitcher........................... $12.00-15.00

Page 46

Top photo:
1. Plate..................... $8.00-10.00
2. Cup & saucer set.... $10.00-12.00
3. Mug..................... $8.00-10.00

Bottom left photo:
1. Bonita cup and
     saucer $10.00-12.00
2. Bonita plate........... $8.00-10.00

Bottom right photo:
1. Elvuelo small bowl.. $4.00-6.00
2. Elvuelo small plate.. $3.00-4.00
3. Elvuelo cup
     & saucer............... $10.00-12.00
4. Elvuelo plate $6.00-8.00

Page 47

Row 1:
1. Plate..................... $35.00-40.00
2. Plate..................... $45.00-50.00
3. Divided plate $30.00-35.00

Row 2:
1. Plate..................... $20.00-25.00
2. Mug
     (matches item 1)... $25.00-30.00
3. Covered pitcher...... $47.00-50.00
4. Mug..................... $35.00-40.00
5. Plate..................... $25.00-30.00

Row 3:
1. Mug...................... $30.00-35.00
2. Mug...................... $30.00-35.00
3. Plate..................... $25.00-30.00
4. Mug..................... $35.00-40.00
5. Mug..................... $25.00-30.00

Page 48

Uncle Wiggily mug.......... $45.00-50.00

Page 49

Row 1:
1. Pitcher $18.00-20.00
2. Sugar $10.00-12.00
3. Creamer................. $10.00-12.00
4. Cup & saucer set.... $15.00-18.00
5. Elsie the Cow mug . $35.00-45.00
6. Bottle warmer $17.00-22.00

Row 2:
1. Plate..................... $25.00-30.00
2. Cup & saucer set.... $35.00-40.00
3. Plate..................... $30.00-35.00

Row 3:
1. Divided plate $20.00-25.00
2. Small divided plate $20.00-25.00
3. Divided plate $20.00-25.00

Row 4:
1. Divided plate $15.00-20.00
2. Divided plate $15.00-20.00
3. Hankscraft
     divided plate......... $15.00-20.00
4. Hankscraft clown
     divided plate......... $35.00-40.00

Page 51

Row 1:
1. Cup $14.00-16.00
2. Custard.................. $12.00-15.00
3. Handled soup bowl.. $20.00-25.00
4. Individual bowl $15.00-20.00

Row 2:
1. Tab handle bowl..... $14.00-16.00
2. Saucer................... $6.00-8.00
3. Plate..................... $10.00-15.00
4. Plate..................... $15.00-20.00

Row 3:
1. Platter................... $25.00-30.00
2. Footed tumbler....... $25.00-30.00
3. Shaker $14.00-16.00
4. Plate..................... $20.00-23.00
5. Coors advertising
     sign $45.00-50.00

Page 54

1. Creamer................. $12.00-15.00
2. Sugar $12.00-15.00

Page 55

Starting with top left of photo:
1. Serving bowl.......... $18.00-20.00

2. Platter..................... $20.00-25.00

3. Covered sugar $12.00-15.00

4. Creamer................... $12.00-15.00

5. Gravy boat $15.00-18.00

6. Oval serving bowl

.... $17.00-20.00

7. Small bowl.............. $4.00-6.00

8. Salad plate $6.00-8.00

9. Dinner plate $10.00-12.00

10. Cup & saucer set.... $12.00-14.00

Page 57

Row 1:

1. Plate....................... $10.00-15.00

2. Utility serving

plate $25.00-30.00

Row 2:

1. Covered batter

pitcher................... $55.00-60.00

2. Syrup pitcher $40.00-45.00

3. Cup & saucer set.... $14.00-16.00

Page 59

Row 1:

1. Silhouette

tumbler $22.00-25.00

2. Creamer................... $14.00-16.00

3. Bowl $20.00-25.00

4. Bowl $15.00-18.00

Row 2:

1. Plate....................... $12.00-15.00

2. Glass tumbler......... $25.00-30.00

3. Pie baker $25.00-30.00

Row 3:

1. Utility plate............ $25.00-30.00

2. Dinner plate $12.00-15.00

Row 4

1. Platter..................... $25.00-30.00

2. Lid........................... $10.00-15.00

3. Saucer..................... $3.00-4.00

Page 60

Row 1:

1. Plate....................... $8.00-10.00

2. Mug........................ $15.00-20.00

3. Large plate $18.00-22.00

Row 2:

1. Plate....................... $10.00-12.00

2. Plate....................... $4.00-6.00

3. Hanging plate......... $12.00-15.00

Page 61

Row 1:

1. Small plate $3.00-4.00

2. Saucer..................... $2.00-3.00

3. Covered sugar $10.00-12.00

4. Saucer..................... $2.00-3.00

5. Small plate $3.00-4.00

Row 2:

1. Pie baker $25.00-30.00

2. Covered bean pot ... $38.00-43.00

3. Covered vegetable .. $25.00-30.00

Row 3:

1. Bowl $3.00-5.00

2. Covered casserole... $25.00-30.00

3. Gravy boat.............. $12.00-14.00

Row 4:

1. Saucer..................... $2.00-3.00

2. Covered casserole... $25.00-30.00

3. Platter..................... $16.00-18.00

Page 62

1. Serving plate $40.00-45.00

2. Divided bowl........... $40.00-45.00

Page 63

Row 1:

1. Cup & saucer set.... $8.00-10.00

2. Bowl $5.00-6.00

3. Creamer.................. $8.00-10.00

4. Creamer.................. $5.00-7.00

Row 2:

1. Dinner plate $8.00-10.00

2. Covered casserole... $22.00-27.00

3. Platter..................... $25.00-27.00

Row 3:

1. Covered bean pot ... $45.00-50.00

2. Coffee server.......... $42.00-47.00

Row 4:

1. Small plate $4.00-6.00

2. Casserole $4.00-6.00

3. Serving bowl.......... $12.00-15.00

4. Soup bowl $6.00-8.00

Page 64

Photo 1: Coffee server... $45.00-50.00

Photo 2: Cookie jar $60.00-70.00

Page 65

Row 1:

1. Small bowl.............. $15.00-18.00

2. Small plate $6.00-8.00

3. Cake server $25.00-30.00

Row 2:

1. Plate....................... $14.00-16.00

2. Plate....................... $14.00-16.00

3. Plate....................... $14.00-16.00

Row 3:

1. Utility plate............ $25.00-35.00

Page 66

Row 1:

1. Dinner plate $8.00-10.00

2. Dinner plate $8.00-10.00

3. Dinner plate $8.00-10.00

Row 2:

1. Dinner plate $8.00-10.00

2. Dinner plate $8.00-10.00

3. Dinner plate $8.00-10.00

Row 3:

1. Pie baker $25.00-30.00

2. Small plate $3.00-4.00

3. Pie baker $17.00-25.00

Page 67

Row 1:

1. Small plate $6.00-8.00

2. Creamer.................. $8.00-10.00

3. Sugar $10.00-14.00

4. Creamer.................. $12.00-15.00

5. Sugar $12.00-15.00

Row 2:

1. Plate....................... $6.00-8.00

2. Cup & saucer set.... $8.00-10.00

3. Plate....................... $6.00-8.00

Row 3:

1. Small plate $4.00-6.00

2. Small plate $3.00-4.00

Row 4:

1. Saucer..................... $1.00-2.00

2. Small plate $1.00-2.00

3. Saucer..................... $1.00-2.00

4. Small plate $1.00-2.00

Page 69

Row 1:

1. Small plate $4.00-5.00

2. Covered sugar $9.00-14.00

3. Cup & saucer set.... $8.00-10.00

Row 2:

1. Plate....................... $6.00-8.00

2. Plate........................ $6.00-8.00

Row 3:

  1. Plate........................ $6.00-8.00

  2. Plate........................ $6.00-8.00

  3. Plate........................ $6.00-8.00

Row 4:

  1. Plate........................ $6.00-8.00

  2. Plate........................ $6.00-8.00

  3. Plate........................ $6.00-8.00

Page 73

Row 1:

  1. Saucer.................... $2.00-3.00

  2. Gravy boat............. $8.00-10.00

  3. Small plate $2.00-3.00

Row 2:

  1. Plate........................ $3.00-4.00

  2. Cup & saucer set.... $6.00-8.00

  3. Platter.................... $8.00-10.00

Row 3:

  1. Vegetable bowl $9.00-12.00

  2. Small bowl.............. $3.00-4.00

  3. Small plate $2.00-3.00

Row 4:

  1. Covered jug............. $90.00-95.00

  2. Bowl........................ $15.00-18.00

Page 75

Row 1:

  1. Small plate $3.00-4.00

  2. Small plate $3.00-4.00

  3. Small plate $3.00-4.00

  4. Small plate $3.00-4.00

Row 2:

  1. Creamer.................. $6.00-8.00

  2. Salt & pepper set. .. $18.00-20.00

  3. Pie baker $22.00-27.00

Row 3:

  1. Plate........................ $4.00-6.00

  2. Plate........................ $6.00-8.00

  3. Pie baker $22.00-27.00

Row 4:

  1. Plate........................ $5.00-7.00

  2. Pie baker $22.00-27.00

  3. Plate........................ $4.00-6.00

Page 81

Row 1:

  1. Plate........................ $14.00-16.00

  2. Luncheon plate....... $10.00-12.00

3. Dessert plate $4.00-6.00

Row 2:

  1. Small bowl.............. $4.00-5.00

  2. Creamer.................. $12.00-15.00

  3. Glass tumbler........ $12.00-15.00

  4. Cup & saucer set.... $14.00-18.00

  5. Bowl........................ $4.50-6.50

Row 3:

  1. Plate........................ $12.00-15.00

  2. Cup and saucer....... $16.00-18.00

  3. Creamer.................. $12.00-15.00

  4. Shaker $10.00-12.00

  5. Covered sugar $15.00-20.00

Page 83

Row 1:

  1. Sugar $13.00-15.00

  2. Shaker $8.00-10.00

  3. Creamer.................. $8.00-10.00

  4. Shakers, pair.......... $12.00-15.00

Row 2:

  1. Plate........................ $10.00-12.00

  2. Cup & saucer set.... $10.00-12.00

  3. Flat soup................. $10.00-12.00

Row 3:

  1. Vegetable bowl $22.00-25.00

  2. Small bowl.............. $8.00-10.00

  3. Salt & pepper set ... $18.00-20.00

  4. Coffee server........... $45.00-50.00

Row 4:

  1. Plate........................ $6.00-8.00

  2. Plate........................ $6.00-8.00

  3. Plate........................ $6.00-8.00

Page 84

Row 1:

  1. Sugar $8.00-10.00

  2. Bowl........................ $15.00-20.00

  3. Creamer.................. $10.00-15.00

Row 2:

  1. Small bowl.............. $4.00-6.00

  2. Saucer.................... $2.00-3.00

Page 85

  1. Plate...................... $10.00-12.00

  2. Bowl........................ $4.00-6.00

  3. Plate...................... $10.00-12.00

Row 2:

  1. Plate...................... $8.00-10.00

  2. Covered sugar $14.00-16.00

3. Cup $6.00-8.00

  4. Saucer.................... $2.00-3.00

Row 3:

  1. Saucer.................... $2.00-3.00

  2. Cup $8.00-10.00

  3. Egg cup.................. $15.00-20.00

  4. Bowl........................ $10.00-15.00

  5. Bowl........................ $3.50-4.50

Page 87

Row 1:

  1. Small plate $4.00-6.00

  2. Small plate $4.00-6.00

Row 2:

  1. Plate........................ $8.00-10.00

  2. Platter.................... $12.00-15.00

  3. Plate........................ $6.50-8.50

Row 3:

  1. Small plate $4.00-5.00

  2. Bowl........................ $3.00-4.00

  3. Small plate $4.00-5.00

Row 4:

  1. Plate........................ $12.00-15.00

  2. Small plate $12.00-15.00

  3. Gravy boat with

    liner $12.00-15.00

  4. Soup bowl $4.00-6.00

Page 89

Row 1:

  1. Shaker $6.00-8.00

  2. Covered sugar $15.00-17.00

  3. Coffee server........... $35.00-40.00

  4. Creamer.................. $12.00-14.00

  5. Shaker $6.00-8.00

Row 2:

  1. Plate........................ $8.00-10.00

  2. Egg cup.................. $12.00-15.00

  3. Bowl........................ $4.00-6.00

  4. Egg cup.................. $12.00-15.00

  5. Plate........................ $8.00-10.00

Row 3:

  1. Creamer.................. $12.00-14.00

  2. Shaker $6.00-8.00

  3. Bowl........................ $5.00-7.00

  4. Liner plate............. $4.00-5.00

  5. Two handle soup $10.00-12.00

  6. A.D. saucer $3.00-4.00

  7. A.D. cup $12.00-14.00

  8. Cup $4.00-6.00

Page 91

Row 1:
1. Cup & saucer set.... $20.00-25.00
2. Sugar $20.00-25.00
3. Small bowl............. $8.00-10.00

Row 2:
1. Covered creamer $22.00-27.00
2. Shaker $15.00-22.00
3. Luncheon plate....... $20.00-25.00

Page 93

Starting with top left of photo:
1. Covered casserole... $40.00-45.00
2. Platter..................... $25.00-30.00
3. Teapot.................... $50.00-55.00
4. Covered marmite ... $30.00-35.00
5. Creamer.................. $15.00-20.00
6. Cereal bowl............. $6.00-8.00
7. Dessert plate $6.00-8.00
8. Soup bowl $20.00-22.00
9. Plate....................... $14.00-16.00
10. Cup $10.00-12.00

Page 95

Row 1:
1. Covered casserole... $25.00-30.00
2. Jug $20.00-25.00
3. Ball jug $35.00-40.00

Row 2:
1. Jug $37.00-42.00
2. Ball jug $50.00-55.00

Row 3:
1. Large jug $40.00-45.00
2. Pie baker $27.00-32.00

Row 4:
1. Baking dish $20.00-25.00
2. Covered jar $45.00-50.00

Page 97

Row 1:
1. Jug $35.00-40.00
2. Jug $30.00-35.00
3. Jug $25.00-30.00

Row 2:
1. Plate....................... $10.00-12.00
2. Platter..................... $20.00-25.00

Row 3:
1. Cup & saucer set.... $14.00-16.00
2. Covered sugar $16.00-18.00
3. Covered vegetable... $35.00-40.00

Row 4:
1. Coffee maker, all china,
   complete $65.00-75.00

Page 99

Row 1:
1. Cup saucer set........ $12.00-14.00
2. Bowl $4.00-5.00
3. Creamer.................. $14.00-16.00
4. Covered sugar $17.00-20.00

Row 2:
1. Covered vegetable
   dish $45.00-50.00
2. Salt & pepper set ... $18.00-20.00
3. Teapot.................... $50.00-55.00

Row 3:
1. Plate....................... $12.00-14.00
2. 3 Tiered tidbit tray. $35.00-40.00
3. Small plate $4.00-6.00

Page 100

Row 1:
1. Creamer.................. $16.00-18.00
2. Sugar with lid $18.00-20.00
3. Coffee urn............... $60.00-65.00
4. Coffee server.......... $45.00-50.00

Row 2:
1. Marmites in chrome
   frame $65.00-75.00
2. Marmites (each,
   without frame) $20.00-25.00

Page 101

Row 1:
1. Creamer.................. $12.00-15.00
2. Salt & pepper set ... $20.00-25.00
3. Ball jug $35.00-40.00

Row 2:
1. Shaker $12.00-15.00
2. Grease pot
   with lid $20.00-25.00
3. Shaker $12.00-15.00

Row 3:
1. Large bowl............. $22.00-27.00
2. Coffee server.......... $35.00-38.00

Row 4:
1. Shaker $14.00-16.00
2. Bowl $12.00-14.00
3. Bowl $14.00-17.00
4. Salad bowl $20.00-22.00

Page 102

Row 1:
1. Loop handle salt
   and pepper, pair... $25.00-30.00
2. Individual
   casserole $10.00-12.00
3. Condiment set
   (lid missing).......... $40.00-45.00

Row 2:
1. Ball jug $35.00-40.00
2. Doughnut teapot $100.00-120.00
3. Jug $25.00-30.00

Row 3:
1. Covered casserole... $30.00-35.00
2. Plate....................... $8.00-10.00
3. Round jar
   (not Hall) $18.00-22.00

Page 103

Individual teapot $1,500.00-2,000.00

Page 104

Fluted vase $1,000.00-1,200.00

Page 105

Row 1:
1. 3 Piece condiment,
   set $42.00-46.00
2. Cream soup $20.00-25.00
3. Cup $12.00-14.00
4. St. Denis cup $20.00-25.00

Row 2:
1. Gravy boat.............. $30.00-35.00
2. Teapot.................... $65.00-75.00
3. One pound butter
   dish $250.00-275.00

Row 3:
1. St. Denis saucer $8.00-10.00
2. Sifter.....................$130.00-170.00
3. Saucer.................... $4.00-6.00

Row 4:
1. Dinner plate $14.00-16.00
2. Bud vase $145.00-175.00
3. Frosted tumbler $18.00-20.00
4. Ball jug $35.00-40.00

Page 107

Row 1:
1. Plate....................... $6.00-8.00
2. Cup $10.00-12.00

3. Creamer.................. $14.00-16.00

4. Small bowl.............. $5.00-7.00

Row 2:

1. Plate....................... $8.00-10.00

2. Teapot..................... $45.00-50.00

3. Coffee server base .. $40.00-45.00

Row 3:

1. Cereal jar................ $60.00-65.00

2. Cereal jar................ $60.00-65.00

Row 4:

1. Loop handle

shaker.................. $15.00-18.00

2. Grease pot $20.00-25.00

3. Covered casserole... $35.00-40.00

4. Marmite.................. $30.00-35.00

Page 108

St. Denis cup and

saucer, set.............. $37.00-42.00

Page 109

Row 1:

1. Creamer.................. $20.00-22.00

2. Sugar $22.00-25.00

3. Beverage mug......... $40.00-42.00

4. Creamer.................. $14.00-16.00

5. Covered sugar $18.00-22.00

Row 2:

1. Gravy boat.............. $22.00-25.00

2. Covered

grease pot $25.00-28.00

3. Handled shakers,

set $24.00-27.00

Row 3:

1. Ball jug $35.00-40.00

2. Teapot....................$110.00-120.00

3. Coffee server........... $40.00-45.00

Row 4:

1. Mixing bowl............ $20.00-22.00

2. Cookie jar $95.00-100.00

3. Covered casserole... $35.00-40.00

Page 111

1. Cup and saucer $14.00-16.00

2. Bowl....................... $4.00-6.00

3. Plate, 6" $4.00-6.00

Row 2:

1. Vegetable bowl $22.00-27.00

2. Oval bowl............... $20.00-25.00

3. Soup bowl $18.00-20.00

Row 3:

1. Breakfast plate, 9". $10.00-12.00

2. Dessert plate, 8"..... $8.00-10.00

3. Salad plate, 7" $6.00-8.00

Row 4:

1. Platter, 13¼"......... $22.00-27.00

2. Small platter, 11¼". $20.00-25.00

Page 113

Row 1:

1. Shelf paper,

each sheet............. $20.00-25.00

2. Rolling pin

(Haker) $125.00-130.00

3. Glass pitcher $125.00-150.00

Row 2:

1. Metal paper

dispenser $30.00-35.00

2. Shakers, pair.......... $20.00-24.00

Row 3:

1. Matchbox................ $35.00-40.00

2. Potato masher........ $12.00-15.00

3. Whisk...................... $12.00-15.00

4. Sifter...................... $50.00-60.00

Row 4:

1. Tray $32.00-37.00

Page 115

I.W. Harper decanter $125.00-130.00

Page 118

Bake set in wire frame .. $42.00-47.00

Page 119

Top-left to right

1. Plate....................... $10.00-12.00

2. Small plate $6.00-8.00

3. Serving bowl........... $15.00-18.00

4. Tab handle bowl..... $8.00-10.00

5. Cream soup $12.00-14.00

6. Creamer.................. $14.00-16.00

7. Dinner plate $10.00-12.00

8. Salad plate $4.00-6.00

9. Cup & saucer set.... $12.00-14.00

Page 121

Row 1:

1. Pitcher $20.00-25.00

2. Shaker $10.00-12.00

3. Pitcher $18.00-20.00

Row 2:

1. Pitcher $40.00-45.00

2. Saucer $2.00-3.00

3. Saucer $2.00-3.00

Row 3:

1. Custard, each $4.00-6.00

2. Tall jar $30.00-35.00

Row 4:

1. Large bowl.............. $35.00-40.00

2. Indent plate........... $6.00-8.00

Page 123

Row 1:

1. Pepper shaker $6.00-8.00

2. Salt shaker $6.00-8.00

3. Cake server $20.00-25.00

Row 2:

1. Pitcher $40.00-45.00

2. Platter................... $10.00-15.00

Row 3:

1. Platter.................... $20.00-25.00

2. Cake lifter $20.00-25.00

3. Cake server $20.00-25.00

4. Rolling pin $100.00-125.00

Row 4:

1. Plate....................... $35.00-45.00

2. Custard.................. $15.00-20.00

3. Bowl....................... $50.00-75.00

Page 125

Row 1:

1. Sugar $8.00-10.00

2. Creamer.................. $8.00-10.00

3. Server $22.00-27.00

4. Custard.................. $8.00-10.00

5. Custard.................. $10.00-12.00

Row 2:

1. Plate....................... $8.00-10.00

2. Plate....................... $4.00-6.00

3. Plate....................... $2.00-4.00

4. Small bowl.............. $4.00-6.00

Row 3:

1. Teapot..................... $35.00-40.00

2. Scoop...................... $45.00-50.00

3. Fork $35.00-45.00

4. Spoon..................... $30.00-35.00

5. Platter.................... $25.00-30.00

6. Rolling pin $100.00-125.00

Row 4:

1. Covered pitcher...... $50.00-75.00

2. Tab handle bowl..... $6.00-8.00

3. Utility bowl $25.00-30.00
4. Stack set w/cover.... $37.00-42.00

Page 126

1. Plate...................... $6.00-8.00
2. Shaker $4.00-6.00

Page 127

Row 1:

1. Bowl $6.00-8.00
2. Shaker $16.00-18.00
3. Lard jar.................. $20.00-25.00
4. Covered jug............ $20.00-25.00

Row 2:

1. Plate...................... $12.00-14.00
2. Spoon $25.00-30.00
3. Bowl $8.00-10.00

Row 3:

1. Utility bowl $35.00-40.00

Row 4:

1. Serving plate $22.00-27.00
2. Serving plate $22.00-27.00

Page 129

Row 1:

1. Server $20.00-25.00
2. Spoon $25.00-30.00

Row 2:

1. Utility bowl $35.00-40.00
2. Small plate $6.00-8.00

Row 3:

1. Covered bowl......... $20.00-22.00
2. Utility plate............ $25.00-30.00
3. Covered jug............ $28.00-35.00

Row 4:

1. Bowl $25.00-35.00
2. Bowl $20.00-25.00
3. Florist bowl $40.00-50.00

Page 131

Row 1:

1. Server $22.00-27.00
2. Casserole
   (individual)........... $4.00-6.00
3. Casserole
   (individual)........... $4.00-6.00
4. Server $22.00-27.00

Row 2:

1. Utility bowl $35.00-40.00
2. Covered bowl......... $30.00-35.00

Row 3:

1. Pie baker $22.00-27.00
2. Rolling pin $125.00-130.00
3. Plate...................... $3.00-4.00
4. Pie baker $22.00-27.00
5. Rolling pin $125.00-130.00

Row 4:

1. Small bowl............. $10.00-12.00
2. Medium bowl.......... $14.00-16.00
3. Large bowl............. $20.00-25.00
   Set of three $44.00-53.00

Page 132

Row 1:

1. Small plate $3.00-4.00
2. Saucer $2.00-3.00
3. Small plate $2.00-4.00
4. Small plate $2.00-4.00

Row 2:

1. Plate...................... $6.00-8.00
2. Plate...................... $6.00-8.00
3. Plate...................... $10.00-12.00

Row 3:

1. Plate...................... $10.00-12.00
2. Plate...................... $10.00-12.00
3. Plate...................... $10.00-12.00

Page 135

1. Cup & saucer set.... $12.00-14.00
2. Covered drippings
   jar......................... $20.00-25.00
3. Shaker $12.00-14.00
4. Cup & saucer set.... $10.00-12.00

Row 2:

1. Plate...................... $12.00-14.00
2. Covered jug............ $16.00-18.00
3. Covered jug............ $18.00-20.00
4. Covered jug............ $18.00-22.00

Row 3:

1. Teapot.................... $30.00-35.00
2. Covered casserole... $35.00-40.00
3. Pitcher $30.00-35.00

Row 4:

1. Utility plate............ $18.00-20.00
2. Platter.................... $20.00-25.00
3. Pie baker $20.00-25.00

Page 136

Row 1:

1. Shaker $10.00-12.00

2. Shaker $10.00-12.00
3. Rolling pin $125.00-130.00

Row 2:

1. Fork $25.00-30.00
2. Spoon $25.00-30.00
3. Bowl $30.00-35.00
4. Sign...................... $30.00-35.00

Row 3:

1. Plate...................... $12.00-14.00
2. Plate...................... $6.00-8.00
3. Plate...................... $5.00-7.00
4. Plate...................... $5.00-7.00

Page 137

Photograph 1:

1. Plate...................... $27.00-32.00
2. Bowl $12.00-15.00

Photograph 2:

1. Clock $65.00-75.00

Page 139

Row 1:

1. Shaker $8.00-10.00
2. Shaker $8.00-10.00
3. Casserole
   (individual)........... $8.00-10.00
4. Creamer................. $12.00-14.00
5. Sugar $10.00-15.00

Row 2:

1. Pitcher $20.00-22.00
2. Ashtray $10.00-12.00
3. Pie baker $20.00-25.00
4. Server $18.00-22.00

Row 3:

1. Utility plate............ $22.00-25.00
2. Casserole set $30.00-35.00

Row 4:

1. Covered bowl......... $15.00-17.00
2. Fork $25.00-30.00
3. Plate...................... $6.00-8.00

Page 141

Row 1:

1. Shaker $18.00-20.00
2. Rolling pin $125.00-130.00
3. Server $20.00-25.00

Row 2:

1. Pitcher $35.00-40.00
2. Fork $25.00-30.00
3. Scoop $35.00-40.00

4. Bowl...................... $35.00-40.00

Row 3:

   1. Pitcher.................. $35.00-40.00

   2. Pitcher.................. $35.00-40.00

Row 4:

   1. Utility plate............ $20.00-25.00

   2. Utility plate............ $20.00-25.00

Page 143

Row 1:

   1. Pitcher.................. $20.00-25.00

   2. Individual

      casserole.............. $8.00-10.00

   3. Sugar

      (if complete).......... $12.00-15.00

   4. Teapot

      (if complete).......... $25.00-30.00

Row 2:

   1. Bowl.................... $30.00-35.00

   2. Spoon.................... $30.00-35.00

   3. Bowl.................... $4.00-6.00

   4. Hot plate................ $30.00-35.00

Row 3:

   1. Bowl.................... $35.00-40.00

   2. Covered pitcher...... $40.00-45.00

Row 4:

   1. Utility plate............ $22.00-27.00

   2. Server.................... $20.00-25.00

   3. Utility plate............ $22.00-27.00

Page 145

Row 1:

   1. Plate.................... $3.00-5.00

   2. Bowl.................... $12.00-15.00

   3. Plate.................... $4.00-6.00

Row 2:

   1. Utility plate............ $15.00-17.00

   2. Small plate............ $4.00-6.00

Row 3:

   1. Pie baker................ $20.00-25.00

   2. Cake plate.............. $22.00-27.00

Row 4:

   1. Plate.................... $6.00-8.00

   2. Pitcher.................. $30.00-35.00

   3. Utility bowl............ $30.00-35.00

Page 147

Row 1:

   1. Creamer.................. $8.00-10.00

   2. Gravy boat.............. $10.00-15.00

3. Creamer.................. $8.00-10.00

Row 2:

   1. Platter.................. $20.00-25.00

   2. Plate.................... $4.00-6.00

   3. Ashtray.................. $8.00-10.00

   4. Teapot.................. $30.00-35.00

Row 3:

   1. Plate.................... $6.00-8.00

   2. Saucer.................. $2.00-3.00

   3. Plate.................... $3.00-5.00

Row 4:

   1. Plate.................... $8.00-10.00

   2. Saucer.................. $2.00-3.00

   3. Saucer.................. $2.00-3.00

   4. Plate.................... $8.00-10.00

Page 149

Row 1:

   1. Creamer.................. $8.00-10.00

   2. Covered sugar........ $10.00-12.00

   3. Creamer.................. $8.00-10.00

Row 2:

   1. Cake plate.............. $15.00-20.00

   2. Server.................... $20.00-25.00

   3. Small plate............ $4.00-6.00

Row 3:

   1. Plate.................... $4.00-6.00

   2. Serving plate.......... $15.00-17.00

Row 4:

   1. Plate.................... $6.00-8.00

   2. Plate.................... $3.00-4.00

   3. Plate.................... $3.00-4.00

   4. Saucer.................. $1.00-2.00

   5. Plate.................... $3.00-4.00

Page 150

   1. Salad bowl.............. $15.00-20.00

   2. Shaker set.............. $10.00-15.00

Page 151

Row 1:

   1. Plate.................... $6.00-8.00

   2. Plate.................... $6.00-8.00

Row 2:

   1. Plate.................... $6.00-8.00

   2. Plate.................... $4.00-6.00

Row 3:

   1. Plate.................... $4.00-6.00

   2. Plate.................... $3.00-5.00

   3. Plate.................... $3.00-5.00

Page 153

   1. Reproduction mug.. $35.00-40.00

   2. Reproduction

      pitcher.................. $55.00-65.00

Page 155

Row 1:

   1. Creamer.................. $8.00-10.00

   2. Sugar with lid........ $10.00-12.00

   3. Sugar with lid........ $10.00-12.00

   4. Cup...................... $4.00-6.00

Row 2:

   1. Plate.................... $4.00-6.00

   2. Plate.................... $6.00-8.00

   3. Bowl.................... $3.00-5.00

Row 3:

   1. Coffee server.......... $32.00-37.00

   2. Bowl.................... $20.00-25.00

   3. Warmer frame for

      bowl.................... $8.00-10.00

Page 156

Row 1:

   1. Covered sugar........ $12.00-14.00

   2. Cup & saucer set.... $10.00-12.00

   3. Creamer.................. $8.00-10.00

Row 2:

   1. Plate.................... $8.00-10.00

   2. Platter.................. $18.00-20.00

Row 3:

   1. Flat soup................ $8.00-10.00

   2. Small bowl............ $4.00-6.00

   3. Bowl.................... $15.00-18.00

Page 157

Row 1:

   1. Covered jar............ $37.00-42.00

   2. Covered casserole... $30.00-32.00

   3. Syrup pitcher........ $20.00-25.00

   4. Batter pitcher........ $30.00-35.00

   5. Utility tray............ $20.00-25.00

Row 2:

   1. Rolling pin.............$120.00-130.00

   2. Bowl.................... $18.00-20.00

   3. Bowl.................... $15.00-18.00

   4. Bowl.................... $12.00-15.00

      3 Bowl set.............. $45.00-53.00

Row 3:

   1. Cup & saucer set.... $10.00-12.00

   2. Teapot.................. $40.00-45.00

3. Small bowl............. $4.00-6.00
4. Creamer................. $12.00-14.00
5. Tab handle bowl..... $8.00-10.00

Row 4:
1. Shaker, each $10.00-14.00
2. Shaker, each $10.00-14.00
3. Shaker, each $10.00-14.00
4. Drippings jar $20.00-25.00
5. Shaker, each $10.00-14.00
6. Creamer................. $13.00-15.00
7. Sugar $14.00-16.00

Page 163

Photograph 1:
1. Pitcher and bowl $100.00-125.00

Photograph 2:
1. Utility plate $20.00-25.00
2. Covered batter jug... $30.00-35.00
3. Syrup pitcher $22.00-27.00
4. Shaker $12.00-14.00
5. Server $20.00-25.00

Page 165

Row 1:
1. Creamer................. $4.00-5.00
2. Sugar with cover $5.00-6.00
3. Small plate $2.00-3.00
4. Saucer................... $2.00-3.00

Row 2:
1. Shaker $10.00-12.00
2. Covered pitcher...... $35.00-40.00
3. Saucer................... $2.00-3.00
4. Plate..................... $2.00-3.00

Row 3:
1. Platter................... $12.00-15.00
2. Bowl...................... $15.00-18.00
3. Plate..................... $6.00-8.00

Row 4:
1. Covered jar $40.00-45.00
2. Pie baker $18.00-22.00
3. Small bowl............. $3.00-4.00
4. Small plate $2.00-3.00

Page 166

Row 1:
1. Coaster $8.00-10.00
2. Shaker $8.00-10.00
3. Teapot................... $48.00-52.00
4. Shaker $8.00-10.00
5. Utility plate............ $20.00-25.00

Row 2:
1. Creamer................. $12.00-14.00
2. Shaker $10.00-12.00
3. Covered casserole... $32.00-37.00
4. Saucer................... $2.00-4.00
5. Saucer................... $2.00-4.00
6. Saucer................... $2.00-4.00

Row 3:
1. World's Fair plate .. $40.00-50.00
2. A.D. cup................. $15.00-17.00
3. Cup $8.00-10.00
4. Dinner plate $10.00-12.00

Page 167

Row 1:
1. Plate..................... $10.00-12.00
2. Bowl...................... $4.00-6.00
3. Coffee server.......... $40.00-45.00
4. Creamer................. $12.00-14.00
5. Sugar $14.00-16.00

Row 2:
1. Plate..................... $4.00-6.00
2. Shaker $8.00-10.00
3. Coffee server.......... $40.00-45.00
4. Shaker $8.00-10.00
5. Plate..................... $4.00-6.00

Row 3:
1. Plate..................... $2.00-4.00
2. Platter................... $10.00-15.00
3. Plate..................... $2.00-4.00

Page 168

Row 1:
1. Soup $14.00-16.00
2. Shaker $10.00-12.00
3. Platter................... $20.00-25.00
4. Cup $8.00-10.00
5. Round vegetable..... $15.00-20.00

Row 2:
1. Plate..................... $3.00-4.00
2. Shaker $8.00-10.00
3. A.D. cup................. $12.00-15.00
4. Covered jar $12.00-15.00
5. Cup $8.00-10.00
6. Plate..................... $2.00-4.00

Page 169

Row 1:
1. Covered sugar $6.00-8.00
2. Creamer................. $6.00-8.00

3. Bowl $3.00-5.00
4. Plate..................... $3.00-5.00

Row 2:
1. Platter................... $12.00-15.00
2. Saucer................... $2.00-3.00
3. Platter................... $12.00-15.00

Row 3:
1. Stack bowls,
    set of 3 .... $18.00-20.00
2. Covered batter
    bowl..................... $37.00-42.00
3. Covered syrup $27.00-32.00
4. Saucer................... $2.00-3.00

Row 4:
1. Utility plate........... $18.00-22.00
2. Bowl...................... $32.00-37.00

Page 177

Row 1:
1. ¼ lb. butter $30.00-35.00
2. Gravy boat............. $18.00-20.00
3. Salt & pepper set $10.00-15.00
4. Cup $6.00-8.00

Row 2:
1. Saucer................... $2.00-3.00
2. Small bowl............. $2.00-4.00
3. Small platter $12.00-14.00
4. Dessert plate $2.00-4.00

Row 3:
1. Platter................... $18.00-20.00
2. Coffee server.......... $32.00-37.00
3. Dinner plate $10.00-12.00

Row 4:
1. Soup bowl $6.00-8.00
2. Handled tray $15.00-20.00

Page 179

Row 1:
1. Covered sugar $14.00-18.00
2. Platter................... $20.00-25.00
3. Covered butter $47.00-52.00
4. Creamer................. $10.00-12.00

Row 2:
1. Bowl...................... $8.00-10.00
2. Coffee server.......... $50.00-60.00
3. Syrup $27.00-32.00

Row 3:
1. Cup $8.00-10.00
2. Teapot................... $45.00-50.00
3. A.D. cup-saucer, set $15.00-20.00

4. Plate...................... $6.00-8.00

Page 181

Row 1:

1. Covered sugar $10.00-12.00
2. Creamer................. $10.00-12.00
3. Creamer................. $12.00-14.00
4. Teapot.................... $30.00-35.00
5. Cup & saucer set..... $10.00-12.00

Row 2:

1. Plate...................... $8.00-10.00
2. Gravy boat............. $10.00-12.00
3. Bowl...................... $3.00-5.00
4. Bowl...................... $2.00-3.00

Row 3:

1. Shaker set $10.00-12.00
2. Plate...................... $3.00-4.00
3. Teapot.................... $22.00-27.00
4. Creamer................. $8.00-10.00

Page 183

Row 1:

1. Sugar $6.00-8.00
2. Gravy boat............. $10.00-12.00
3. Covered sugar $10.00-12.00
4. Plate...................... $4.00-6.00

Row 2:

1. Plate...................... $8.00-10.00
2. Plate...................... $5.00-8.00
3. Bowl...................... $4.00-5.00
4. Small bowl............. $2.00-3.00

Row 3:

1. Platter.................... $15.00-20.00
2. Platter.................... $20.00-25.00

Row 4:

1. Plate...................... $6.00-8.00
2. Plate...................... $6.00-8.00
3. Plate...................... $6.00-8.00

Page 185

Row 1:

1. Gravy boat............. $25.00-28.00
2. Covered vegetable.. $35.00-40.00
3. Butter and cover $57.00-67.00

Row 2:

1. Cup and saucer $12.00-14.00
2. Platter.................... $25.00-30.00
3. Egg cup $20.00-25.00
4. Covered sugar $20.00-25.00

Row 3:

1. Teapot.................... $35.00-40.00

2. Plate...................... $6.00-8.00
3. Butter $32.00-37.00
4. Creamer................. $12.00-17.00

Page 187

Row 1:

1. Small plate $3.00-4.00
2. Sugar $12.00-14.00
3. Sugar $12.00-14.00
4. Sugar $12.00-14.00
5. Small plate $4.00-5.00
6. Creamer................. $10.00-12.00

Row 2:

1. Plate...................... $8.00-10.00
2. Small plate $3.00-4.00
3. Plate...................... $4.00-5.00
4. Dinner plate $8.00-10.00

Row 3:

1. Pie baker $20.00-25.00
2. Saucer.................... $2.00-3.00
3. Creamer................. $8.00-10.00
4. Tea or coffee
   server..................... $27.00-37.00

Row 4:

1. Dinner plate $6.00-8.00
2. Gravy boat & liner.. $12.00-14.00
3. Dinner plate $6.00-8.00

Page 189

Row 1:

1. Small bowl............. $6.00-8.00
2. Utility bowl $22.00-27.00
3. Covered casserole... $30.00-32.00

Row 2:

1. Pie baker $20.00-25.00
2. Utility plate........... $20.00-22.00

Row 3:

1. Platter.................... $20.00-25.00
2. Lid only.................. $8.00-10.00

Row 4:

1. Utility bowl $32.00-37.00
2. Platter.................... $17.00-22.00

Page 190

Priscilla teapot............... $40.00-45.00

Page 191

Row 1:

1. Covered sugar $14.00-16.00
2. Saucer.................... $2.00-3.00
3. Creamer................. $10.00-12.00

Row 2:

1. Pie baker $22.00-27.00
2. Plate...................... $10.00-12.00
3. Bowl...................... $8.00-10.00

Row 3:

1. Covered casserole... $25.00-30.00
2. Utility bowl $25.00-30.00

Row 4:

1. Coffee server.......... $40.00-45.00
2. Large utility bowl .. $40.00-45.00

Page 193

Row 1:

1. Bowl...................... $5.00-7.00
2. Sugar $12.00-14.00
3. Creamer................. $12.00-14.00
4. Cup $6.00-8.00
5. Bowl...................... $6.00-8.00

Row 2:

1. Small plate $4.00-6.00
2. Saucer.................... $2.00-4.00
3. Saucer.................... $2.00-4.00
4. Small plate $3.00-5.00

Row 3:

1. Plate...................... $10.00-12.00
2. Plate...................... $10.00-12.00
3. Plate...................... $10.00-12.00

Row 4:

1. Platter.................... $25.00-30.00
2. Platter.................... $25.00-30.00

Page 195

Row 1:

1. Gravy boat............. $15.00-17.00
2. Salt & pepper set ... $16.00-20.00
3. Egg cup $18.00-20.00
4. Creamer................. $12.00-15.00
5. Sugar and cover $16.00-18.00

Row 2:

1. Butter and cover $55.00-75.00
2. Pitcher $45.00-50.00
3. Covered casserole... $35.00-40.00

Row 3:

1. Plate...................... $8.00-10.00
2. Cup & saucer set.... $12.00-14.00
3. Flat soup $12.00-14.00
4. Pie baker $20.00-25.00

Row 4:

1. Set of three bowls... $50.00-55.00
2. Pickle dish $15.00-18.00

3. Platter..................... $20.00-25.00

Page 197

Row 1:
1. Plate........................ $3.00-4.00
2. Plate........................ $3.00-4.00
3. Plate........................ $3.00-4.00
4. Saucer..................... $2.00-3.00

Row 2:
1. Plate........................ $3.00-4.00
2. Saucer..................... $2.00-3.00
3. Saucer..................... $2.00-3.00
4. Creamer.................. $10.00-14.00
5. Saucer..................... $2.00-3.00

Row 3:
1. Plate........................ $8.00-10.00
2. Plate........................ $8.00-10.00
3. Plate........................ $8.00-10.00
4. Small plate $4.00-6.00

Row 4:
1. Bowl........................ $20.00-22.00
2. Platter..................... $10.00-12.00
3. Small plate $2.00-3.00

Page 199

Row 1:
1. Covered sugar $13.00-15.00
2. Salt & pepper set ... $12.00-14.00
3. Creamer.................. $12.00-14.00
4. Creamer.................. $12.00-14.00

Row 2:
1. Plate........................ $8.00-10.00
2. Dessert plate $4.00-5.00
3. Saucer..................... $1.00-2.00
4. Bread and butter
   plate...................... $3.00-4.00

Row 3:
1. Covered casserole... $20.00-25.00
2. Gravy boat with
   liner $12.00-14.00

Page 201

Row 1:
1. Bowl........................ $6.00-8.00
2. Sugar and cover $20.00-22.00
3. Sugar and cover $20.00-22.00
4. Bowl........................ $6.00-8.00

Row 2:
1. Small plate $6.00-8.00
2. Small plate $8.00-10.00

3. Creamer.................. $12.00-14.00
4. Small plate $6.00-8.00
5. Small plate $6.00-8.00

Row 3:
1. Plate........................ $10.00-12.00
2. Plate........................ $12.00-15.00
3. Plate........................ $10.00-12.00
4. Plate........................ $10.00-12.00

Row 4:
1. Cup & saucer set.... $13.00-15.00
2. Platter..................... $20.00-25.00
3. Cup & saucer set.... $13.00-15.00

Page 202

1. A.D. cup-saucer,
   set $15.00-20.00
2. A.D. plates, each $4.00-6.00
3. A.D. cup-saucer,
   set $15.00-20.00
4. A.D. coffeepot not
   shown.................... $30.00-35.00
   (also with decals)

Page 203

1. Platter..................... $22.00-27.00
2. Covered bowl $32.00-37.00
3. Gravy boat.............. $20.00-25.00
4. Liner $10.00-12.00
5. Flat soup................. $12.00-15.00
6. Plate........................ $8.00-10.00
7. Sugar and cover $16.00-18.00
8. Cup and saucer $10.00-12.00

Page 205

Row 1:
1. Plate........................ $6.00-8.00
2. Saucer..................... $2.00-3.00
3. Pickle dish or
   platter................... $6.00-8.00

Row 2:
1. Plate........................ $8.00-10.00
2. Sugar and cover $8.00-10.00
3. Cup & saucer set.... $6.00-8.00

Row 3:
1. Plate........................ $6.00-8.00
2. Plate........................ $4.00-5.00
3. Plate........................ $4.00-5.00

Row 4:
1. Plate........................ $5.00-6.00
2. Plate........................ $5.00-6.00

3. Plate........................ $5.00-6.00

Page 206

Row 1:
1. Sugar $6.00-8.00
2. Creamer.................. $6.00-8.00
3. Gravy boat & liner.. $10.00-12.00
4. Creamer.................. $8.00-16.00

Row 2:
1. Plate........................ $8.00-10.00
2. Small bowl.............. $3.00-4.00
3. Saucer..................... $4.00-6.00
4. Platter..................... $15.00-20.00

Row 3:
1. Calendar plate $12.00-15.00
2. Plate........................ $8.00-10.00
3. Plate........................ $8.00-10.00

Row 4:
1. Plate (stamped
   Harker & HLC).... $8.00-10.00
2. Plate........................ $6.00-8.00
3. Plate........................ $6.00-8.00

Page 211

Row 1:
1. Liner plate............. $6.00-8.00
2. Covered sugar $14.00-16.00
3. Cup and saucer $10.00-12.00

Row 2:
1. Hot plate Farberware
   frame $25.00-30.00
2. Cup $8.00-10.00
3. Hot plate................. $25.00-30.00

Row 3:
1. Covered
   casserole $30.00-35.00
2. Ice bucket $40.00-45.00

Row 4:
1. Plate........................ $8.00-10.00
2. Tidbit tray,
   metal handle $17.00-22.00

Page 212

Row 1:
1. Cup & saucer set.... $14.00-16.00
2. Plate........................ $14.00-15.00
3. Candy dish $17.00-22.00

Row 2:
1. Nut bowl $20.00-25.00
2. Plate warmer.......... $25.00-30.00

Row 3:
  1. Tidbit tray,
      metal handle $22.00-27.00
  2. Tidbit tray $30.00-35.00

Page 213

Row 1:
  1. Platter..................... $20.00-25.00
  2. Teapot..................... $37.00-42.00
  3. Gravy boat............. $18.00-20.00
Row 2:
  1. Plate...................... $10.00-12.00
  2. Plate...................... $6.00-8.00
  3. Small bowl............. $4.00-6.00
  4. Cream soup $12.00-15.00
Row 3:
  1. A.D. saucer............. $2.00-3.00
  2. A.D. cup $10.00-12.00
  3. Butter and
      cover..................... $37.00-47.00
  4. Creamer................. $10.00-12.00
  5. Sugar and cover $14.00-16.00

Page 215

Row 1:
  1. Plate $12.00-14.00
  2. Bowl...................... $10.00-12.00
  3. Cup $8.00-10.00
  4. Vegetable bowl $20.00-25.00
Row 2:
  1. Creamer................. $10.00-12.00
  2. Creamer................. $10.00-12.00
  3. Sugar $10.00-12.00
  4. Sugar $10.00-12.00
  5. Sugar $10.00-12.00
Row 3:
  1. Plate...................... $4.00-5.00
  2. Sugar $8.00-10.00
  3. Creamer................. $8.00-10.00
  4. Cup $4.00-6.00
  5. Bowl...................... $4.00-6.00

Page 217

Row 1:
  1. Creamer................. $6.00-8.00
  2. Gravy boat............. $10.00-12.00
  3. Sugar $6.00-8.00

Row 2:
  1. Plate...................... $8.00-10.00
  2. Covered serving
      bowl.................. $18.00-22.00

3. Plate...................... $6.00-8.00
Row 3:
  1. Platter.................... $12.00-15.00
  2. Platter.................... $14.00-16.00

Page 219

Row 1:
  1. Plate...................... $8.00-10.00
  2. Cup $5.00-7.00
  3. Casserole with
      frame $27.00-32.00
  4. Plate...................... $6.00-8.00
  5. Cup $4.00-6.00
Row 2:
  1. Plate...................... $4.00-6.00
  2. Serving plate $8.00-12.00
  3. A.D. cup and saucer,
      set $12.00-15.00
Row 3:
  1. Plate...................... $10.00-14.00
  2. Plate...................... $8.00-10.00
  3. Plate...................... $4.00-6.00
  4. Plate...................... $4.00-6.00

Page 221

Row 1:
  1. Covered sugar $16.00-21.00
  2. Shaker $10.00-12.00
  3. Teapot.................... $50.00-55.00
  4. Saucer.................... $2.00-3.00
  5. Creamer................. $15.00-17.00
Row 2:
  1. Dinner plate $10.00-12.00
  2. Dessert plate $6.00-8.00
  3. Dinner plate $10.00-12.00
Row 3:
  1. Cream soup $15.00-17.00
  2. Covered casserole... $35.00-40.00
  3. Candleholder.......... $15.00-20.00
  4. Cup & saucer set.... $12.00-16.00

Page 223

Row 1:
  1. Platter..................... $17.00-22.00
  2. Oval bowl............... $17.00-22.00
Row 2:
  1. Plate...................... $10.00-12.00
  2. Bowl...................... $6.00-8.00
  3. Plate...................... $10.00-12.00
Row 3:
  1. Covered sugar $14.00-16.00

2. Creamer.................. $10.00-12.00
  3. Plate...................... $6.00-8.00
  4. Shaker $4.00-6.00
  5. Gravy boat.............. $12.00-17.00

Page 225

Row 1:
  1. Salad plate $3.00-5.00
  2. Dessert plate $3.00-5.00
  3. Salad plate $2.00-4.00
Row 2:
  1. Covered sugar $8.00-10.00
  2. Creamer................. $7.00-9.00
  3. Teapot.................... $32.00-37.00
  4. Plate...................... $3.00-5.00
Row 3:
  1. Covered casserole... $18.00-20.00
  2. Bowl...................... $12.00-16.00
  3. Covered casserole... $25.00-27.00
Row 4:
  1. Plate...................... $2.00-3.00
  2. Bowl...................... $1.00-2.00
  3. Plate...................... $1.00-2.00
  4. Plate...................... $1.00-2.00

Page 226

Damaged "Autumn Leaf" Paden
Bak-Serv plate, if perfect...$37.00-42.00

Page 227

Row 1:
  1. Plate...................... $2.00-3.00
  2. Plate...................... $2.00-4.00
  3. Bowl...................... $2.00-3.00
Row 2:
  1. Plate...................... $8.00-10.00
  2. Plate...................... $5.00-7.00
  3. Cup and saucer $10.00-12.00
  4. Creamer................. $8.00-10.00
  5. Covered sugar $10.00-12.00
Row 3:
  1. Plate...................... $6.00-8.00
  2. Salad plate $4.00-5.00
  3. Saucer.................... $1.00-2.00
  4. Plate...................... $1.00-2.00
Row 4:
  1. Platter.................... $15.00-17.00
  2. Salad plate $3.00-4.00
  3. Bread-butter plate . $1.00-2.00
  4. Cup and saucer $6.00-8.00

Page 229

Row 1:
1. Sugar $6.00-8.00
2. Creamer.................. $6.00-8.00
3. Cup & saucer set.... $6.00-8.00
4. Small plate or
   bowl..................... $2.00-3.00

Row 2:
1. Platter.................... $10.00-12.00
2. Bread-butter plate . $2.00-3.00
3. Dinner plate $6.00-8.00

Row 3:
1. Dinner plate $4.00-6.00
2. Dessert plate $2.00-3.00
3. Individual
   casserole $4.00-5.00
4. Teapot.................... $27.00-32.00

Row 4:
1. Serving plate in
   aluminum frame ... $27.00-32.00
2. Large utility plate.. $25.00-30.00

Page 231

Row 1:
1. Creamer.................. $10.00-12.00
2. Sugar and cover $13.00-15.00
3. Creamer.................. $10.00-12.00
4. Sugar $13.00-15.00

Row 2:
1. Plate...................... $6.00-8.00
2. Small plate or bowl. $3.00-4.00
3. Platter.................... $8.00-10.00

Row 3:
1. Plate...................... $6.00-8.00
2. Saucer.................... $2.00-4.00
3. Plate and bowl........ $6.00-8.00

Row 4:
1. Plate...................... $6.00-8.00
2. Luncheon plate....... $4.00-6.00
3. Plate...................... $10.00-12.00

Page 233

All Pfaltzgraff pieces are currently
available.

Page 234

1. Dinner plate $8.00-10.00
2. Small plate $4.00-6.00
3. Bowl $3.00-4.00

Page 237

Row 1:
1. Covered syrup $18.00-22.00
2. Syrup-lid missing... $14.00-17.00

Row 2:
1. Holland jug............. $25.00-30.00
2. Jug-lid missing....... $25.00-30.00
3. Ball jug $28.00-30.00

Row 3:
1. Covered jar $40.00-45.00
2. Pie baker $20.00-25.00

Row 4:
1. Salad bowl $27.00-32.00
2. Covered casserole... $27.00-32.00

Page 239

Row 1:
1. 12 oz. tumbler $18.00-20.00
2. 6 oz. tumbler $18.00-20.00
3. Shaker set $16.00-20.00
4. Shaker set $16.00-20.00
5. Cup & saucer set.... $18.00-20.00

Row 2:
1. Covered
   sugar jar $45.00-50.00
2. Salad plate $17.00-22.00
3. Cookie jar $45.00-50.00

Row 3:
1. Dutch jug............... $30.00-35.00
2. Covered drippings
   jar....................... $20.00-25.00
3. Small jug $12.00-17.00

Page 241

Row 1:
1. Teapot.................... $35.00-40.00
2. Cup and saucer $10.00-12.00
3. Dinner plate $10.00-12.00

Row 2:
1. Creamer.................. $12.00-14.00
2. Covered sugar $13.00-16.00
3. Gravy boat &
   liner..................... $12.00-17.00

Page 247

1. Salt & pepper set ... $17.00-20.00
2. Creamer.................. $15.00-20.00

Page 251

Row 1:
1. Saucer.................... $3.00-4.00

2. Dessert plate $3.00-5.00
3. Ashtray set in
   frame $15.00-20.00

Row 2:
1. Plate...................... $3.00-5.00
2. Plate...................... $4.00-6.00
3. Plate...................... $3.00-4.00

Row 3:
1. Small plate $2.00-3.00
2. Butter plate $6.00-8.00
3. Salad plate $3.00-4.00
4. Plate...................... $4.00-6.00

Page 253

Row 1:
1. Covered sugar $12.00-14.00
2. Creamer.................. $10.00-12.00
3. Cup & saucer set.... $8.00-10.00
4. Small bowl............. $4.00-6.00

Row 2:
1. Covered sugar $12.00-14.00
2. Creamer.................. $12.00-14.00
3. Cup $4.00-6.00
4. Plate...................... $8.00-10.00

Row 3:
1. Platter.................... $8.00-10.00
2. Small plate $2.00-3.00
3. Plate...................... $3.00-4.00
4. Square plate $2.00-3.00

Row 4:
1. Plate...................... $8.00-10.00
2. Shaker $6.00-8.00
3. Small plate $3.00-4.00
4. Dinner plate $6.00-8.00

Page 263

Row 1:
1. Cup & saucer set.... $10.00-12.00
2. Bowl $3.00-5.00
3. Small plate $3.00-5.00

Row 2:
1. Plate...................... $6.00-8.00
2. Covered vegetable
   bowl..................... $25.00-30.00

Row 3:
1. Teapot.................... $25.00-30.00
2. Gravy boat............. $10.00-12.00
3. Dessert plate $4.00-6.00

Row 4:
1. Platters.................. $15.00-17.00

Page 264

1. Plate........................ $25.00-30.00
2. Cup & saucer set.... $20.00-25.00
3. Covered casserole... $55.00-60.00

Page 265

1. Cup $10.00-12.00
2. Small bowl.............. $6.00-8.00
3. Small plate $10.00-12.00
4. Dinner plate $14.00-16.00

Page 267

Variety of Southern Pottery plates,
  each........................ $12.00-14.00

Page 268

Row 1:
1. Large plate $14.00-16.00
2. Small plate $12.00-14.00
3. Tea or coffee pot $95.00-100.00

Row 2:
1. Egg cup $32.00-35.00
2. Jam jar & liner....... $25.00-30.00
3. Muffin cover $105.00-130.00

Page 269

1. Plate........................ $35.00-40.00
2. Teapot.................... $95.00-110.00
3. Cup & saucer set.... $25.00-35.00
4. Plate........................ $35.00-40.00

Page 271

Dinner plate.................. $10.00-12.00

Page 275

Row 1:
1. Stetson
    decorated $2.00-3.00
2. Stetson
    decorated $2.00-3.00
3. Illinois China......... $3.00-4.00
4. Illinois China......... $3.00-4.00

Row 2:
1. Platter.................... $15.00-20.00
2. Sugar $7.00-9.00
3. Plate....................... $8.00-10.00

Row 3:
1. Small bowl.............. $4.00-5.00
2. Small bowl.............. $4.00-5.00
3. Utility bowl $8.00-10.00

Row 4:
1. Square plate $4.00-6.00
2. Plate....................... $3.00-4.00
3. Small plate $2.00-4.00

Page 277

Row 1:
1. Creamer.................. $12.00-15.00
2. Bowl $4.00-6.00
3. Salt & pepper set ... $12.00-14.00

Row 2:
1. Covered sugar $10.00-12.00
2. Teapot.................... $30.00-35.00
3. Creamer.................. $8.00-10.00

Row 3:
1. A.D. cup saucer, ... $18.00-20.00
2. A.D. cup saucer, ... $18.00-20.00
3. A.D. cup saucer, ... $18.00-20.00
4. A.D. cup saucer, ... $18.00-20.00
5. Snack set $10.00-14.00

Row 4:
1. Plate only $4.00-6.00

Page 281

Row 1:
1. Pitcher.................... $45.00-50.00
2. Tumbler $18.00-20.00
3. Pitcher (juice)........ $35.00-40.00
4. Tumbler $14.00-18.00
5. Utility/cake plate ... $22.00-27.00

Row 2:
1. Plate (gray higher). $6.00-7.00
2. Gravy boat............. $17.00-20.00
3. Muffin cover $75.00-80.00
4. ¼ lb. butter $22.00-27.00
5. Egg cup $15.00-18.00

Row 3:
1. Teapot.................... $35.00-45.00
2. A.D. cup-saucer, ... $12.00-17.00
3. A.D. coffee server ... $55.00-65.00
4. A.D. creamer $20.00-22.00
5. A.D. sugar.............. $22.00-24.00

Page 282

Row 1:
1. Tab handle soup..... $8.00-10.00
2. A.D. covered sugar . $45.00-50.00
3. A.D. coffee server ...$110.00-135.00
4. A.D. creamer $35.00-40.00
5. "Leaf" plate............ $6.00-8.00
6. "Leaf" cream soup .. $10.00-12.00

Row 2:
1. Plate....................... $10.00-12.00
2. Plate....................... $4.00-6.00
3. Calendar................ $15.00-17.00
4. Utility plate $22.00-27.00

Page 283

1. Creamer.................. $10.00-12.00
2. Cup $6.00-8.00
3. Shaker $4.00-5.00
4. Plate....................... $2.00-3.00

Row 2:
1. "Leaf" plate............ $6.00-8.00
2. Cream soup $6.00-8.00
3. Gravy or sauce
    boat $12.00-14.00

Row 3:
1. Plate....................... $4.00-6.00
2. Handled bowl $6.00-8.00
3. Cup $2.00-3.00
4. Plate....................... $2.00-3.00
5. Bowl $3.00-4.00

Row 4:
1. Plate....................... $4.00-5.00
2. Plate....................... $2.00-3.00
3. Plate....................... $4.00-5.00

Page 285

Row 1:
1. Sugar w/out cover .. $8.00-10.00
2. Creamer.................. $10.00-12.00
3. Covered butter $12.00-16.00
4. Covered sugar $6.00-8.00

Row 2:
1. Plate....................... $3.00-4.00
2. A.D. cup $12.00-14.00
3. A.D. coffee server,
    lid missing $20.00-25.00
    if complete............ $25.00-30.00
4. Plate....................... $4.00-5.00

Row 3:
1. Small plate $3.00-4.00
2. Small plate $3.00-4.00
3. Small plate $3.00-4.00
4. Small plate $3.00-4.00

Row 4:
1. Calendar plate $8.00-10.00
2. Plate....................... $8.00-10.00
3. Plate....................... $4.00-6.00

Page 287

Row 1:
1. Plate........................ $14.00-16.00
2. Serving plate......... $35.00-40.00
3. Cup & saucer set.... $15.00-17.00

Row 2:
1. Creamer.................. $14.00-16.00
2. Sugar and cover $20.00-25.00
3. A.D. cup-saucer, set $20.00-25.00
4. Egg cup $17.00-22.00

Row 3:
1. Pitcher $45.00-50.00
2. Shaker $12.00-14.00
3. Teapot.................... $50.00-55.00
4. Shaker $12.00-14.00

Page 292

Tumbler........................ $37.00-42.00

Page 293

Row 1:
1. Saucer
   (Wheelock)........... $5.00-7.00
2. Shaker $12.00-14.00
3. Shaker $12.00-14.00
4. Shaker $12.00-14.00
5. Bowl $5.00-7.00

Row 2:
1. Teapot.................... $30.00-35.00
2. Batter jug $75.00-80.00
3. Creamer.................. $15.00-17.00

Row 3:
1. Server $20.00-25.00
2. Pitcher $100.00-110.00
3. Ice tea tumbler....... $27.00-32.00
4. Salad bowl............. $27.00-32.00
5. Fork and spoon
   (in bowl) set $47.00-52.00

Row 4:
1. Plate........................ $10.00-12.00
2. Serving plate......... $30.00-35.00
3. Tablecloth.............. $75.00-85.00

Page 295

Row 1:
1. Glass shaker set..... $35.00-40.00
2. Sugar w/o lid $8.00-10.00
3. Set of glass
   shakers $22.00-27.00

Row 2:
1. Pitcher $35.00-40.00

---

2. Side handle jug $32.00-35.00
3. Milk or utility
   pitcher.................. $20.00-22.00

Row 3:
1. Refrigerator jug...... $25.00-30.00
2. Shaker $8.00-10.00
3. Set of bowls $17.00-22.00
4. Cookie jar (not
   correct lid) $50.00-55.00

Row 4:
1. Platter.................... $22.00-27.00
2. Plate........................ $4.00-5.00
3. 1 lb. butter............. $45.00-50.00
4. Scales.................... $35.00-40.00

Page 296

Row 1:
1. Salad bowl $18.00-20.00
2. Utility bowl $10.00-12.00
3. Salad bowl $17.00-22.00

Row 2:
1. Plate........................ $4.00-5.00
2. Bowl $3.00-4.00
3. Plate........................ $6.00-8.00

Page 297

Row 1:
1. Plate........................ $2.00-3.00
2. Shaker $6.00-8.00
3. Gravy boat.............. $10.00-12.00

Row 2:
1. Milk pitcher........... $20.00-25.00
2. Bowl $4.00-6.00
3. Plate........................ $4.00-6.00

Row 3:
1. Pitcher $25.00-30.00
2. Stack set w/covers.. $25.00-30.00
3. Covered casserole... $20.00-25.00

Row 4:
1. Pie baker $17.00-22.00
2. Canteen jug $18.00-22.00
3. Plate........................ $6.00-8.00

Page 299

Row 1:
1. Sugar cover
   missing $4.00-5.00
2. Shaker $3.00-4.00
3. Shaker $3.00-4.00
4. Creamer.................. $5.00-7.00
5. Bowls, each............. $3.00-4.00

Row 2:
1. Plate........................ $4.00-5.00
2. Plate........................ $2.00-3.00
3. Pie baker $12.00-15.00

Row 3:
1. Utility plate........... $12.00-15.00
2. Small plate $3.00-4.00
3. Small plate $3.00-4.00

Row 4:
1. Covered utility
   bowl..................... $8.00-10.00
2. Shaker $6.00-8.00
3. Utility plate........... $15.00-17.00

Page 301

Row 1:
1. Gravy boat.............. $12.00-14.00
2. Salt $4.00-6.00
3. Pepper.................... $4.00-6.00
4. Covered sugar $12.00-14.00
5. Creamer.................. $8.00-10.00

Row 2:
1. Covered utility jar.. $18.00-20.00
2. Relish dish............. $8.00-10.00
3. Plate........................ $2.00-3.00

Row 3:
1. Plate........................ $6.00-8.00
2. Oval bowl............... $8.00-10.00
3. Salad plate $3.00-4.00

Row 4:
1. Cup & saucer set.... $6.00-8.00
2. Soup bowl $3.00-4.00
3. Utility tray $15.00-20.00

Page 302

Serving tray in frame.... $35.00-40.00

Page 303

Row 1:
1. Syrup jar (God
   Bless America) $30.00-40.00
2. Refrigerator set of 3
   bowls w/cover $25.00-30.00

Row 2:
1. Canteen jug $20.00-25.00
2. Covered cookie jar,
   (lid missing).......... $30.00-35.00
3. Coffee server.......... $20.00-25.00

Row 3:
1. Coffee base, complete
   w/dripper $25.00-30.00

2. Jug $18.00-20.00
3. Coffee base, complete
   w/dripper $25.00-30.00
Row 4:
   Refrigerator jugs, ea. $20.00-25.00

Page 305

Row 1:
1. Plate....................... $3.00-4.00
2. Shaker $8.00-10.00
3. Shaker $8.00-10.00
4. Saucer.................... $1.00-2.00
Row 2:
1. Utility plate............ $22.00-25.00
2. Plate...................... $4.00-6.00
3. Dinner plate,
   if good $8.00-10.00
Row 3:
1. Custard.................. $4.00-6.00
2. Small covered
   bowl...................... $10.00-12.00
3. Medium covered
   bowl...................... $12.00-17.00
4. Large covered
   bowl...................... $17.00-22.00
Row 4:
1. Covered pitcher,
   hinge lid............... $37.00-42.00

2. Tab handled bowl
   (large) $12.00-14.00
3. Tab handled soup... $6.00-8.00
4. Milk/utility pitcher.. $20.00-25.00

Page 307

Row 1:
1. Plate....................... $8.00-10.00
2. Bowl $10.00-12.00
3. Egg cup $17.00-20.00
4. Plate....................... $3.00-5.00
Row 2:
1. Covered sugar $12.00-14.00
2. Creamer.................. $10.00-12.00
3. Gravy boat.............. $12.00-15.00
4. Cup $6.00-8.00
5. Shaker $4.00-6.00

Page 308

Row 1:
1. Bean pot $30.00-35.00
2. Syrup $32.00-37.00
3. Teapot.................... $40.00-45.00
4. Shaker $10.00-12.00
5. Ball jug $32.00-37.00
Row 2:
1. Spoon $22.00-27.00
2. Shaker $8.00-10.00

3. Teapot.................... $30.00-35.00
4. Utility pitcher $17.00-22.00
Row 3:
1. Plate....................... $6.00-8.00
2. Handled mug.......... $16.00-20.00
3. Canteen jug $20.00-25.00
4. Bowl $6.00-8.00
5. Bean pot $4.00-6.00

Page 309

Row 1:
1. Plate....................... $13.00-16.00
2. Teapot.................... $55.00-60.00
Row 2:
1. Covered sugar $25.00-30.00
2. Creamer.................. $17.00-22.00
3. Cup & saucer set.... $15.00-20.00

Page 310

Marcrest
1. Cookie jar $30.00-32.00
2. Snack plate............. $5.00-7.00

Page 311

Bottom of page
1. Bird bowl $52.00-57.00
2. Bird bowl $32.00-37.00
3. Bird ladle............... $42.00-47.00

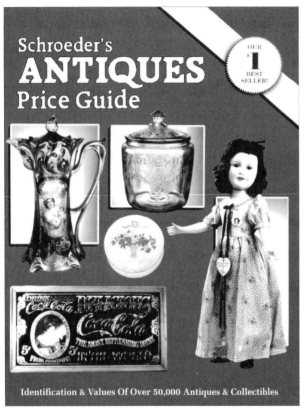